POLITICAL DYNAMICS OF WOMEN

Political Dynamics of Women

Edited by

Puran Chandra

AKANSHA PUBLISHING HOUSE
NEW DELHI - 110 059 (INDIA)

AKANSHA PUBLISHING HOUSE
R-37B, Vani Vihar, Uttam Nagar
New Delhi - 110 059
E-mail: ektabooks@yahoo.com

Showroom
4649/21B, Ansari Road
Daryaganj, New Delhi - 110 002
PHones: 23263193, 9811582579

Political Dynamics of Women

First Published, 2005

ISBN 81-8370-002-0

PRINTED IN INDIA

Published by M.P. Misra for Akansha Publishing House, New Delhi - 110 059 and Printed at Mehra Offset Press, Delhi.

Contents

Preface

> "Women are not sufficiently represented in politics or government. If politics is the art of government—and it is—and if government is public housekeeping—and it is—then women's place is quite logically in politics."
>
> —Mary Donlon.

Till today, to many women, politics is a vague expression, which has traditionally been the business of men. Women participate to a lesser degree than men in all political activities. Women are still very inadequately represented in national and international political processes. Despite women exercise franchise today but the percentage of women voters remains comparatively low.

In the modern civilised society 'Politics' is chiefly a skill controlled area. Persons skilled enough to control the environment are definitely active in politics.

In the yore days, the position of Hindu women in early Vedic times was very different from the lower status to which they were degraded after about 300 BC. However, matriarchy was replaced by patriarchy with the Vedic Aryan which seems to have overtuned the image of the women which prevailed from this. And degradation continued all through the Christian era till now. Though some women leaders emerged at different times—to name as Chand Bibi, Razia Sultana, Rani Laxmi Bai of Jhansi, Ahilyabai, and more recently Indira Gandhi, who made debut in the field of politics—i.e. heading the governance of State. However, as in other fields of life women have been treated inferior to men.

This book, as suggested by the name of the title.

depicts the dynamics of women in politics. The text is supported by facts and figures gathered from various authoritative sources. The main topics, given elaborate treatment herein are—Women soldiers in political war; Women and politics: A theoretical perspective; Women and politics: An intellectual discourse; Reservation for women in Parliament and State Assemblies; Women in local bodies; Decision-making and political participation; Political dynamics of women: A case study; Women in politics; Communism and women; Women uprising during the freedom struggle; Politics of women and Panchayati Raj; Political dynamics of women and Congress constructive programme; Women representation in political life; Women in politics and trade unions: global scenario; etc.

We have tried to present the political dynamism of women taking instances from all over the world. Actually source of information is all secondary i.e. the Abstracts, reports, journals, books, individual studies and Govt. records. As no claim for originality. All credit for this goes to all great men of letters whose painstaking research findings are cited or substantially made use of.

We owe a deep sense of gratitude to them for sharing their views. We are equally thankful to all the editors, publishers, copyright holders of different publications. We are grateful to our friends, well-wishers, and family member for their constant moral support and inspiration. Finally, Mr. M.P. Misra, our publishers deserve all appreciation for materialising our endeavours.

We will feel amply rewarded, if this could prove of some benefit to those for which this is meant.

—Editor

1 Women Soldiers in Political War

Politicians are as good as you are, for the way you vote creates politicians."

I GLOBAL SCENARIO

Till today, to many women, politics is a vague expression meaning the government of the country, which has traditionally been the business of men. As such women participate to a lesser degree than men in all political activities. To make an assessment of women's participation in politics is a difficult task due to lack of statistics and information on the subject. The literature on women's participation in practice is uneven.

The political participation of women as an issue was given importance in the Nairobi Forward-looking Strategies for the Advancement of Women. The strategies note, for instance, that women are still very inadequately represented in national and international political processes dealing with peace and conflict settlement (paragraph 24) and that efforts should be into satisfied to overcome prejudices, stereotyped thinking, denial to women of career prospects and appropriate educational possibilities, and resistance by decision-makers to the changes that are necessary to enable equal participation of women with men in the international and diplomatic services (para 253).

Women as Voters

In a democracy the right to franchise is the first basic right, but it is surprising that in a majority of countries women did not enjoy the right to vote until the end of World War II. There are great regional disparities in this regard. In

most of the developed regions women enjoyed the right to vote from the nearly 20th century. New Zealand was the first country which had granted the right to vote to its women as early as in 1893, followed by Australia in 1901. Up to 1945,

TABLE 1: RIGHT TO VOTE TO WOMEN

Name of the Country	*Year of Women's Right*
Albania	1945
Bulgaria	1944
Canada	1918
Czechoslovakia	1920
Denmark	1915
Finland	1906
Japan	1945
Poland	1918
Sweden	1921
Switzerland	1971
U.S.S.R.	1917
United Kingdom	1918
United States	1920
Algeria	1962
Mexico	1953
Afghanistan	A recent development
China	1949
India	1950
Indonesia	1945
Iran	1963
Iraq	1980
Argentina	1952
Brazil	1934
Pakistan	1947
Thailand	1932
Vietnam	1946

Source: The World's Women 1970-1990) Trends and Statistics, U.N.N.Y. 1991, pp. 39, 40.

35 countries out of 96 had granted the right to vote to women, but these were mostly developed regions. In developing regions it took a long time for women to women exercise this fundamental right. In most of the African states, women got the right to vote only in the sixties, seventies and eighties. In South Africa it was given only in 1979 and in Iraq in 1980.

Despite women exercise franchise today but the percentage of women voters remains comparatively low. This may be due to various reasons; first of all the exercise of franchise is a right and not a duty. Hence many people do not exercise this right it is more so in the case of women, due to their household responsibilities. Generally the negative or indifferent attitude of male members is also responsible for this state of affairs. The lack of interest of women in politics is another reason.

A number of studies have been made on voting pattern/behaviour, though not on gender basis. Hence it is difficult to make any generalisation on this issue. But on the basis of observation it can be concluded that in countries where women do not enjoy much freedom, their voting pattern is not different from men, as the man dictates the terms, whereas where women are more educated and independent, and care for their individuality, the voting behaviour differs.

On taking account, percentage of women voters, it will reveal that it is higher in rural areas than in urban. This may be attributed to the personal contact between the voters and the candidates. In urban areas, the impersonal relation and the lack of homogeneity of the groups are mainly responsible for indifference towards voting pattern.

Women Contestents/Elected Members of Parliament, State Assemblies and Local Bodies

Though, the percentage of women voters has considerable increased in all the countries yet their representation in parliaments is not that proportional. In 1987 only 10% of countries' parliamentarians on an average were women. The strength of parliamentary representation by women varies

according to the political system and the historical period. In 1987, the highest representation to women in parliaments was in eastern Europe and the erstwhile U.S.S.R.—nearly 28%. But of late the number has been decreasing.

Amazingly, in a large number of developed countries, like the United Kingdom (6.3%) the United States (5.3%) France (6.4%) and Japan (1.4%), the representation of women in parliaments is extremely poor. This may be attributed to historical, social and cultural factors. But it also reflects the negative attitude of a male-dominated world. As compared to the developed regions some of the developing countries like India have made good progress (8.3%).

A number of factors are responsible low representation of women in national parliaments. Women in general do not have much interest in politics. This is supported by studies made by psychologists on women's aptitude and behaviour. The declining moral value, the increasing use of money to achieve political power and the crimilisation of politics are some of the factors which do not encourage women to take an active part in politics.

Again, party attitudes are also responsible for this state of affairs. Generally political parties do not favour nomination of women candidates as they are not sure of their success. Moreover political parties generally select their candidates from fields like law and journalism where the percentage of women is comparative low. Today party tickets are given on various considerations such a religion, caste and money. Polities is a game of power which depends on right calculations and while nominating candidate political parties do not find women as successful pawns in the game of politics. In the decision-making process at the party level women are generally kept at a distance.

The political parties normally in their election manifestos do not give importance to women's issues, which need special representation of women. Most of the parties do not set aside quota for women or provide for reservation of seats. In Indian

TABLE 2: POLITICAL PARTICIPATION OF WOMEN IN DEVELOPED AND DEVELOPING COUNTRIES

Name of the Country	*Parliamentary Seats occupied by women*	
	1975	*1987*
Albania	33.2	28.8
Bulgaria	18.8	21.0
Canada	3.4	9.6
Czechoslovakia	26.0	29.5
Denmark	15.6	29.1
Finland	23.0	31.5
Japan	1.4	1.4
Poland	15.9	20.2
Sweden	21,4	28.5
Switzerland	7.5	14.0
U.S.S.R.	32.1	34.5
United Kingdom	4.3	6.3
United States	3.7	5.3
Algeria	—	2.4
Argentina	8.6	4.7
Brazil	0.3	5.3
Mexico	5.0	10.8
Afghanistan	—	—
China	22.6	21.2
India	4.3	8.3
Indonesia	7.2	—
Iran	—	1.5
Iraq	—	13.2
Kuwait	—	—
Pakistan	4.1	8.9
Saudi Arabia	—	—
Thailand	1.1	3.5
Vietnam	—	17.6

Source: The World's Women 1970-1090 Trends and Statistics—U.N.N.Y., 1991

many parties promise a 30% quota for women but do not implement this in practice). Many a time they nominate

women candidates where they are not hopeful of success or they would like to encash a wife's ticket if her husband his been killed in order to gain public sympathy.

In the light of foregoing discussion, it can be safety to concluded that, the world picture of the political participation of women in politics is far from satisfactory. The status of women is directly related to the decision making process, and unless women are associated more closely this process, equality and justice to women cannot be achieved.

II

POLITICAL PARTICIPATION OF WOMEN: INDIAN SCENARIO

Undoubtedly, an all out effort is being made to enhance the status of women in India. But status is related to the exercise of power, both political and administrative. And unless women are able to exercise this power in large numbers, their status in society will not change significantly.

The women's political participation in India is increasing steadily at a slow pace. While the number of female electors has varied between 80 to 90%, the percentage of voters has been considerably low. This of course is not very surprising as it reflects the social culture of our society. But what is significant is that there is a continuous increase in the percentage of women voters (from 58.3 to 78.8%). This reflects the increasing political consciousness among women.

Despite the fact that the percentage of women to men voters has gone up to 80%, the number of contestants, both to the Lok Sabha and the Rajya Sabha, is far from satisfactory. From 1952 to 1984 the percentage of female to male contestants has been varying between 2.3% to 3.17%. It is astonishing that though there is a tremendous increase in the number of women voters, there seems to be no correlation between the number of voters and the contestants. It is evident from the result of the recent elections ot the Parliament and some states asseblies.

TABLE 3: NO. OF ELECTORS AND VOTERS TO THE LOK SABHA (SEX-WISE) FROM 1952 TO 1984

Year	*Electors*			*Voters*		
	M	*F*	*Percentage (F/M)*	*M*	*F*	*Percentage (F/M)*
1952	95267500	77946135	31	50975832	29733270	58.3
1957	102205638	91446431	89	55924441	35405424	63.3
1962	113944234	102427981	89	70703050	47764170	67.5
1967	130423737	102173708	78	86460463	66264048	76.6
1971	143474831	130619662	91	87382907	64153895	73.4
1977	167019151	154155176	92.3	109609940	84653975	77.3
1980	185210315	170380385	91.9	115133649	87271764	75.8
1984	196730499	182810109	92.9	134122952	107123935	79.8

Source: Women in India—A Statistical Profile (1988). Government of India.

TABLE 4: NO. OF CONTESTANTS AND THOSE ELECTED TO THE LOK SABHA (SEX-WISE) FROM 1952 TO 1984

Year	*M*	*F*	*%age (F to M)*	*M*	*F*	*%age (F to M)*
1952	1831	43	23	475	14	2.94
1957	1474	45	5.05	467	27	5.78
1962	1915	70	3.6	4.59	35	7.62
1967	2300	69	3.0	489	31	6.4
1971	2693	86	3.2	497	21	4.2
1977	2369	70	2.95	523	19	3.6
1980	4478	142	3.17	514	28	5.5
1984	5149	164	3.2	486	42	8.64
1987	—	—	—	491	46	9.4

Source: Women in India: A Statistical Profile (1988), Government of India.

One main impedinent to the advancement of women is the prevailing unequal division of household and childcare responsibilities. Women's double burden combined with the long and non-flexible hours of work required for political participation come as hindrance in the way of many otherwise embitious women. The time factor is one of the major obstacles to women's participation in parliaments. Other more significant fact is the lack of interest shown by various political parties while nominating candidates. Even the Congress party has not been fair to the fair sex. Though some parties supported the idea of 30% seats for women, in practice this was never implemented. Women continued to be bypassed on the issue of distribution of party tickets more so in recent elections.

It is also true that many women do not come forward for these positions. And in many cases their chances of success to not seem to be very bright and hence most of the parties do not want to take the risk of losing seats.

The percentage of female to male has gone up from 7.5% (1952) to 13.6% (1980). Though there was a decline (10.8%) in 1982, it has again gone up to 13%. This sharp difference

between the membership of the two houses may be due to the difference in the procedure of election. The election to the Rajya Sabha is indirect (by the respective Legislative Assemblies) whereas for Lok Sabha it is direct. It is obvious that many women are prepared to participate in the political process provided they are saved from the hazardous process of going through a direct election. The increasing violence and criminalisation of politics and other such obstacles hinder women participating in elections.

TABLE 5: MEMBERS OF THE RAJYA SABHA (SEX-WISE)

Year	*M*	*F*	*Percentage*
1952	201	15	7.5
1957	212	20	9.4
1962	218	18	8.2
1967	215	24	11.1
1972	225	18	8
1976	212	24	11.3
1980	213	29	13.6
1982	213	23	10.8
1984	209	24	11.5
1986	215	28	13

Source: Women in India: A Statistical Profile (1988), Government of India.

The fact true of the Lok Sabha elections of the State Assemblies. The percentage of women contestants varied between 1.55% to 3.43%. It is surprising that instead of an increase, there is a decrease in the percentage. The highest was in 1957 (3.43) and the lowest in 1967 (1.55 percent). As compared to the contestants the percentage of those who were elected to the State Assemblies is comparatively better. But it is disheartening to note that there has been a continuous decline in the percentage of women elected to Assemblies, specially from 1974-75 (2.76); except in 1979-80 when it was slightly better (4.51%). The reasons for the poor representation of women in the State Assemblies are more or less the same as that for the Lok Sabha—lack of encouragement of political

parties, and the criminalisation of politics coupled with heavy responsibilities at home front.

Women in Panchayati Raj Bodies

An effort is being made to involve women in politics at the grass-root level, as there is a difference in the political complexion and culture of urban and local government organisations. Women for different reasons are not actively involved in urban local bodies. But the involvement of women in Panchayati Raj institutions specially at the lowest level has been increasing. The recent legislation of Parliament on Panchayati Raj, ensures a 30% reservation of seats for women (constitution 73rd Amendment Act). There is no doubt that rural women have become more politically conscious than women in urban areas. But there are many teething troubles. Reality on the ground is yet very dismal.

Men try to dominate the scene even in PRI. In many meetings, the women's presence does not seem to be necessary and their signature/thumb impression is taken after meeting. Many women have no idea about the local issues or the decision taken in the meetings. Their presence is more or less symbolic. But these difficulties can be overcome by making women more conscious of their rights and duties, through different ways such as awareness camps.

Obviously, a permanent change in the political and social complexion needs a strong foundation and hence an all out effort should be made to innovative more and more women in this process of decision-making.

It is necessary for the very survival of a democracy that the process of election should be fair. The increasing criminalisation of politics is of setback not only to the increasing participation of women but for the very development of a democratic society. Hence, these is an urgent need for political parties, the Election Commission and the voters to join hands in order to fight this menace and to make the election atmosphere less violent and more transparent.

A representative democracy should be able to 'represent' the various segments of society in a more or less proportionate way. But the per cent state of affairs is a clear violation of this principle. Hence there is a need to reserve certain seats (on the same analogy as for S.T.'s and S.C.'s) for women also so that all political parties may be compelled to nominate women candidates to certain seats. The competition among women contestants may also increase women's political awareness.

Political parties have still to realise that the issue pertaining to women are not issues to be dealt with separately by women only. They are to be discussed and decided at the national level. The progress of the nation depends on the development of manpower-which includes 50% of women power. Reservation of women in Parliament and state legislature, which has been brought in Parliament as a Bill many a time could not be passed as yet. This shows the inactive mentality and indifference of all political parties who have yet to accept it as the core of heart.

2

Women and Politics: A Theoretical Perspective

Modern democratic systems governance provide ample opportunities for participation. Effective participation of the people is an indicator of true democracy. Therefore, the institutional organisation plays a major role in developing the sense of efficacy. The family, peer group, membership of various associations and political parties help in developing the sense of efficacy. As the institutional and associational affiliation help in developing the sense of efficacy, the absence of these may also retard it. But whatever may be the system educated persons being efficacious, feel that they have the capacity to mould the environment. In this it is opt to quote Almond and Verba who state, "irrespective of autocratic or democratic socialisation experiences, the well-educated person feel more politically competent than the less educated individual."

In fact, education and socio-economic status are inter-related. Persons with higher socio-economic status posses more self-confidence. They have personal control as well as control over the external environment. Consequently their involvement in politics, beginning from simple political activities like voting, to the more complex form like decision-making is effective and meaningful. Membership of a majority group generally reinforces efficacy. In order to safeguard group interest, persons belonging to such groups develop mental dispositions to become more assertive. Thus, participation in the political process sometimes may be due to necessity.

Political efficacy being a feeling in the individual to have sufficient mastery in the political sphere the 'locus of casuality' may be fixed on the self and not on the environment. De Charms has categorised people into 'origin' and 'pawn' on the basis of their perception to social casuality, he says, him a person is termed as 'origin' who perceives his behaviour to be the outcome of his own choice. On the other hand, a 'Pawn' is a person who believes that his behaviour is determined by external forces beyond his control. Rotter states the internal controls of an individual are the rewards which follows from the individual's own behaviour. The various external controls are the result of luck, chance, fate, as under the control of powerful others, or as unpredictable because of the great complexity of process surrounding him."

On the other hand to quote Rotter, a reinforcer is that which changes behaviour in some way by either increasing or decreasing the potentiality of its occurence. These include both internal and external reinforcements. The internal reinforcements as defined by him are an individual's perception that an event has had some value for him. The external reinforcements are the acts or events which have predictable reinforcements value for the group or culture to which the individual belongs. Rotter has defined external control to be the rewards which are contingent upon the external control to be the belief that reinforcements were contingent upon the individuals' own behaviour.

In the modern citilized society 'Politics' is chiefly a skill controlled area. Persons skilled enough to control the environment are definitely active in politics. Therefore, political efficacy and personal control are closely related, individuals having personal control perceive the political systems to have great influence on their socio-economic and other personal pursuits. For them (1) the political system is the only source from which they can get certain benefits, (2) the decisions of the political system may also be viewed as interfering their various pursuits, and (3) they have an obligation to be concerned with the political process. The first category of belief is

termed as the political reward salience. Individuals having such belief view the political system as the sole accomplisher of certain which no other institution can do it has enough resources which are not available elsewhere. The varied problems of the society can be dealt with by the political system. The second category of individuals view the political system not so much a means to problem solution, as it is the problems itself.' 'They desire that the government should perform less so that their individual goals may pursued inhindered. Both types of individual feel that government has great impact on their lives, whether they assign it more work and expect rewards or assign less work and desire that it should govern the least.' The 'obligated' are the third category of individuals who believe that their good citizen roles demand obligation which they are morally bound to discharge. This perception has close link with rewards from the political system. Persons having the three types of dispositions towards the political system involve in political activity. But persons who assign an activist role to the government and have a reward salience, generally become politically active.

II

It is significant note here but since independence more and more number of women in have been educated and entered public life. The Constitution has guaranteed equal civil and political.rights to both. But these provisions have not helped them play a direct and dominant role in whatever capacity they participated. 'An enormous disparity exists between women's formal political equality and their meaningful exercise of political power. (V. Rajlaxmi). The external environment has provided opportunities but women in general, have not been able to develop the ego strength and the capacity to control the external environment, (to 'exercise meaningfully the political power'). Efficacy being a psychological disposition, a questionnaire to measure this was circulated among the two hundred and fifty-seven women.

Women belonging to other categories attach less importance to voting and their say in the affairs of the state the office holders are much less in the positive side. The other categories are not very clear in their opinion but as revealed from their number, they do not consider that they have much to say in the affairs of the State.

External Environment

Despite development in certain areas, in underdeveloped countries like India, the traditional outlure has not changed substantially as to do away with the dichotomous division of society. The private world with its narrow restricted boundary (i.e. home) is still considered as the right place for women. Feeling of mastery over the self and the outside world is nurtued in which is reinforced or restricted by the society. The childhood socialisation of a girl is very much different from a male child. The restriction on her movement, engagement in domestic work obstructs her exposure to the outside world. Even in the absent of these restrictions, her exposure is not as much as that of a boy. Certain vocations are still preferred for men as a general rule.

Still today, in Indian families the voice of a daughter counts less in family decision making. Thus a girl is deprived of the feeling since her childhood that she can influence decisions. This creates a sense of ineffectiveness. Even after marriage she does not have much effective role in her in-laws family. Much political apathy may have its origin in a general feeling that, after all matters of apparent choice have probably fixed in advance—a state of affairs which becomes fact, indeed. Its influential parts of the electorate acquire in it because they have learned to view the world as a place where grown-ups take of choice but fix things so as to avoid overall friction.

The pattern of child rearing in our country, particularly a female child is to adjust to the skill of others and performing social roles as per the norms of the society. A breach of the societal norm may be excusable for a male but not for a

female. A primary concern and responsibility for the young tends to focus attention upon engendering in them on suitable morality. In addition there is some suggestion that the custody of moral values is often acquired as a consolation prise for exclusion from these activities which have the highest value in the society.

In Indian society, the primary role of women is still considered as wives, mother, child bearers and rearers, whatever may be their level of education and professional career. In a developing country like ours where scarcity of jobs compel men to hunt for jobs, they are unwilling to encourage females coming into public spheres, pursue power and assume position. The weak socialisation process during childhood and continuously determining environment in their adulthood prevent in developing enough control, both internal and external to be efficacious. Not only in political but also in other public spheres, women are always subdued.

In comparison to inactive, politically active, women have a different background. In most cases their politicisation occurs in the family which served as a spring board to enter politics. But most of the politically active women have little dominance over their male counterparts which is symbolic of their inefficacy. Leaving aside Mrs. Indira Gandhi, Mayati in U.P., Jayalalitha in Tamil Nadu, Vasundhra Raje in Rajasthan and Smt. Nandini Satpathy in Orissa and their like other women ministers have little dominance over their male counterparts. Even the portfolios held by women ministers in the central council of ministers were not very important. Till 1956 the Health portfolio had always been given to the sole women Cabinet Ministers. In 1957 External and Home affairs were assigned to two female deputy ministers. In 1958 economic affairs and in 1959 Finance portfolios gives to women ministers with no independent charge. In 1964 Information and Broadcasting, and social security portfolios were assigned. During the Prime Ministership of Mrs. Gandhi, she had the portfolios of Atomic energy, External affairs, Planning etc. During her Prime Ministership Law, Civil

Aviation was assigned to women ministers. Their representation almost remained disproportionate to their strength in the Legislature. Till 1961 there were three female ministers. From 1962 to 1969 there were five ministers. From 1970 it decreased to four and in 1973 only three were included. Their number cause to 2 in 1977 and remained as such till 1979. In 1983 there were five, in 1984 there were four women Ministers. More recently in present Govt. of India led by Dr. Manmohan Singh, pathetically women ministers are given less important portfolio. His predecessor, Vajpayee is also no exception.

Katz and Lazrasfeld found not only that upper status women are more likely to be political opinion leaders than lower status but that women with small families are also more likely than women with large families to be opinion leaders of this kind. Leisure increases outside contact and involvement in activities outside ones family and home. Similarly financial security also helps in involving in politics. Elizabeth Douvon and Economic viability of upper class women can be accounted for higher rates of 'political participation'. Low social status due to low education and income result in lack of self-confidence. Therefore, their participation, in politics is comparatively less." The lack of self-confidence in the lower-status groups is, in fact, reflected in the lower sence of political effectiveness.... and interest in politics follows the same class pattern. Lack of self-confidence is, more over, associated with fewer groups membership, in as much as a refusal to join parch-teacher organisation or even fraternal groups. Where persons of different status mingle often is the product of fear of how one will appear to others of somewhat higher status.

The markers of participation are voting, working for political parties, influencing the authorities by pressure tactics which require sufficient knowledge of the political system and the power holders. Voting is a regularised procedure for chosing leaders and transference of power. But as an index to measure political participation it is inadequate, particularly

in India where elections are largely manipulated. Electorate turn out is due more to mobilisation than political awareness. It is seen during elections that female electorate turnout is more compared to men. Similarly rural women vote more frequently than urban women. But their participation is not qualitatively superior, neither do they excel in education, awareness and exposure compared to their urban counterparts.

Psychological Disposition and Internal Control

Efficiency being a psychological disposition, the traits in women which influence participation will help understanding their control over themselves and the environment. Certain motives of a person create interest in an area which he or she pursues with enthusiasm. When the need for participation in politics is considered, most of the needs of women are fulfilled in the private world rather than the public. Certain problems which are discussed in male gatherings with seriousness are solved before she is aware of it. Problems like the rising cost ofl iving, transportation, taxation are perceived as personal problems rather than as social problems. Resultantly, they do not assign much importance to its repercussion on the Society.

Alport has defined twenty-one variables in a personality, one of which is political interest. Laswell states pursuit of 'power' to be the essential base of political man. The conception of political type is that some personalities are power seekers, searching out the power institutions of the society into which they are born and devoting themselves to the capture and use of government. A person with power motive attaches great importance to imposing himself on others." Leaving aside the female gladators in politics, generally women have little interest in politics. This is one of the reasons for confining themselves in the domestic circle, imposing their will on the family members but leaving the males to involve in the public sphere. It is observed that power motive is an essential determinant for involving oneself in politics. He must have sufficient skill to master over others. However dominant women may be in their private or non-political world, generally

they are less power oriented in the public (political) field. As pursuit of power is intrinsically related to interpersonal skill and generally women lack political efficacy, they are much less successful in influencing decisions and participate actively.

Self-esteem, rises and falls with the 'fortunes' of ego involved objects. The socially determined sources of self-esteem have been termed 'status' and the individually determined sources as 'self-integrity.' In reinforcing self-esteem from these sources, people fall back upon rationalisation as protective devices, as well as upon repose, reception, withdrawal, denigration of the opposition and so forth. An individuals' desire for personal status is insatiable. Whether we say that he longs for prestige, for self-respect, autonomy or self-regard a dynamic factor of this order is apparently the strongest of his drives." Irrespective of being a male or female human life is devoted to the protection of ego and the promotion of the self. In a very important sense, life is devoted to the protection of the ego, 'the care and promotion of the self. Nor is the definition of what is ego or ego involved is confined to the body: or even to wholly personal attributes. Contratily it tends be extended to people symbols, ideas and objects with is in some way are associated with some aspect of the person. The selection of the ego involved objects is the product both of the social designation and ideosyncratic personal preference, the operation of the two factors making for individuality with a common framework.

Remarkably, self-esteem of woman is not enhanced by political involvement particularly in India. Ego gratifiation of women in India is not contigent upon political pursuit. The self-esteem that women commands the domestic sphere in other public activities is not attached to political participation. During and after the freedom movement women exhorted to participate in politics which had a different attribute and objective then. It was a matter of principle, an ideal and with a motive to sacrific that people joined the movement. Though the number of educated women was very few and society was more traditional plunging into politics was held with high

esteem. Present day politics has become a murky profession where personal rewards, are adhered to rather than principle. Women generally attach high regard to morality and profession devoid of this attribute appears less alluring for them. Political objects become ego-involved for a person whom (a) society invests them with status attribute accepted by the individual and (b) whenever the individual identifies with such objects in the pursuit of private ends.

The office holders attach status and esteem to political office but majority express inability to challenge the external environment. Party members and workers are still few in number to challenge the environment. To assert oneself against the environment is associated with controlling one's internal impulses and external events which is gradually acquired by an individual. Even this gradual acquisition of ego strength is not the form with all human beings.

Women in India, assign a major role to luck, chance, and powerful others which control external environment. They assume that mastering one's destiny is difficult which is a reflection of ego weakness. The dominant person tends to be 'stronger' in 'face to face' situation..... to have feelings of safety, security, personal rightous and self-confidence. Political organisations are predominated by males where female have little scope to assume leadership. The attributes required for asserting oneself and assuming leadership roles are contingent upon personal control with few exceptions women lack in the psychological traits and therefore, less of political involvement and play minor roles compared to their male counterparts when politically involved.

But recently a change is being noticed. With the expansion of education women even from lowest strata of society are gaining political consciousness. Let us hope for a better and bright future.

REFERENCES

1. Allport, "The Psychology of Participation," *Psychological Review*, 52 (1945), p. 122.

2. Allport, G.W., *Personality, A Psychological Interpretation* (New York; Holt, 1937), pp. 29-30.
3. Centril, Hadly, *The Psychology of Social Movements* (New York; Wiley, 1941), pp. 30-52.
4. Erikson, E.H., *Childhood and Society* (New York; Newton 1950), pp. 260-70.
5. Katz Elitr and Lazrasfeld Paul F., *Personal Influence* (Glancoe, Ill: Free Press, 1955), pp. 273, 291.
6. Lipset, Segmaour M., "The Sources of Radical Right," in Danniel Bell, ed. The Nic.
7. Reisman, David, "Orbits of Tlerance Interviews and Elits," *Public Opinion Quarterly*, 20 (1950), pp. 49-73.

E3

Women and Politics: An Intellectual Discourse

The present chapter explores the pros and cons of etiology of women and politics. The reproduction of this long discourse, will benefit the serious readers immensely in penetrating the core of the feminism. In bringing feminist imperatives to a critical exploration of the tradition of Western political thought and going on to locate the insights and concerns of political theory in the heart of the feminist enterprise, we implicitly and, at times, explicitly indicated that we had an alternative to offer which would forge links between the Western tradition and feminist thinking in a way that served to illumine the past, instruct the present, and presage a reconstructive future. WIn our parlour age it is not enough to critique what is, vital as that task may be. The political thinker, as witness, must imagine a livable future, must proffer coherent proposals for reordering our public and private worlds if he or she is to make a claim on the attention of others. One telling critique of Marxist politics, for example, has been its "persistent readiness to allow intensity of moral distaste for a present state of affairs to excuse a weakening of the determination to understand (or even to reflect seriously upon) the causal properties of the future social order with which it is hoped to supplant the present." That criticism is justifiably levelled at much contemporary feminist politics: too often the present is assailed but proposals for the future are neither specified with coherence nor consistent with one another or the ends being sought. Wildly visionary futures are portrayed but no cogent way to move from the horror of the present to the heaven of the future is provided.

We have no heaven to offer perhaps because we have not discovered in ordinary reality the irredeemable hell many feminists have seen in present social arrangements and experiences. Yes, there is much that is unconscionable and cries out for relief. There is much that is ugly, sordid, and violent; tragic, pathetic, and heartbreaking. There are events that arouse horror, outrage, and disbelief. There are realities that encourage cynicism, disconcern and despair. At times one is overwhelmed by madness and corruption in high places and like a wrathful, avenging god one would topple the secular temple, call down lightning upon the unjust, humiliate the arrogant who gamble with the lives of the innocent, and rid the world of opportunistic ruthlessness, whether it calls itself democratic, socialist, revolutionary, or holy. Nothing, at such times, seems sweeter than vengeance. Nothing, at such times, seems more fitting than cold wrath. Nothing, at such times, seems more enchanting a prospect than an "apocalypse now." It is at precisely such times that the political imagination must come to life and the moral sentiments awaken from slumber not simply as personal exigencies, to save oneself from cynical escapism and corrupting delusions of death and glory, but as a *public imperative and responsibility*.

Our century is piled high with bodies: victims of the deadly politics of the right (fascism), the left (Stalinism and other so-called Marxist regimes that create burying grounds and call them people's republics), and the less immediately fatal but ultimately coarsening and life-denying politics of liberal complacency and benign neglect. The task of the political imagination must be to serve as witness for the victims, all those the final solutions, ends-of-history, and politics-as-usual either eliminate, manipulate, degrade, or deny, without at the same time falling into a political identity, language, and mode of practice that sentimentalises their victimization and repeats the terras of their degradation. From the Biblical warning that those who live by the sword shall perish by it to the rock group Who's expression of postrevolutionary working-class cynicism, "Meet the new

boss/just like the old boss," warnings have been issued to social-changers and their would be beneficiaries to eschew a politics of violence and coercion, to be suspicious of false promises, and to be unremittingly skeptical of boldly stated but thinly defended claims. Feminists and their political constituents, being human, are no more exempt than anyone else from the lures of vanguardism or the false comfort of delusory faith.

Those with a need for absolute certainty must force intractable human material into the mold of their hubris in order that life mesh with abstraction. The search for what is called the "totality" is uncomfortably close to this century's term for unmitigated political terror, totalitarianism. Life is too various, diversity too dear, to give it over to a single definition or purpose. There are no ultimate solutions though there are those arrogant or dangerous enough to attempt them. In calling for a reconstruction of public and private. We do so within the frame of a theory and a politics of limits, not because We can envisage only limited possibilities from politics but precisely the opposite: because we know that politics too easily becomes an engine of limitless, destructive possibilities as the face of Leviathan dons an executioner's mask. For feminism to save its soul it can have nothing to do with the creation of a new order that *requires* sacrificial victims for its achievement.

We must actively urge individuals to act in common to agreed upon and worthy ends. We must unalterably and with a clear voice oppose ends that are unworthy, that in the name *of future* justice or freedom destroy human beings in the present. Without illusions, we are neither world-weary nor abject. As for charges of pessimism, we offer Camus's response as my own: "The idea that a pessimistic philosophy is necessarily one of discouragement is a puerile idea." Part of the struggle involves reflecting on whether our current misery and unhappiness derive entirely from faulty and exploitative social forms that can, and therefore must, be changed or whether a large part of that unhappiness derives

from the simple fact of being human, therefore limited, knowing that one is going to die. In these matters and others, as Wittgenstein put it, "Light dawns gradually over the whole." Every reflective person who has struggled to see more clearly knows the truth of this saying. Light dawns, but only if one persists. The discussion which follows is divided into two sections in which we attempt to discover and illumine for others a number of vexing, interconnected puzzles and problems from a stance informed by feminism and political thought. In the first section we take up the question of feminist theory and the project of creating a reflective feminist discourse. The activity of theory is, literally, about seeing. *Theorein, the* Greek word from which our own derives, meant to watch or to look at. "Seeing" is a complex activity, transformed, like mind, over time. Although it is impossible to reproduce precisely one's own process of seeing for others, we shall try by looking first at the activity of the theory itself. In the second part of this chapter, we move imaginatively from particular to universal, from concrete to abstract, from public to private as we envisage a reconstructive ideal of public and private.

The terrain traversed in this chapter is not *about* political theory but is itself an example of what it means to *do* political theory in our time. Too often scholars in the field of political theory devote themselves entirely to the task of probing the texts of "the fathers." Too often this yields works of filiopiety rather than original rethinking and confronting the political problems we face at present. We are not urging that we kill the fathers but that we recognize that we cannot remain forever in the house of the fathers. Lincoln said it best:' 'The dogmas of the quiet past are inadequate to the story present.... As our case is new, so we must think anew, act anew. *We must disenthrall our selves*" (emphasis mine). Although the past was by no means quiet for our ancestors in political theory, that past, as dogma, is a refuge for us now compared to the storm of the present: hence our call to disenthrallment.

POLITICAL DISCOURSE AND ITS DISCONTENTS

This is what we need: we need an account of women's liberation which can incorporate the self-understanding of the female subject as an essential feature of its overall logic of explanation. We need to be able, cogently, to articulate the bases and steps in the creation of female identity, public and private. We need a way to explore female speech and language along public and private vectors. We need to create a mode of political thinking that helps women redescribe social reality from a vantage point that allows for, and sustains, critical reflection. We need to conceptualise plausible alternatives. We need to avoid powerful tugs toward repetition of the compulsions of the past, including the sentimentalization and oppressions of women under some new guise. This is a large order indeed.

There is no single, overarching logic of explanation which can do everything for us. Those who make monistic claims fail to distinguish between explaining and interpreting human life in all its diversity and denying or quashing the diversity as they "explain" human life. There are times when we need to examine the individual female subject in her particular social location and probe her inner and outer realities; there are other times when the individual female subject will be submerged within some aggregate category like sex, race, or class, because our theoretical aim is the explanation of systemic or structural features of an overall social order. Psychoanalytic theory can no more account for the political economy of women under capitalism than Marxist economic theory can offer a coherent understanding of women's psychology and sense of self-identity.

The search for the female subject is simultaneously a quest for a form of inquiry that serves the ends of explanation, understanding, and critique along public and private vectors. This means that the theorist must reject out of hand any mode of explanation which requires or sanctions the imposition upon the female subject of the theorist's own views as to who she is, what she wants, and what she should have in advance

of any attempt to probe that subject's self-understanding. To take a human being as the object of political inquiry without patronising, manipulating, or distorting her world must be every critical feminist thinker's concern. Too often those whose chief delights include abstract formulation, as Freud ironically reminded us, wind up treating real "objects," including human beings, as abstractions and treating abstractions as if they, not human beings, had real existence, agency, and importance in the world. One cannot survey the human race from a great and learned distance, proclaiming loudly that one has found the truth for the good of all the nameless, faceless abstractions one has nevery really bothered to take seriously, and go on to provide the account of women's liberation we have called for.

One must first *locate the* female subject in creating a feminist political theory *for* and *about* her. One must refuse to accept the political silencing of women under terms that either take their social position, traditionally a particular, local and concrete one, for granted or label it and move on to other, more "important" matters. One must find out how the female subject in our time sees herself, or would, were she given the opportunity to provide a spoken account of her existence. The feminist political thinker aims to transform her discipline as well as her social world in important ways. This necessitates locating the woman as subject or political and social inquiry, moving away from the abstracted, disembodied "product" of social forces featured in much contemporary social science. This female subject, as the object of inquiry, must be approached as an active agent of a life-world of intense personalization and immediacy.

As the female subject explores her life-world, dimensions of her daily existence which fell previously under the interdiction of silence will be opened to scrutiny. This dynamic of consciousness poses a serious problem for the political analyst: How active and intrusive a part should she play in the process of the self-discovery of others? Dorothy Smith, a feminist sociologist, locates herself at the activist end of a

range of alternatives when she writes: "We might attempt to develop *for* women analyses, descriptions, and understandings of their situation, of their everyday world, and of its determinations in the larger socioeconomic organization to which it is articulated. This is a task the subject cannot undertake alone as the very terms of her privatization and particularity prevent her from making the conceptual linkups Smith would develop *for* her. Smith's approach avoids the arrogant presumption that the analyst, in advance of either seeing or listening to her subjects, can proffer an accurate description of their world. Instead, she promulgates what we shall call a part-whole-part hermeneutic in which inquiry begins with the self-descriptions of subjects in context, a discourse made possible only after silences are broken. This is followed by the analyst's rendering of those self-descriptions in a manner that makes them more widely and generally accessible by assimilating them into a theoretical framework that gives them explanatory power at a more abstract level of understanding. We suggest a third step though Smith does not. The conceptual formulations based upon the subjects' self-interpretations should then be shared with the subjects to elicit whether, on their view, the analysis seems intelligible and responsible, or whether it is distorting in some serious or, most unhappily, demeaning way. This raises many problems, including the force of *resistance* by subjects based on distortions of their own self-understanding, or, simply, on the need to "defend" themselves. These are not easily dealt with but they must be faced, not denied.

There is one final vexation Smith hints at but shies away from confronting and that is: Why should a personalised, localised, particular female subject be brought into the more abstract, rationalised, universal mode? To be sure, the realm of particularity, which we will recast here as the private, exists in a determinate relation with a wider social organization whether private subjects recognize this or not. But the private world also exudes its own values and imperatives in part because it *is* the theater of particularity and everyday concrete meaning. If that mode were suppressed altogether in favour

of the exigencies and demands of abstract personhood and the pull towards rationalization, technological definition, and universalism, who would tend to the little world, keeping alive its life-redeeming joys and tragedies? In other words does Smith, or does any feminist political thinker, really want to so relocate female subjects and reconstruct the matrix of their traditional identities by substituting the terms of universal, bureaucratic socio-economic imperatives that, as women achieve a public identity, they lose this other world and the values imbedded with it entirely?

If we can bear to turn our thoughts to this problem we shall perhaps come close to seeing, perhaps experiencing within ourselves a queasiness or twinge of regret in sympathy with the fears and ambivalences of many women about the feminist movement and a proposed way of being that, it is claimed, shall serve as their liberation, shall "free" them from their domestic prisons. It may help us to understand what the militant activist's single-mindedness disallows: that there are no gains without losses; that assaults on a given order sweep along, in their trail much that makes life livable, diverse, and charming as well as that which makes it exploitative and unjust. And the truth of the matter is that no one can predict the fruits of major social change, though all social changers want their potential constituencies to focus only on the most optimistic possible outcomes.

An illuminating contrast-model to a mode of inquiry that incorporates female self-understanding as central, having both as method and aim helping women become conscious of themselves through a process they actively undertake, is the form of social analysis undertaken by a renowned world-changer, Simone de Beauvoir, in her feminist classic, *The Second Sex*.. At first glance it might seem that de Beauvoir and we are engaged in similar activities: both of us have the modern woman-in-society as our concern: both of us want that woman to alter her inherited and, in some ways, restricting or damaging views of herself; both of us want change in a direction that would transform her world for the better. But

de Beauvoir's analysis emerges from a stance of great distance cast in a mode of disquieting abstractedness. The difference between political inquiry *for* women and de Beauvoir's theory *about* women is apparent when de Beauvoir chooses as her central terms of social description and analysis Sartrian categories which have no meaning in ordinary discourse, terms that are unavailable to social participants themselves. To be sure, the woman who makes her way through de Beauvoir's lengthy tome may pick up the language of "Immanence" and "Transcendence." But if she then wishes to state her case to others, to persuade them of her point of view rather than pummel them with her superior knowledge, she *must* be able to make that case in terms of personal, political, and social discourse that are commonly shared.

Rather than beginning with the female subject's self-understanding, de Beauvoir labels her subject by fixing her in that cement she calls Immanence, a variant on Sartre's Being-in-itself (not, by the way, the Being-to-be). With Sartre, she identifies woman with nature, the practice-inert, the sphere of Immanence. This world of everyday life is first treated as an abstraction and then condemned as a morass, a bog, noncivilization. De Beauvoir contrasts Immanence with all that is light, worthy, civilised the work of men!), the realm of Transcendence (Sartre's; Being-for-itself, definitely the Being-to-be). De Beauvoir's subjects are pictured in a matrix of the local and particular. But rather than framing her analysis from the point of view of the subject's self-understanding, de Beauvoir compares them unfavourably to men who undertake "free projects" in the realm of Transcendence Although de Beauvoir declares women free and autonomous a priori (a metaphysical construction having no bearing of their social identities, a noumenal category, sundered from phenomenal reality), she consigns them to a region declared to be one of determination, totally lacking in autonomy."

De Beauvoir launches volleys against her subjects in the of liberating them. Women are consistently and invidiously

pared with men. For example, de Beauvoir approvingly cites the claims of one male writer who hit upon the notion that the body of man had its own integrity and "makes sense" apart from woman; however, the woman's body, what Sartre called women's "unfortunate anatomy," is a body that " 'seems wanting in significance by itself." This narcissistic male view, reminiscent of the Greek misogynists who saw women as misbegotten men and not fully human, is repeated by de Beauvoir as a serious piece of wisdom rather than probed as the male's "advertisement for myself."

As the price of admission to the realm of Transcendence de Beauvoir's female subjects must shuck off their female identities. Civilization de Beauvoir declares to be male and men its essential parts; women, the flip side of the coin, lie outside civilization and are inessential. The formulation is an existentialist recasting of the Aristotelian typologies of "necessary conditions for" and "integral parts of." The reader who objects that our critique of de Beauvoir is misplaced because she is simply describing "what is" has failed to appreciate the insistence, argued and exemplified throughout this book, that description is never from a neutral point of view. Instead, description may be framed from a moral or critical point of view that allows us to question and to probe "what is," or description may be framed from an abstract, all-knowing point of view that explicitly aims to liberate humanity but in the process demeans, labels, or undermines human dignity, self-identity, and the social bases of our humanity.

De Beauvoir's choice of descriptive terms carries moral and political implications for the female subject she characterises as stuck in Immanence within a body "'wanting in significance by itself." De Beauvoir adopts a set of terms that silences the vast majority of women in advance or gives them an implicitly coercive alternative. They can either speak the language of Immanence, in which case they remain outside civilization babbling, as it were, from the bog, or they can begin to speak in the voice of civilization which is a *male* voice, framed by, for, and about males. Given these alternatives, de Beauvoir

enjoins women to throw off the veils of Immanence, enter the world of Transcendence, and become as Sartrian men who declare that the world is theirs to do with as they will. Rather than a slow process of self-discovery and reflection on the terms of their life-worlds, de Beauvoir holds out the lure of the world-historic figure as a way to force women to recognize the pettiness of their own existence. She proclaims:

> The men we call great are those who—in one way or another—have taken the weight of the world upon their shoulders; they have done better or worse, they have succeeded in re-creating it or they have gone down; but first they have assumed that enormous burden.... To *regard the universe as one's own... one must belong to the cast of the privileged: it is for those alone who are in command to justify the universe by changing it...* (emphasis added).

Her adoption of the male mode as normatively superior is complete when de Beauvoir urges women to take up the instrumental use of sex now practiced by "busy men." A busy woman, she writes, one who "expends her energy, who has responsibilities, who knows how harsh is the struggle against the world's opposition, needs—like the male—not only to satisfy her physical desires but also to enjoy the relaxation and diversion provided by agreeable sexual adventures." Women are urged to maintain their dignity throughout, however.

This celebration of male heroes, sexual instrumentalism, and modes of male-defined identity is framed within a work that concludes with a call for the "complete economic and social equality of women"; the precondition of that equality is the "inner metamorphosis" of women. The problem is that de Beauvoir knows in advance the trajectory of that metamorphosis. Like the terms under which Plato admitted female Guardians, de Beauvoir's require female self-denial.

De Beauvoir's capitulation to silencing terms and female self-denial is painfully evident in her discussion of "The Data of Biology" which opens *The Second Sex,* She holds female embodiment at arm's length as if it were repugnant to her

and distant from her. Woman is portrayed as "the victim of the species." Man is portrayed as imbued with a sense of virile domination that extends to reproductive life (for example, the life of the male is "transcended" in the sperm, and so on). The female subject, simply by being born female, suffers an alienation grounded, not as Marx would have it, in oppressive and exploitative social structures and arrangements, but in her biological capacity to bear a child. Pregnancy is described in foreboding terms as the alienation of woman from herself (the woman is not "transcended" through her procreative capacity as the male is through his sperm).

The fetus is characterised as a "tenant," a parasite upon the mother's existence. Menstruation is horrific and disgusting. Nursing merely exhausts the mother—de Beauvoir nowhere acknowledges that it, or any other female reproductive or nurturant activity have meaning or profound emotional importance to and for the subject herself. One particular statement reveals the depth of de Beauvoir's loathing, projected onto all of female humanity. She calls a woman's breasts "mammary glands" that "play no role in woman's individual economy: *they can be excised at any time of life*" (emphasis mine). A male physician who expressed such cavalier disregard for the sensibilities of a woman about to undergo the ordeal of mastectomy would, correctly, be denounced for his sexism. No analyst who approaches her subject from the stance of abstractedness, peevishness, and disdain evinced by de Beauvoir could begin to truly see and to hear her subjects as they broke silence on matters of particular concern to them—for women this invariably includes, as thousands of women in consciousness-raising learned, reflecting upon one's body and one's feelings of socially induced shame or repugnance about that body, and how to attain a sense of biological integrity through self-affirmation, not denial.

Rejecting de Beauvoir's approach for one that incorporates the self-understandings of female subjects as central does not, in itself, tell us what political discourse is for. How can political discourse embody as an essential feature, a means

and an end, a process of arriving at transformative knowledge of self and other—truth not as a thing-in-itself abstractly couched but as the action creation of meaning between two or more people? If the search for truth or meaning is not to replicate those approaches, whether feminist or not, in which passive subjects simply receive "truth" as uncovered by some expert or visionary, it must be construed as a dynamic, social search for transformative and reconstructive knowledge.

This suggests another rich way feminists, particularly those concerned with feminism as a process or a means as well as an end, may draw upon psychoanalytic discourse, grounded as it is in a theory which embodies a moral and theoretical imperative of truth-telling and truth-seeking. For example: Wolfgang Loch, a psychoanalyst and philosopher, describes truth as the active *construction* of something that makes sense and permits the subject to rely on it, to live a life wide-awake, not sleep-walking. To reach this truth, with its profound implications for political discourse and political action, a particular sort of dialogue that is itself a feature of the truth that finally emerges must be undertaken. The means of truth-seeking cannot be bifurcated from the ends of truth-construction. For Loch, this dialogue's vital end is to reach a truth from, by, and for the subject-herself, but within a social frame of uncoerced communication which becomes, as in the Hebrew tradition; a rock to stand on. This dynamic process includes but is not merely interpretation, the drawing out of a hidden meaning; instead, it implicates both subject and analyst (or political thinker by analogy) in the construction or reconstruction of truths whose trajectory aims toward the future.

This means that political discourse aimed at the construction of new meanings, at enabling subjects to become more intelligible to themselves, must take place within an arena in which human speech or discursive reflection is undominated, uncoerced, un-manipulated, in an approximation of Jurgen Habermas's "ideal speech situation." The salience of this ideal for a critical account of women's liberation is that it offers a motive *for* that liberation framed from the

point of view of the individual subject as one actively seeking meaning and purpose. This search will be distorted if it occurs under manipulative, coercive, or silencing conditions. The implication for political discourse is simply this: the political thinker who wants to find out "the truth" must approximate as closely as possible in her work the uncoercive terms of the psychoanalytic dialogue as a locus of "ideal speech." The relevant features of the "ideal speech situation" for political discourse include the repudiation of shaming, guilt-inducing moralisms, and the absence of abstracted assessments. To those who insist that our terms would make political discourse nearly impossible, we would argue that the notion is offered up as a worthy picture of reality and as a standard against which, we can assess our own efforts. Although we can never realize perfectly the "ideal speech situation," our construction of transformative meaning through political discourse requires such an ideal as a mode of inquiry and an end in itself.

The feminist analyst who takes the self-understanding of the female subject as a central feature of political inquiry and goes on to affirm an ideal of noncoercive human discourse as a touchstone from which to assay silencing considerations, is, for example, ideally equipped to explore critically the anti-abortion Right-to-Life movement in the United States. This movement has encouraged thousands of never-before-political women to take an active role in organizing, marching, leafletting, petitioning, politicking, maintaining vigils, sitting-in, lobbying Congress, even heckling and harrassing (though much less of that than feminist targets of Right-to-Lifers claim from their own spirit *of parti pris).* Right-to-Life women have been assailed by many feminists, or those sympathetic to the pro-abortion or "pro-choice" position from a stance of superiority and portrayed stereotypically as reactionaries and right-wingers; ignorant dupes of the Catholic Church; fanatics; misguided and male-identified opponents of progress, enlightenment, and all that is rational and good. One recent article by a feminist on the "pro-life" movement termed them "neo-fascists."

We are not suggesting that there is no truth in the charges lodged by feminists and their supporters. But we are saying, and this is the crux of the matter: without allowing Right-to-Life women to speak the truth as they understand it; without engaging them from a stance that respects their human possibility for the creation of meaning through uncoerced dialogue, which requires of the investigator a stance of empathy, openness, and a willingness to entertain and explore alternatives she may not share, we will continue to treat them in distorted, presumptuous, and prejudicial ways (there is a vein of anti-Catholic prejudice to be found in pro-choice characterizations of Right-to-Lifers as robotised minions of the Church).

A sympathetic willingness to see and to hear the Right-to-Life woman and understand her position as she herself perceives it as the beginning point, remember, not the end point of critical exploration, prompts a second suggestion for theoretical investigation. It would be enlightening to explore feminist orthodoxies on the abortion question by determining whether feminists share the arguments for abortion made in the case of *Roe versus Wade* which guaranteed abortion rights. This exploratory inquiry would probe feminist self-understanding on the abortion question; whether, for example, this self-understanding includes a vision of the human being as a possessor of self, cut off from ties that bind her to a community or tradition, or a commitment to a militant notion of privacy that undercuts any serious political claims launched from a moral point of view by deploying a notion of tolerance construed as the insistence that the private opinions of others can exert no claims over us. Our point is that the proabortion and Right-to-Life positions may both be unreflectively held and thus require probing and exploratory reexamination. Our further point is that the current *political* situation that pits these two groups of women against one another as implacable and hostile foes embodies the mirror image of the ideal speech situation: it is a highly charged milieu riddled with coercive, manipulative, and silencing considerations on both sides in which each accuses the other of placing herself

against liberation, justice, equality, choice, freedom on the one hand, and morality, human community, family ties and values, and the reaffirmation of the sanctity and importance of human life or potential life as unassailable on the other.

Finally, one must find a way to move coherently from self-understanding and the social construction of reality and meaning, to critique. Brian Fay offers a set of criteria for a critical account of women's liberation. We have drawn on that account for our own purposes. Fay's arguments are dense and we shall offer a condenzation of their central features. First, he argues that ideas help to make us and our social worlds what we and they are. Second, he claims that any action by a human agent is motivated and can be interpreted. Third, and related to the first two, that it is through action—Fay stresses *political* action, presuming, as he does, that politics has some primary claim on us among diverse human activities—that human beings reveal themselves to one another; therefore, such action is essential to becoming and being seen as a person. Fourth, that our actions, ideas, and the activities which flow from them may, in trivial or important ways, be muddled, distorted, or confused. Fifth, and Fay's bedrock, that there are real human needs, as well as wants, purposes, intentions, and desires; that these needs have motivating force; that they can be distorted and damaged; that they are essential even if distorted; finally, that they serve as the presuppositional basis for *any* form of social existence and, it follows, for transformative social possibilities as well.

To make good on his tall order. Fay begins by insisting, as we did in our critique of de Beauvoir, that the knowledge claims of the critical thinker must in principle be translatable into ordinary language and that it must be possible for those claims to be grounded in the human subject's self-understanding even if one's critical aims are, finally, to persuade these subjects to conceive of themselves and their situations in different ways. Fay resolutely rules out vanguardism as a stance which can have a place in a critical venture from a

moral point of view. His critical posture includes neither coercion nor manipulation of the lives of those he is struggling to alter. Fay's social theorist is a kind of educator, who draws upon an image of the "ideal speech situation" as a contrast to coercive and manipulative models and goes on to connect understanding and critique to human potentialities and democratic aims.

The dimension of Fay's account we shall look at more closely here is his notion of "ideology critique," the process of unmasking the distorted modes of self-understanding and probing the twisted forms of self-identity of his subjects. Ideology critique is a central pillar in Fay's proposed agenda for a critical theory of women's liberation, for any such theory must articulate the ways in which a sexist social order has damaged and deformed individual women, and go on to clarify the ways in which they, and it, can be changed and liberatory possibilities opened up.

The most provocative dimension of Fay's ideology critique is his insistence that ideology is never merely or simply a distortion or falsehood, but that expressions of ideology, like neurotic symptoms to the psychoanalyst, are clues to and features of a complex structure comprised of manifest and latent, apparent and more deeply rooted exigencies. No analyst who disregarded a symptom as the expression of a totally false belief (for example, the conviction on the part of a patient that his left ear had fallen off though it was demonstrably attached to his head), to be ignored as he treated the disorder, would get very far. The symptom, like all our beliefs however muddled, inconsistent, incoherent, magical, or merely misinformed, is our entree to underlying motivations, authentic needs, and less distorted views of self and others. The political theorist must listen carefully and observe sympathetically for everything that individuals do, say, or believe is important and has meaning. This uncovering of true or less distorted meaning, ideology critique, is a process of reclamation.

An example may clarify this important point. Many women, particularly feminists, find a phenomenon which calls itself "total womanhood" shocking, stupid, even repugnant and an expression of female "false-consciousness." The movement's founder, Marabel Morgan, wrote a book in 1973 called *The Total Woman* that became one of the ten bestsellers of the decade (by the end of 1979 103,000 hardcover and 2,700,000 paperback copies were in print). The "total woman" movement appears to enlist thousands of restless, unhappy, bored, confused, dissatisfied, and resentful women who are then encouraged to "talk out" their miseries after which they are offered a prescription for ending their woes. From a critical, feminist perspective the cure looks suspiciously like a heavy dose of what helped to make the woman miserable in the first place. Women are enjoined to become "happy housewives" as well as seductive sexpots, to approach every vexation with an understanding smile, a soothing voice, and a boundless capacity for selflessness. Ignored, so far as we can tell, by social thinkers and condemned by feminists, we can only hazard plausible guesses as to *why* so many women have signed up to become "total women's what meaning this movement offers that was previously denied them and how it has helped them to attain a self-identity they can use as the basis for living their lives.

A critical inquiry into the total women" would draw out from its participants their own motivations as these propelled them into the movement. To presume that the "total woman" ideology is *thoroughly* debased would be not only a bad beginning point that would preclude a sympathetic stance for listening to participants, but also a way to do social theory that is presumptuous. If, with Fay, we see ideology as a clue to underlying meaning and truths, investigation of "total womanhood" could help us assay the hopes, fears, desires, aims, anxieties, boredom, purposelessness, confusion, or despair that have spurred so many to seek to become "total women." These beliefs and attitudes, uncovered through dialogue and probing, would be taken seriously. Finally, it

might be possible to persuade a "total woman" of the contradictory or inconsistent nature of the beliefs she espouses, in part because life in modern society is such that no woman could ever live up to the "total woman" ideal or find a secure locus for herself and social identity 'within it. This is a possibility, but it demands as a preliminary step encouraging the subject to reach down into her own self-understanding and to draw out aspects of her own social situation. In this way we may come to see the structural pressures on her family and herself and how these became implicated in her felt misery and her desire to change herself.

If she decided, after revealing herself in speech, and having another revealed to her who held a different view of women in modern society, that what "fulfilment" is supposed to mean for the "total woman" and the organization of contemporary social life were fundamentally at odds, the onus of her restlessness would undergo a shift to consideration of those social forces that lay at the basis of her own confusion. If she did not move from self-understanding to critique, it would not be the theorist's prerogative to compel or manipulate her in any way. Although on the basis of tests of coherence, internal consistency, and plausibility, the political thinker may have the better case, if that case isn't accepted by the subject whose life-world and self-identity it aims to interpret, explain, and move, towards transformation, to coerce agreement would subtly but irreparably undermine the connection between means and ends the critical thinker must preserve. One recalls Eugene O'Neill's "The Iceman Cometh" and Mickey's dogged and fanatical insistence that his illusion-ridden comrades learn to face the painful truth about themselves and their situation. The result is disaster. Some illusions may be necessary, for some people, at some times, just to keep on living.

RECONSTRUCTING THE PUBLIC AND PRIVATE

The readers can be asked to picture in their minds' eyes, a time long ago and far away, the scene described by Richard

E. Leakey and Roger Lewin in *Origins*. Perhaps this passage may serve as a benchmark amidst the confusions and tumult of the present.

> ....from the Shanidar Cave in the Zagros Mountain highlands of Iraq.... on a June day *some sixty thousand years ago a man was buried* in unusual circumstances.
>
> The humidity of the cave was far from favourable for preserving the bones of the dead man; but pollen grains survive very well under these circumstances, and researchers at the Musee de L'Homme in Paris who examined the soil around the Shanidar Man discovered that *buried along with him were several different species of flowers*. From the orderly distribution of the grains around the fossil remains, there is no question that the flowers were arranged deliberately and did not simply topple into the grave as the body was being covered. It would appear that the man's family, friends, and perhaps members of his tribe had gone into the fields and brought back bunches of yarrow, cornflowers, St. Barnaby's thistle, groundsel, grape hyacinths, woody horsetail, and a kind of mallow (emphasis added).

This deliberate burial, with its nonutilitarian sensibility and delicate specificity, is described by Leakey and Lewin as an act by human survivors that "betrays a keen self-awareness and a concern for the human spirit." Later, the coauthors remark that the sociality of human beings runs like a vital thread through our most distant origins. The human being, they declare, is "an animal with its own unique reasons for living in communities." What all this means is not simply that we are social beings but that we are, profoundly, beings with certain needs or yearnings of spirit as well as body. We possess an inborn imperative, power as *potentia,* to find and to create meaning.

We begin our final reflections with several presumptions that may be taken as axiomatic though they are neither arbitrary nor the end product of a formal exercise in abstract logic. First, human beings have a need to live with and

among others in relations of concrete particularity, in space, extending over and through time. It we are deprived of such relations we are damaged and distorted in body and spirit. Our second presumption is that human beings, and here the evidence stretches from prehistory through the present, experience an imperative—Freud termed it an epistemic instinct—to discover, to understand, and to create meaning. That drive, too, can be damaged and deflected and to the extent that it is we become less fully human. Clearly those ancestors of ours, as they gathered their offerings of thistle and hyacinth, horsetail and groundsel, had no utilitarian calculus in mind; they didn't plan to eat the flowers and grains nor feed them to animals. No, they scattered these remembrances in orderly fashion over the grave of a loved one: a family member, a tribesman, one of their own. This action can only be explained with references to our presumptions or similar reasons which might plausibly form the basis of human morality and social existence.

In thinking of the present and recasting the future there are those, and one finds feminists in their ranks, who see past epochs as so much human waste, perhaps a remorseless tale of patriarchal horror or pervasive class conflict. They would create a future in which there will be no more of whatever it is that makes human history, for them, a litany of debasement, and the present an unconditional war against enemies. We are not one of these. The struggle over tradition—what is it, how ought we to regard it— is central to reconstructive notions of public and private. Those we disassociate ourself from believe history has no claim upon us at all. There are others to whom tradition embodies sanctity, has unchallenged claims on us, and serves as a sanctuary from the present. Our ideal neither repudiates the present in toto nor seeks, nostalgically, to return to the past but faces the more difficult task of evaluating its claims upon us. Does the fact that a particular social form, the family for example, is traceable to prehistory, all of recorded history, and is present in all known societies, constitute an important claim on us because it can be presumed to express something so

fundamental about human beings that to reject it is either folly or madness? This question cannot be answered abstractly. Rather one must take up evidence from the past, like the burial in the Shanidar Cave, as clues to a vast and awesome mystery that embodies, at one end of a range of alternatives, authentic human imperatives, those basic notions with which this inquiry began.

Stuart Hampshire has sketched a nonutilitarian starting point for reflection on human beings and their universe—we have already cited one clue, 60,000 years old, that human motivations cannot be subsumed within utilitarian categories or calculations—and that is that *every way of life* will be built up on notions of morality that contain "prohibitions, barriers to action, in certain quite distinct and clearly marked areas of action; these are the taking of human life, sexual functions, family duties and obligations, and the administration of justice according to the laws and customs of a given society..... A morality is, at the very least, the regulation of the taking of life and the regulation of sexual relations." Each way of life will embody within its social forms a cluster of basic notions as the moral grounding required, in the first instance, for the creation and sustenance *of any way of life.* Without such a set of moral rules and prohibitions, basic notions and symbolic forms, no *human* society could exist.

The free-floating pictures of human life that emerge from such feminist texts as Firestone's or Daly's present an abstract plan of a society to come that is not threaded through and through with the warp and woof of a set of basic moral notions and prohibitions that tie us to past and present. Thus their pictures of present and future become rhetorical in relation to social and human reality; everything is cast too much in the abstract, is alternately visionary and banal with respect to the concreteness of what is, of what human beings not only are but must in some ways remain. The exercise of the political imagination must take root in those moral concepts and categories in which people think and which serve as the touchstones of respective ways of life. This means one must

repudiate rhetorical claims that the past can be quite overcome and declarations that it must be, in order to preserve the complexity involved in moral reevaluation, in distinguishing between the notions, rules, and prohibitions essential to any way of life and those that embody a *particular ideal of a way of life.* For example, one must distinguish relations between women and men in public and private spheres that one finds, in some ways, destructive and incompatible with an ideal of a way of life, and the inescapability of *necessary* relations between men and women if social life in any form is to survive.

To make these distinctions one must first accept the reality of limiting conditions; one must recognize that we are not thoroughly untrammeled in our imaginings, though we may self-indulgently entertain the view that we are. In this way one not only opens up the possibility for, but accepts the irrevocability of conflict, given our diverse assessments of the moral imperatives embodied in ideas of ways of life. Too often, feminist utopians and revolutionists throw out not the baby *with the* bathwater, but the baby *rather than the* bathwater. That is, they junk all notions of what is essential, of limiting conditions, in the creation of the future by concentrating exclusively on what must, they believe, change in order for women to be "free." They will brook no disagreement for to disagree is to exhibit the poison of "male identification." Yet conflicts involving moral claims are part of what it means to be human. To end all such debates, as some feminists would by articulating a single, overarching lodestone of Truth, is to undermine that restless urge towards the creation of meaning as an ongoing adventure of the human spirit.

Thus when we think about public and private and its reconstruction, if we are to avoid the presumptuous and the abstracted, we are thinking about a multiplicity of moral claims and about competing human values concerning what an ideal way of life ought to be. Such conflict is unavoidable. A harmony of purposes, ends, virtues, and identities is achievable *only* if we so thoroughly erode the bases of human

existence that we willingly engage in radical and destructive social surgery. In our own century, the Nazi and Stalinist experiments have been the most destructive instances of this sort. If every thing, every basis of human existence, every rule and prohibition, not excluding the incest taboo, is "up for grabs," those who unscrupulously grab will inherit the earth and we will no longer have the earth as our inheritance.

The upshot of such reflection is a recognition that each succeeding generation must respect some moral necessities, must have some "taken for granteds," rules without which even the minimal aspects of a human existence that propelled our prehistoric ancestors to place flowers on the graves of their beloved, will be jeopardised. Tradition does have claims on us; history does limit us. But moral debate, hence political conflict, can and should arise concerning competing *ideals* of human existence: these may be debated, rethought, overridden so long as the debate makes reference to, and builds upon, a necessary moral foundation. The horror of fascism was its total overtuning of all fundamental prohibitions. The great emblem of that terror, the symbol of all such exercises in horror and hubris, is the death camp.

It is on the basis of our recognition of the existence of limiting conditions and the inescapability of moral rules in fundamental areas of human existence, together with our presumptions concerning human sociality and the imperative to create meaning that we turn, first, to a reconstructive ideal of the private world. We shall treat the private not in instrumentalist terms, as the necessary condition for some other ideal or end embodying no good or end in itself, nor as a taken-for-granted, nor as something to be overcome in order to attain unity in the ideal state of total social justice, but as a locus of human activity, moral reflection, social and historical relations, the creation of meaning, and the construction of identity having its own integrity.

To talk of an ideal of the private world within the context of contemporary American society is to talk about the family. The family is the linchpin in all visions of future alternatives,

often as something to be reformed or overthrown. It is the institution singled out must frequently by feminists as one of the keys to female oppression. The image which has emerged from feminism's treatment of the family, although shifts are now being signalled, reflects a distortion symptomatic of the diseases of the present it seeks to cure. One of the key symptoms of our present disease— our "legitimation crisis"— is a widespread draining of our social institutions, public and private, of their meaning and significance. In stripping away the old ideological guises that celebrated motherhood yet denigrated women, extolled an ideal of private life yet disallowed parents the means with which to live in decency and with dignity, feminists and other social critics have played a vital role.

But unmasking ideological distortions is not synonymous with constructing an alternative that does not incorporate its own silencing and repressive effects. What reconstructive ideal of the private can serve as an alternative to the romantic ideologies of the past that required and rationalised a picture of women as inferior or as beings engaged in second-rate, albeit necessary activities, and to feminist ideologies in the present that promote the erosion and meaning of private family life in the absence of any viable alternative? To envisage such an ideal one must examine the question on several levels. First, because there are those who adamantly insist the family is not a necessary feature of human life, one must demonstrate coherently that some form of familial existence is a presuppositional feature of social existence. Second, one must go on to articulate a *particular ideal* of family life that does not repeat the earlier terms of female oppression and exploitation. We shall treat the most fundamental level first for it is the foundation of any reflective, reasoned inquiry into the question. We ask readers to return once again to a previous epoch, in this case the eighteenth and early nineteenth centuries. The savants and philosophers of that time, heirs of the Enlightenment, were not timid men. They posed, quite unabashedly, the most fundamental of questions: What is the nature of man? The question admits, as we have seen, of

no easy answers for the human being is, from birth, a being profoundly influenced by culture. How is one to disentangle man's natural nature from his social nature? Few opportunities for direct observation, for what scientists call "controlled experiments" ever present themselves. (Though, in a sense, families and alternatives to families including institutionalization provide constantly powerful evidence with observable results.) Contests raged between those who held to the notion that man in the state of nature was a Rousseauian "noble savage," pure in heart, affectionate, as yet untainted by a corrupt society and those who argued that apart from human social relations there would be no "human" nature at all. The case of "le jeune sauvage de l'Aveyron," the wild boy of Aveyron, promised to help settle, once and for all, the nature of man.

The wild boy of Aveyroa was captured in 1800 in a district of southwestern France. After a series of escapes and recaptures during which a naturalist made a detailed description of him which has survived, the wild boy was placed in the Institute for Deaf Mutes in Paris under the tutelage of Abbe Sicard, an authority on the retraining of the deaf and a member of the Society for Observers of Man which had taken a special interest in the case. The society believed that the wild boy would help to resolve their philosophic speculations concerning human nature, the relationship between nature and nurture, whether there were innate ideas, and so on.

The abbe himself shortly gave up on the wild boy as hopeless. This being who had aroused such initial curiosity and enthusiasm rapidly invited disinterest and disgust. For, rather than the incarnation of Rousseau's noble savage, what those who observed the wild boy discovered was a "disgustingly dirty child affected with spasmodic movements and often convulsions who swayed back and forth ceaselessly like certain animals in the menagerie, who bit and scratched those who opposed him, who showed no sort of affection for those who attended him; and who was in short, indifferent to everything

and attentive to nothing."

At this juncture a remarkable young man, a twenty-six-year-old doctor, Jean-Marc-Gaspard Itard, enters the picture. In 1800 he undertook responsibility' for the wild boy's education and developed a rigorous programme for the approximately twelve-year-old youth who had been deprived of human company, as closely as could be determined, from the age of three on. Those, like the Abbc Sicard, who had given up on the wild boy, insisted that he had been left in the wild because he was an idiot. Itard took precisely the opposite tack: he saw in the wild child one who was an idiot *because* he had been left in the wild. Itard's arduous, painful, finally despairing efforts to educate and humanise the wild boy of Aveyron are among the most poignant records left us from that epoch.

Itard discovered that outside human social relations and cut off from the organizing structure of language, even the most basic human senses of sight, touch, and hearing remain unfocused and unintegrated, centered upon the stomach only. He had to attend to each of Victor's (as the wild boy came to be called) sensory modalities separately—first to arouse or tap them and then to organize them. But with the onset of puberty all these efforts came to an abrupt halt. Unfocused, unbound sexuality proved to be too much; earlier efforts were swamped and the boy regressed back into a "'wild," unsocial, unreachable condition. Itard finally gave up. Victor was turned over to an institution where he lived out the remainder of his less-than-human existence. This extraordinary tale powerfully suggests that outside the bounds of human nurture human beings would not be like the beasts—who are adroit and adept within their habitats—but less-than-human human beings. Our debt to nurture extends even to our most elementary sensory discriminations.

Cut-off from human society and language we could neither identify objects, nor establish categories, nor engage in social relations. But surely, the reader will cavil, no contemporary social critic ever advised that we return to a presocial existence,

ever advocated a new state of nature. Perhaps not, at least not in such terms. But the past fifteen years have seen a number of visions of family-less, asocial existence celebrated. These have taken several forms, including one in which, not having biological, nuclear families, all individuals, including children, would be "free" to look for the best contractual deal in living arrangements. Firestone, for example, egregiously negates any legitimate moral claims of children on others, or moral obligations of adults to children, not only by her strategy for technocratic child-rearing by experts, but by celebrating the "good old days" in which a concept of the child did not exist—and, one might add, in which children were systematically exploited, crushed by back-breaking labour, physically and psychologically abused as a matter of course rather than a matter of concern, and stunted in their human capacities from birth. She romanticises ghetto life because in it black children live unrepressed lives unlike their ap-tight, less fortunate white counterparts. Surely, this is a contemporary version of the state of nature, looking backwards to a mythic golden age in which children were "free from" adults and finding in the present, in a patronising celebration based on racist stereotypes, a state of nature enclave in the midst of the oppression of blacks in the ghettoes of America's cities in which a large minority of our fellow citizens are condemned to unemployment, welfare dependency, marginal existence, and inferior education.

A second variation of the end-of-family ideology grew out of the counterculture commune movement in the 1960s, one to which many social rebels turned as an alternative to the nuclear family. The motivations for these moves lay primarily in restructuring male-female relations and presuming, from a stance lacking in moral concern and reflexivity, that these changes would a fortiori be "good for the children" as the child would be the "child of all" and not the "possession of two." The force of this ideology is apparent in a study on the children of the counterculture in which the authors provide "an overall portrait of children almost uniformly neglected, deprived, and tormented; many are uneducated, disorganized,

and disturbed; a pervasive boredom and lack of joy and serious problems of mal-or undernourishment were prevalent. After such a sad portrait, it comes as a shock to find the authors concluding that communes are a success in child-rearing because they have done away with materialism and competitiveness." This is reminiscent, though it is a far less coherent claim, of Chodorow's insistence that communal alternatives are *presumptively* preferable to private familial child-rearing because they result in less "individualism."

Another claim and aim of social critics in family elimination or radical transformation is an instrumentalist one: in order for other political ends to be achieved. The idea here is that devotion to the family and to private ties and purposes not only takes the edge off radical commitments to change (coopting is the favoured term with which to describe and simultaneously disparage) but also means one is pressed into service by a society that has the family as one of its structural supports. By implication, and here a counterfactual argument is implied, *in the absence of any viable private life public life would be transformed for the better.* We shall take up this claim, as we link public and private, at the conclusion of the chapter.

We begin with a reaffirmation: familial ties and modes of child-rearing are essential to establish the minimal foundation of human, social existence. What we call human capacities could not exist outside a familial mode; for human beings to flourish a particular ideal of the family is necessary. We shall take up that challenge in a moment. But first, the family's status as a moral imperative derives from its universal, pan-cultural existence in all known past and present societies. We are not dealing with a tangential, episodic cultural form but a transhistorical one. To state a presumptive case for familial ties, to argue that they are required to make us minimally human, is *not* to detail the specific forms within which the creation and nourishment of humanity may take place. Aristotle and all the other political theorists down through the centuries who asserted the primacy of politics, and viewed man (the male, at any rate, if not generic humanity)

as preeminently a political animal even as they downgraded or simply took for granted the private sphere, were guilty of a serious distortion. It is the family which "pervades all our perceptions of social reality." It is the family that constitutes our "common humanity," for our use of language, the basis of that humanness, has its origin in family forms. This makes the family "the universal basis of human culture.... As language constitutes the essence of man as a species, and not reason, so the family and not the social order, is the setting that humanises him."

Those who claim that humanization and the creation of identity could be done as well in some alternative to familial ties ignore the counterevidence provided by abandoned, neglected, or abused children, many of whom exist in shells that are families in the formal sense alone; children reared totally in institutions; children separated from their families during critical periods because of war or social-calamity; children neglected under the guise of not "hanging them up" in counterculture communes; together with a vast body of evidence from history, anthropology, social theory and psychoanalytic case studies. To be sure, the feminist political thinker must sift what gets' "packed into" the family as understood by non-or anti-feminist thinkers. But to ignore the evidence because she would alter a familial form in the direction of more egalitarian relations between the sexes is likely to result in a dauntingly optimistic image of the future which feeds on a distortion of the present and a silencing of discourse on vital moral imperatives. This is reminiscent of the suppression of debate on a whole range of issues by nineteenth-century Suffragists under the felt demand that they be both social rebels and "ladies." Feminism, until recently, has tended to view as anti-feminist or, minimally, as suspect, open, reflective discussion of heterosexual ties and eroticism, the needs and identities of children considered as ends-in-themselves and not merely as means, and accounts of the normative meaning and richness of being a parent.

Children will incur an assault to their humanness, an

affront they will know in the tissue of their bio-psychic beings, if they suffer from the diseases of neglect and nonattachment. A being without a presumptive need for attachments of a special kind— concrete, particular, and continuing—*would not suffer distortion and damage if such relations were absent.* Just as Marx's theory of alienation presupposes an ideal of human existence that holds, or would hold, in the absence of damaging exploitative and oppressive social structures, so the knowledge we now have of what happens to children *in the absence of strong, early attachments to specific adult others,* allows us to assert that we are dealing with a categorical imperative of human existence.

If children are to be morally and socially responsible and potentially self-reflective adults, they must be reared in a highly charged emotional setting in which they are loved in a manner that establishes basic trust. This requires the continuing presence of specific beloved others. It is only through powerful, eroticized relations with specific others, parents or their permanent not temporary surrogates, that children will be nurtured and protected in a way that allows their creation of self and other to be structured and mediated by parental care and concern. It is only through the child's internalization of specific others that he or she can later identify with nonfamilial human beings. These powerful early ties serve as the template of conscience that makes possible adult empathy, the qualities of pity and compassion of which Rousseau spoke. These ties cannot emerge, *pace* Plato and Firestone, in abstract, diffuse, nonfamilialised settings. In the absence of special, specific ties, familial feelings cannot be suffused into or displaced throughout a wider social network. The child will have lost the capacity for human identification. Not every neglected and abused child becomes a Charles Manson, but every Charles Manson was an abused and neglected child. "The jail house was my father," Charles Manson cried. For us to ignore these as the rantings of a madman is for us to repress moral reflection on the most basic things of all. One needs a family history to have a social history. As Stanley Hauer was puts it:

> ... the family is morally crucial for our existence as the only means we have to bind time. Without the family, and the inter-generational ties involved, we have no way to know what it means to be historic beings. As a result we become determined by rather than determining our histories. Set out in the world with no family, without a story of and for the self, we will simply be captured by the reigning ideologies of the day.

The child's helplessness, Freud once remarked, is the first stirring of moral motives. Deprivation of deep and profound emotional ties in infancy causes irreparable damage to our later capacities for creating and sustaining human bonds and social concern. If these are not developed very early in life they cannot be reclaimed. The poor wild boy of Aveyron is an extreme case, but every twelve-year-old adolescent who murders without remorse is a stark reminder of this truth: the diseases of nonattachment lead to the inability of the child to modify his or her aggressive impulses and to find "alternative modes of expression that are sanctioned by love." Selma Fraiberg writes: "The distinguishing characteristic of the diseases of non-attachment is the incapacity of the person to form human bonds... the other striking characteristic of such people is their impoverished emotional range. There is no joy, no grief, no guilt, no remorse. In the absence of human ties, a conscience cannot be formed; even the qualities of self-observation and self-criticism fail to develop."

Totally institutionalised forms of child care, or modes that call themselves familial but replicate family ties through hollow, sentimentalised repetition of terms for family relations—"brother," "sister," "family"—rather than a serious attempt to recreate and resituate genuine intergenerational, not simply peer or generation-specific bonds, have damaging effects upon children that result from the diseases of nonattachment. Child-rearing in which children are raised primarily by and within institutionalised structures, perhaps with the family serving an adjunct function, avoids some of the diseases of nonattachment but is more likely to create obedient, oversocialised rule-followers who unquestioningly do their

"duty" and do not challenge authority as adults. To push children prematurely into a group context results in more, not less, pressure for adaptation to conformist pressures given the routinization of tasks, regimentation of schedules, and group-dominant values which underlie these settings in the first place. Children who grow up in institutionalised structures frequently have a diminished capacity forempathic identification with others, for they have "internalised" an abstract, diffuse authority' not amenable to the reality-testing, the tumultuous "with" and "against," "love" and "hate," of parental and sibling attachments.

It is to be thoroughly muddled, confounded in fact, to assume that it is easy to separate out what one sees as the "good" that may inhere in family life from what one decrees "bad," either by eliminating biological familial ties altogether or "recreating" them in quite different social arrangements. To call some abstract structure, or a loose collection of like-minded, unrelated peers "families" is to treat our most basic human relationships frivolously, as mere historic accidents, or as the excreta of oppressive relations having no deep inner logic, meaning, or purpose of their own. "The minimum guarantee for the evolution of the human bond is prolonged intimacy with a nurturing person" or persons. Fraiberg concludes on a solemn note: "But to a very large extent the diseases of non-attachment can be eradicated at the source by ensuring stable human partnerships for every baby. If we take the evidence seriously we must look upon a baby deprived of human partners as a baby in deadly peril. This is a baby who is being robbed of his humanity." The feminist political thinker must similarly ask at what price she would gain the world for herself or other women, utterly rejecting those victories that come at the cost of the bodies and spirits of human infants. Unless this reflexivity is ongoing and central, feminism is in peril of losing its soul.

The feminist concerned with a reconstructive ideal of the private sphere must begin by affirming the essential needs of children for basic, long-term ties with specific others.

Only then should she move to a second level of exploration and challenge by pursuing the creation of her ideal on this moral foundation. The second level begins with the articulation of a rich, concrete description of contemporary social reality. The American feminist who looks at the "real world" finds that families are centrally responsible for rearing children in cur society. We are familial, with, statistics sometimes cited to 'prove" that only seven per cent or only fourteen per cent of American women live in the "ideal-typical nuclear family of husband-earner and wife non-earner with two dependent children." Such figures are misleading if they are taken as evidence that the family is on the way out. They are misleading because they imply that families with a female wage-earner are somehow not families at all. They are misleading because they suggest that those single parent families required by the repressiveness of the welfare system don't count as families. Finally, they are misleading because they take *all* women as the base from which to calculate and this includes millions of unmarried young women who continue to live in their parents' homes; moreover, to cite contestable statistics is not the same as posing serious alternatives. This 'evidence" in family breakdown is frequently cited with glee as "proof" of family decomposition, as if this boded only good for the future. Even if the statistics were unquestionable, one could interpret them as evidence of the extent to which contemporary, capitalist society has so undermined our capacities or our ability to act upon our deepest human imperatives, that it has made the sustenance of rich, long-lasting, cross-generational ties difficult or impossible for many to attain.

The reflective feminist, then, begins her considerations with the important, not trivial, fact that Americans remain committed to family life and that it would require major social coercion and manipulation to destroy that commitment. Those thus committed include children as well as adults. Accounts of the search of displaced, abandoned, or neglected children for "mothers" and "fathers" is one of the most heartbreaking and telling one can imagine of the familial-imperative and the deep, emotional operations of familial

imagery. Studies done by such observers as Robert Coles and Myra Bluebond-Langner demonstrate the pervasive force of "family," either as daily reality or as fond dream, and give powerful evidence of familial commitments. The concrete reality of the lives of American children, their self—and social understanding, includes a devotion to an ideal of the family that sometimes implicates them in criticisms of their own. But the salient point is their affirmation of the ideal to be preferred: it is not a family-less or nonfamilial ideal, but a familial one. The reflective feminist must be as concerned with the concrete existences and self-understandings of children as she is with female subjects. Her mode of theorising and posing alternatives must locate this concern as central.

To attain and affirm an ideal of family life as the locus of humanization is, contrary to certain unreflective radical orthodoxies, to put pressure upon social structures and arrangements, not to affirm them. For to the extent that the public world, with all its political, economic, bureaucratic force, invades and erodes the private sphere, it, not the private world, should he the target of the social rebel and feminist critic. To promote a politics of displacement that further erodes the terms of the private sphere and all that stands between us and a coarse power or market-ridden definition of all of life, is to repress discourse on public, political issues even as one simultaneously takes the symptoms of its destructive effects as thc "good news" that radical change is just around the corner.

It is the isolation and debasement of women under terms of male-dominated ideology and social structures that must be fought, not the activity, the humanising imperative, of mothering, or of being a parent, itself. Too frequently mothers has been overassimilated to what feminists call "the shitwork." Mothers were demeaned under the guise of "liberating them. In many early feminist accounts mothering was portrayed as a condition of terminal psychological and social decay, total self-abnegation, physical deterioration, and absence of self-respect. Women, already victims of an image that denigrated

their social identity under the terms of the male American success ethos, now found themselves assaulted by the very group that would liberate them. "I'm only a mother" is a comment we have heard from many women not engaged in professional activity, and it reflects this socially decreed diminution of self-respect.

Back in the late 1960s a friend and I, struggling with our identities as mothers and graduate students, an anthropologist- and political theorist-in-becoming, decided to attend a feminist group being formed which billed itself as dedicated to transformative purposes in thought and action. At the first session each of us was asked, in turn, to give her reasons for being there, to briefly tell the story of how she came to this place at this time. When our friend's turn came, and she began to speak of her conflict over public and private values, commitments, and purposes, of her guilt and her confusion over whether that quest was a reflection of male-dominated social values, or a genuine response to an ambiguous situation, she was cut off abruptly and publicly shamed with this silencing declaration from the group's "facilitator": "We will have no diaper talk here. We're here to talk about women's liberation." Our friend and we left, for we could not treat our children as abstractions, as nuisances to be overcome, or as evidence of our sad capitulation to the terms of patriarchy. Fortunately, we later found and became part of a consciousness-raising group that did not require, as the price of entry, the disarticulation of our moral sensibilities and the denial of our diverse and sometimes conflicting public and private purposes. We were able to engage in "truth-telling" of a special and powerful kind. It is interesting that many feminists now deny that the prevalent force of feminism was ever— save for a few "fringe lunatics"— antifamilial and see such claims as anti-feminist. This convenient forgetting of the immediate past, sadly, makes such feminists no different from those who want to put Vietnam and other conflicts "behind us." That is another term for repression. That is another way to silence debate.

To affirm a vision of the private-familial sphere as having its own dignity and purpose is to insist that particular experiences and spheres of social relations exude their own values and purposes, and have ends not attainable by, or within, other spheres. To assert the continued necessity of such relations and a particular notion of their reconstructed vitality is to recognize that we are all impoverished if all of life falls under a single set of terms. It is to adopt a perverse version of the Platonic epistemology that calls for other ways of seeing to be suppressed, literally exiled, or taken as inferior when compared with a supreme, powerful way of seeing beyond and above everyday human existence. We are here calling for the *redemption of everyday life,* a recognition of its joys and vexations, its values and purposes, and its place in becoming human. We are embracing what George Steiner calls the " 'personal lexicon' in everyone of us" which "inevitably qualifies the definitions, connotations, semantic moves current in public discourse.... The language of a community, however uniform its social contour, is an inexhaustibly multiple aggregate of speech-atoms, of finally irreducible personal meanings. The element of privacy in language makes possible a crucial, though little understood, linguistic function.... Obviously, we speak to communicate. But also to conceal, to leave unspoken. A world without the possibility for concealment, a world, as the Nazi imperative had it "without shadows," with no hiding places, nor refuge, nor solace, nor alternative to the force of the public-sphere, is a world that invites barbarism or sterility or both. Helene Cixous argues that women's "political urgency" must be "caring about what seems to be of no importance, to be the insignificant, to be the well-known, the familiar..." Compared to the heady power of de Beauvoir's World Historic figures this seems paltry-stuff. But "seems" is not "is" and the fact it seems so indicates our continued enchantment by certain public imperatives, male-created, sustained, and celebrated that we ostensibly would repudiate or alter radically.

If it is the case that women have a distinct moral language, as Carol Gilligan has argued, one which emphasises concern

for others, responsibility, care, and obligation, hence a moral language profoundly at odds with formal, abstract models of morality defined in terms of absolute principles, then we must take care to preserve the sphere that makes such a morality of responsibility possible and extend its imperatives to men as well." If Gilligan finds women's inner lives more complex, and learns that women have a greater ability to identify with others, to sustain a variety of personal relationships and to attain genuine reciprocity in those relationships, and locates these qualities and capacities in women's involvement with families and the protection of human life, we must think about what would be lost if the private sphere erodes further or if we seek to alter our intimate relations entirely.

One moral and political imperative that would unite rather than divide women, that would tap what is already there but go on to redeem and transform it, would be a feminist commitment to a mode of public discourse imbedded within the values and ways of seeing that comprise what Sara Ruddick has called "maternal thinking." Such thinking need not and must not descend into the sentimentalization that vitiated much Suffragist discourse. For women to affirm the protection of fragile and vulnerable human existence as the basis of a mode of political discourse, and to create the terms for its flourishing as a worthy political activity, for women to stand firm against cries of "emotional" or "sentimental" even as they refuse to lapse into a sentimental rendering of the values and language which flow from "mothering," would signal a force of great reconstructive potential. It would require of feminists moves toward those women they now tend to classify, along with men, as "Other." Feminists should be among the first to recognize that individuals who are put on the defensive, made to feel inadequate, as women-as-mothers now feel, will respond in defensive, even reactionary ways unless or until others begin to approach them as ends-in-themselves rather than simply pawns in the game or enemies in the war.

There is, of course, an irritant in the image as we have thus tar presented it, and that is that in order to provide trust and security for their children parents, in turn, must experience trust and security themselves in their relations with one another and with the "outside world." Parents who are frustrated and Demeaned, rendered dependent and helpless in work-life and citizenship, will have difficulty instilling such bedrock belief and ways of being inside their families. Conflicts that originate outside" get displaced "inside," perhaps into the very beast of the family's emotional existence. We know, for example, that the incident of wife and child-battering rises in times of unemployment and economic recession. That is all too often our current reality. What this means is that political thinkers, including feminists, devoted to the family reconstructive mode cannot carry out their supremely important tasks unless or until there are structural changes in American life. That is where the heart of politics and the family" should lie—not in over politicising our most intimate relations and turning the family into the war of all against all to be negotiated by contract, but in fighting the pressures at work from the outside which erode, impoverish, or preclude the Housing of our most basic human ties. Richard Sennett argues that the erosion of a strong public life... deforms the intimate relations which seize people's wholehearted interest." It is to public life and possibilities for its reconstruction that we now turn.

We shall spend somewhat less time discussing a reconstructive notion of the public because it stands in less need of a defense and reaffirmation within feminist political discourse than our besieged sphere of the private. In moves to treat the existence of a particular disjuncture between public and private that has in the past and remains in the present unacceptable to a feminist vision, some feminists have explored alternative societies to ascertain how they interrelate or oppose public and private. Anthropologists have taken the lead in this effort and we shall briefly take up the argument from anthropology, as articulated by Michelle Zimbalist Rosaldo. Then we turn to the tradition of political

theory, examining what we find it necessary to repudiate and important to reclaim. We conclude with an exercise of the political imagination that "dwells in possibility," the possibility of what we shall call the "ethical polity."

Rosaldo uses the term "domestic" to refer to the institutions and modes of activity organized around mothers and children. "Public refers to activities, institutions, and forms of associations that link, rank, organize, or subsume particular mother-child groups" within a larger, frequently overarching framework. Rosaldo insists that examination of these twin loci provides the "necessary framework" for evaluating male-female roles in society, an insistence we share from our own perspective as a political thinker. Rosaldo's anthropological model leads her to conclude that women's status "will be the lowest in those societies where there is a firm differentiation between domestic and public spheres of activity and where women are isolated from one another and placed under a single man's authority in the home," a conclusion we would not quarrel with. But then she adds that "perhaps the most egalitarian societies are those in which public and domestic spheres are only weakly differentiated, where neither sex claims much authority and the focus of social life itself is the home, Later, she concludes that an egalitarian ethos turns on men taking on domestic roles, as she has defined them. Finally, she compares American society unfavourably with a tribe which still practices head-hunting with this statement: "Unlike the Ilongot, however, American society is in fact organized in a way that creates and exploits a radical distance between private and public, domestic and social, female and male."

Our quarrel is not with the accuracy of Rosaldo's anthropological description and her characterization of her tribal contrast model; rather, we question the use of such a model in the first place. Even if one ignores the fascinating fact that Ilongot men, or some of them, are head-hunters and women are not, surely an activity that expresses certain destructive human possibilities in a manner that may plausibly

have as part of its underlying motivation an assertion of "maleness" and "male-differentness" given the greater assimilation of domesticity and the public in Ilongot society that Rosaldo praises, a tribe cannot provide us with a viable model. As human social forms and the human mind grow more complex, nuanced, and structured within civilization, filled with multiple identifications and envisagements (mind), and multiple possibilities and roles (social forms), and this brings in its wake altered public and private modes of expression and action, one cannot revert to a simpler way of life as a serious alternative. In holding the Ilongot up as a preferred contrast model to our own arrangements between the sexes, Rosaldo is forced by the logic of her argument to downplay the *qualitative,* not merely quantitative differences between our way of life and theirs.

Soren Kierkegaard once remarked that politics in the modern age was imperilled and doomed because the modern subject had become too complex to be merely represented. The shifts involved in moving from tribal forms to our sprawling, vast, literally mind-boggling technological, industrial, political-economic-social order are *qualitative,* not simple quantitative alternations. We have, to take up Rosaldo's formulation via Kierkegaard, become too complex to establish a *simple* set of egalitarian terms of division of labour and exchange. Our divisions of private-public contain within them a whole range of meanings unavailable to the Ilongot, plus, to be sure, a set of pan-cultural, bedrock imperatives involving the nurturing and caring for infant children by specific others in space and over time.

Packed into our concept of the private or domestic is a complex set of recognitions of the perils and pitfalls of child-rearing experts who cajole, warn, instruct, and applaud us. The Ilongot woman doesn't need her well-thumbed copy of Dr. Spock. The contemporary American parent requires it, or similar assistance and assurance. Ilongot society didn't spawn a league devoted to encouraging and supporting women in breast-feeding their infants. It doesn't require the whole edifice of modern medicine, or a struggle against that edifice

with its depersonalization and its robbing women of the process of giving birth. It didn't need years of protest and agitation to enable women to be surrounded by kin, at least the husband, as a supportive environment for birth. It didn't require a protest spearheaded by women rebels, including but not exclusively feminist, to allow women to keep their babies with them following birth, rather than packing them off to a central nursery. It didn't require court cases and social struggle for fathers to assert their rights to domestic involvement. The "equality" the Ilongot experience bears such a thin relation to whatever concepts finally characterise relations between men and women in our society that we doubt Wittgenstein would see it as bearing a "family resemblance" to our own.

If we cannot be "retribalised," can we be repoliticised? The question requires consideration of the terms of repoliticization. Recalling quickly the alternatives in Western political thought: Plato's archetypes represent not a re-but a depoliticization, creation of an earthly world in which no voice is raised in dissent and the Guardians may lie because they know better. We know many will find this unacceptable because Plato is a profound thinker, a great writer, and a man of vision, but, whatever Plato's justifications, the fact is that the Guardians lie in order to deceive the public, or to prevent it from being unnecessarily aroused or tormented by doubt. Whatever Plato's motives, there is little doubt that the frequently less than profound practitioners of modern politics would have but one aim in mind: keeping and maintaining themselves in power and treating adult citizens as infants to be cajoled or lied to "for their own good." That is what is called "the bottom line." Bypassing Aristotle and Christian political thinkers for a moment, there can be no wavering on the fact that the terms of the Machiavellian "deal," with its coarsening effects for both public and private life, must be repudiated. Once again, the bottom line, despite all attempts to show that Machiavelli either meant less than he said or said less than he meant, is tortuous and finally deceiving.

Any one who accepts or opts for a "Machiavellian deal," including those feminists who incorporate as central a "Machiavellian moment"—Atkinson with her ontic enemies and sex-war or Brownmiller with her militarised Sparta and learning to love to "fight dirty" —have already given themselves over to nihilism. The perversity of Machiavellianism is not simply or only its vision of public life but the fact that promulgation of that vision helps to bring about Machiavellian methods at their most destructive. Taking one's opponents as enemies, for example, as a recent American president did, viewing every political debate or conflict as a personal assault equivalent to an assault on the state, led to the Nixon administration's inglorious use of "reasons of state" and "executive privilege" for cynical and thoroughly despicable purposes; moreover, our embrace of an implicit Machiavellianism in our public and private evaluations meant that Nixon's assault upon the foundations of American constitutional integrity, his criminal offenses of covering-up, lying, and obstruction of justice, were finally pardoned or glossed over by many citizens because "the man has suffered enough" and, despite overwhelming evidence to the contrary, because he had "meant well," or had the bad luck to "get caught."

A muddling of public and private purposes, terms, and moralities was also in evidence when revelation of the late President Kennedy's alleged involvement with a number of women not his wife was treated by some as "proof" that "he was as bad as Nixon." Kennedy's alleged peccadilloes were given a status identical in their import and seriousness for the future of American democratic social forms as Nixon's creation of enemies lists, plumbers, a secret police force, plundering of public funds, subversion of the Constitution, and so on. This confusion also explains the late J. Edgar Hoover's simultaneous obsession with possible "communist" infiltration of the Reverend Martin Luther King's Southern Christian Leadership Conference and with the details of Dr. King's sex life as being equally the justification for defaming him and declaring him unworthy of the public trust. It

should be noted that a cramped and cribbed, narrow-minded set of Christian moralisms frequently affixes itself to the terms of the Machiavellian deal: a marriage not made in heaven. Under the guise of bringing morality to politics this deal only brings moralisms to the private lives of political figures and ignores a public morality altogether. As Sennett puts it, "... confusion has arisen between public and intimate life; people are working out in terms of personal feelings public matters which can be properly dealt with only through codes of impersonal meaning."

Liberal political theory demands a more complex, ambiguous response. It turns on the public-private distinction and the *particular* terms of that distinction, forged in liberal drought and practice, are unacceptable as the bases of a reconstructive idea. They require too much precious exclusion of the private sphere: they turn on too little recognition of the invasion of politics itself by great forces of unaccountable public power, largely economic, that make a mockery of the politics liberalism professes to embrace. Liberalism's public-private split, as Marx devastatingly pointed out, denies real social distinctions and artificially bifurcates politics and economics whose pas de deux (some would say *danse macabre)* has been the predominant feature of Western society since the triumph of Calvinism.

But a reconstructive ideal indebted to liberalism also demands what Ronald Dworkin calls "taking rights seriously." Too often radical social critics and activists, with what seems an unerring eye for opening moves that immediately cancel out their proclaimed ends, call "rights" the phony rationalization of bourgeois ideology, or the last refuge of pernicious individualism. Yet we cannot do without a robust and vibrant understanding of rights unless we are prepared to accept the dangerous presumption that individuals are nothing more than the products of social forces, having no dignity, meaning, or inherent presumptive force of their own against abuses of public power. Feminist political discourse needs a defense of rights within the framework of a reconstructive public sphere.

Women have struggled for too long to be included within the range over which rights operate, and the understanding of persons' rights implies, to junk "rights" as mere ideology without substantive value and meaning. Finally, liberalism, imperfectly, nurtures the conviction that life consists of a plurality of worthy activities and ends and that these—art for example— must not be brought under the domination of political power.

Rousseau's ambivalent legacy offers us a public life as the vibrant focus of citizenship, the locus of the highest human ideals, and a troubled and troubling picture of that pervasive, inescapable *force majeure,* human sexuality and the emotions attendant upon it. Hegel provides a dialectic of self-consciousness as the dynamic concatenation of mediated private and public meanings. We need not accept his precise characterization of the household, civil society and the state which finally gives much too much to the state, fails to come to grips with the corrosive effects of civil society, and treats the family both as the stepping stone to universal ethics and the realm in which women are consigned to a shadow world, to call upon his account of mind and embodied selfhood. From Marx we can draw little for an explicit political vision but we can learn much about linkages between diverse social spheres and the pervasive force of ideological distortions which justify exploitative and inegalitarian social relations.

Marx's category "class" can be adopted variously depending upon one's reconstructive aims. As a powerful tool of social analysis, a category necessary in any critical assessment of social reality, class is inescapable. But as the basis for a theory of political renewal in contemporary America, class has limited critical purchase. Americans do not see themselves primarily as members of a class even as they are aware of what the Marxist would call "class-divisions" in the larger social order and in their personal lives. The Marxist feminist, if she is genuinely interested in reaching a potential constituency in and through politics rather than creating an ideal order "in speech" alone, must take the self-definition of

that constituency into account. If she does she will find that the pervasive, rock-bottom sense Americans have of being "individuals" is not to be eradicated by fiat or through a few intensive years of Marxist political education. We concur with Monique Wittig's critique of the Marxist sacrifice of the historical subject and share her insistence that individuals must constitute themselves as subjects, as active agents of their own destiny. They must not be reduced, as Camus once cried, to historical terms. Efforts can and should be made to take the edge off the predatory aspects of individualism, but to sacrifice the concept of the *individual* is to guarantee in advance the failure of one's reconstructive ideal and to invite unchecked political terror. Class does not and cannot characterise individuals in their political aspects as *citizens* because, through the lens of class, they are seen as non-individuated members of an abstract, collective category. To call for class to exclusively define the individual's terms of entry into public life is to limit and confine one's concerns to those considered members of one's own class and to neglect visions of the "common good." If, however, class analysis leads to the demand for a revitalised and more egalitarian polity in which citizens can debate the public business on the basis of greater equality of respect and treatment than pervasive class inequity allows, it serves the reconstructive purposes we have in mind.

American social identity is not only profoundly individual, it is also intensely linked to the belief that being an American means or ought to mean "something." It means one has claims against a society that refuses to treat one with respect. It means this country has historically stood for certain worthy ideals. In 1962 when the Students for a Democratic Society issued their challenge to the public world, they did so as Americans urging their fellow citizens to fully implement our own ideals by revitalising a participatory ethos and making possible genuine responsibility, of citizens, over the decisions that affect their lives. They recalled Jefferson, Lincoln, and John Dewey. They did not, in 1962, fall into the orgy of self-contempt, social loathing, and mindless arrogance

characteristic of later enemies of "Amerika," the "pig society." Martin Luther King and the great social movement he represented most forcefully fought for a specific, concrete American dream and asserted their rights, as Americans, to human dignity and to equality of respect and treatment. Strangely, few feminists have couched their political vision in terms of what it means to be an "American" or a "citizen" save in a thin, instrumentalist sense ("How to get yours"). Where is a feminist analogue of Dr. King's "I Have a Dream"? In whose behalf is the feminist dream being dreamt?

Interestingly, it is more frequently among the feminist rank and file, those "ordinary women" who support the ERA and embrace some aspects of traditional femininity, that one finds both the affirmation of a feminist identity as a specifically American identity and the demand that America make good on its commitments to human rights and equal justice. The struggle is to do what our revolutionary forebears did during the early days of the American Revolution; what slaves and abolitionists did during the dark, tragic, yet profoundly ennobling struggles of the Civil War: what working men and women did as they fought for decent wages and a "fair deal"; what the ancestors of slaves and many American young people, including feminists, did in the 1960s to insist with Camus that they would love their country and also love justice. In all these cases it is the individual who is the basic unit of action even as the ideal of politics is a participatory one. The Christian social gospel, a potent force in American consciousness and history adds force to this ideal for it sees individuals, not as lost in some aggregate abstraction, but as unique, irreplaceable beings with inalienable human dignity as well as immortal souls. A robust rather than insipid, reactionary, or moralistic Christian social language as part of a revitalised political discourse would satisfy our insistence that the terms of this discourse be neither abstract nor a historical but concrete, available to social participants, involving a potentially transformative dimension and critical edge.

We earlier embraced those aspects of Aristotelian thought

that turned on the imperative that acting in common together with others to agreed upon ends is a worthy form of human life. We shall simply reiterate that Aristotelian moment here. Unfortunately, the most pervasive manner in which Aristotelianism enters discussions of citizenship and a "public space" involves a sentimental rendering of the Greek tradition. More importantly, it requires putting at the heart of one's political vision a great void, the absence of something (a Greek "public space") as one's contrast to "all lesser" forms of citizenship, including democratic citizenship. There never was a "public space" as celebrated in romantic notions of the Greek way in any case: that space was pervaded by the terms of Greek social existence, including the privatization and misogynist treatment of women, the presence of despised but "necessary" slaves and underclasses, and the condemnation of non-Greeks as *"barbaroi,"* less than human beings to be dominated, plundered, or destroyed. It is important to remember, as one shines a light through the romantic mists obscuring Aristotle's Greece, that most of the debates in the "public space" had little to do with great or noble ends, and much to do with jockeying for position and pelf, raising monies "by any means necessary," and going to war under the conviction that to be a hero, one of those warriors Arendt celebrates as he displays himself before his fellows, one must die young and leave a beautiful memory.

To pursue the trail of this nostalgia leads to the conclusion that "There is no longer a public space," or that our "public space" is infected and thereby undermined by social concerns. To lament the absence of a "public space"—even the notion of a "space" conveys an aura of pristine; exclusion, apart from, floating above the concerns of everyday life—becomes a self-fulfilling prophecy as well as self-indulgent nostalgia. It means one is blinded to authentic instances of citizenship within one's own society. It means one nurtures the concept of the "citizen" in a hothouse of purity so as to keep it untainted by the struggles of the present. Citizenship, like a robust social gospel, must dirty its hands in the tasks of the present.' It must, with Lincoln, "disenthrall itself"; it must

cast off the image of noble figures disinterestedly debating final ends. Perhaps the most cogent way to put our objection to attempts to hold on to and reclaim the concept of politics as a "public space" and "citizens" as those who inhabit it, is to state that it is as inappropriate to the realities of the present as that tribal analogy we critiqued earlier. Public imperatives, competing public claims, public morality, public duties, responsibilities, goods, yes: a "public space," no. The public world we are claiming for our reconstructive vision is very much *in* and *of the* world, not cut asunder from it in a presumption of its own uniqueness, not parasitic on spheres it despises as those of necessity even as it drains them of dignity and meaning.

In our own time we have seen America's handicapped citizens, a minority dispossessed and deprived of most basic dimensions of human existence—dignity, the right to work, the right to use of public transportation and buildings, the right to education, the right to intimacy—organize themselves into a viable political force and break through invisible walls of public unconcern and private disgust, barriers of silence and shame, stigmata of helplessness and dependence that we forced upon them. Are these not citizens? When they march in public or stage a sit-in—some in wheelchairs, others on crutches, some blind, others minus limbs—have they not created a politics that aims simultaneously to attain their group ends and to reach out so that others may identify with them as individuals and citizens? Their movement transcends a politics of self-interest for it represents in practice a powerful participatory ideal and embodies a less exclusionary definition of the moral and political community. The handicapped movement is an exercise in democratic political education. What of Ralph Nader and the consumer movement he initially catalysed and has spearheaded? This movement from its inception has been a grass-roots one, organized around issues of both local and national concern, and is not reducible to a politics of self-interest or self-aggrandisement. Are these not citizens? Have they not created a politics, a "space" populated by real, engaged people rather than exhibitionistic warriors?

Once we political thinkers escape the iron cage of the agora, we can say, paraphrasing a religious ideal. "Where any number of citizens is gathered in the name of acting together in common towards ends they debate and articulate in public, there is citizenship." The quadriplegic who wants simple entrance and egress from the public buildings accessible to us all, just like the black youths who sat in at the lunch counter twenty years ago, or the women straggling for equal respect, are heroes and heroines of another mold, not militarised citizens, not world-historic leaders who take the world as "their own," but individuals who fit another mold different from the Greek one.

Women have a stake in all of this because the Greek way and its nostalgic re-creation exclude and debase them and because its maintenance means most of women's traditional concerns, passions, and responsibilities will fall outside the grid of a "public space." The activation of a female participatory capability must begin with her immediate concerns, go on to give a robust account of them, and then bring these concerns to a transformed vision of the political community. The vision of citizen of which we speak is inclusive, not exclusive: it reaches out to include the young, the old, the infirm, to enlist all on terms of an equality guaranteed by their humanness that does not, at the same time, deny the inegalitarianism of the society in which that equality of participation is affirmed. Such an ideal, and again women's stake is great, must embrace a strong, dignified vision of nonviolence that holds that even as one may find it necessary to break particular laws, one must simultaneously affirm the moral law openly, in the light of day, not under cover of darkness and without public debate and scrutiny. In the words of Dr. King:

A nonviolent army has a magnificent universal quality. To join an army that trains its adherents in the methods of violence, you must be of a certain age. But in Birmingham, some of the most valued foot soldiers were youngsters ranging from elementary pupils to teen-age high school and college students. For acceptance in the armies that maim and kill,

one must be physically sound, possessed of straight limbs and accurate vision. But in Birmingham, the lame and the halt and the crippled could and did join up. Al Hibbler, the sightless singer, would never have been accepted in the United States Army or the army of any other nation, but he held a commanding position in our ranks.

The armies of nonviolence, participatory citizens informed by reconstructive ideals that grant inalienable dignity to human beings and to their everyday lives as well as to their political commitments and ends, are ideally suited for women to join their ranks. Camus cried that perhaps we cannot prevent a world in which children are tortured by we can lessen the number of tortured children: If you do not do this who will do this'? Given the concrete realities of their social life-worlds, women are uniquely placed to affirm this imperative and make it binding on others. Finally, a reconstructive ideal must fight the enchanting lures of resentment and the poisonous destruction of rage. Martin Luther King expressed, unyieldingly, moral outrage but he never raged at others for he hoped to draw them into his moral and political vision. A feminist politics that does not allow for the possibility of transformation of men as well as women is deeply nihilistic; it does not truly believe in transformative possibilities nor the ideal of genuine mutuality.

A politics of compassion may not be the stuff that leads us to excoriate enemies or march in assurance of our own rectitude to do battle with foes, but it does allow for the possibility of good faith and it does recognize that no good can come from the widespread dehumanization and destruction of others. Hate is easy; arousing the regressive urges and instincts of one's fellow men requires little more than a capacity for spite. What is difficult, what is the most daunting task of the political imagination in our time, is to fight the allure of hate, particularly when it comes to us in the name of the revolution.

One of the best examples from our recent past of a situation in which a politics of compassion sought to draw

out from others a spirit of renewed commitment to a set of moral and political ideals was Sen. Robert F. Kennedy's extemporaneous remarks in Indianapolis, Indiana, in the heart of that city's black community, on learning of the death of Martin Luther King. Kennedy first acknowledged the bitterness, hatred, and desire for revenge his audience would feel and the polarization between white and black that we, as a country, could be moving towards. He indicated to his listeners that he could "feel in my own heart the same kind of feeling [of hatred and distrust] at the injustice of such an act," after the assassination of his older brother. After first acknowledging, and neither denying nor belittling these powerful urges and reactive forces, he carried his listeners to an ideal "beyond these rather difficult times," to an insistence that what was needed was not hatred or violence "but love and wisdom, and compassion toward one another, and a feeling of justice toward those who still suffer within our country, whether they be white or they be black."

So as not to make things easier or simpler than they were, he reminded his fellow citizens that difficult times lay ahead; that they had not seen the end of violence and disorder. Finally, coming full circle and reaffirming the ideal of the man who had died, Kennedy stated: "Let us dedicate ourselves to what the Greeks wrote so many years ago: to tame the savageness of man and to make gentle the life of this world. Let us dedicate ourselves to that, and say a prayer for our country and for our people.' Those who can see in these words only cynical political advantage or a mushy refusal to face the dire facts have fallen into the despair and cynicism that a politics of compassion must most robustly and firmly oppose, for we can have no illusions about its seductiveness.

None of us lives in what we shall here call the "ethical polity." But we can conceive of that possibility. And if our thinking refuses to capitulate to coercive terms, to be condescended to or hectored, if we refuse to be drawn into Utopian pipe-dreams or bullied prematurely into action, our reflections may yet become part of a reconstructive vision of

a future social world in which civility and complexity prevail. Such a world would require private spheres bearing their own intrinsic dignity and purpose tied to moral and aesthetic imperatives, all the textures, nuances, tones and touches of a life lived intimately among others. A richly complex private sphere requires, in order that it survive, freedom from some all-encompassing public imperative, but in order for it to flourish the public world itself must nurture and sustain a set of ethical imperatives, including a commitment to preserve, protect, and defend human beings in their capacities as private persons, and to allow men and women alike to partake in the good of the public sphere on an equal basis of participatory dignity and equality. Rather than an ideal of citizenship and civic virtue that features a citizenry grimly going about their collective duty, or an elite band of citizens in their "public space" cut off from a world that includes most of the rest of us, within the ethical polity the active citizen would be one who had affirmed as part of what it meant to be fully human a devotion to public, moral responsibilities and ends.

Our ideal is the preservation of a tension between diverse spheres and competing ideals and purposes. There is always a danger that a too strong and overweening polity would swamp the individual, as well as a peril that life as lived in a polity such as our own, faced with delegitimation, will decivilise us. That is, the crises of our time may erode within us the possibility of civic virtue as we increasingly come to substitute private pleasures and asocial inwardness for any sort of public involvement and obligation to others. Within an ethical polity the individual would, or could, have many irons in the fire. The prevailing image of the person would be that of a human being with a capacity for self-reflection as to the ends and means of public and private action. Such persons could tolerate the ineradicable tension between public and private imperatives, thought and action, aesthetic standards and ethical principles. He or she could distinguish between those conditions, events, or states of affairs which are part of a shared human condition—grief, loss through death, natural disasters, and decay of the flesh—and those man-made injustices

which can be remedied, or which one can work to remedy. Above all the human being within the ethical polity never presumes that ambivalence and conflict will one day end, for he or she has come to understand that such ambivalence and conflict is the wellspring of a life lived reflectively and that we are all enriched by the messy reality which is our lot. A clear notion of what ideals and obligations are required to animate an authentic public life, an ethical polity, must be adumbrated: authority, freedom, public law, civic virtue, the ideal of the citizen—all those beliefs, habits, and qualities which are integral to a political order.

We will have kept the moral wager and affirmed our humanity only if, with Camus, we refuse to capitulate to the plague. We must embrace a politics of limits. There are things we must not do for in so doing we will not only further cheapen already fragile human ties in the present but undermine the very humanitarian ends we claim to seek. Each of us has the responsibility of making judgments between competing visions of the political imagination, rejecting those which tap primitive rage from those which have as their template our earliest memories of needs met and succor provided within a social context that was our secure universe. Only in this way can envisagements of hope and compassion—private and public—ideals the more clamorous pictures of the rageful would expunge from our world—be kept alive. It is, of course, possible that our language of political inquiry, including its emerging feminist variant, is not adequate to the task of uniting the material and the spiritual, the public and the private, by achieving a dialectics of choice, variability, and possibility grounded in a conviction which disallows absolute certitude and the destruction it brings in its wake. The task of the political imagination is possible if civility is not utterly destroyed, if room remains for playful experimentation from deep seriousness of purpose free from totalistic intrusion and ideological control. For even when notions of sexual equality and social justice are not realized and seem far-off ideals, freedom preserves the human discourse necessary to work toward the realization of both. One day as

our children or their children or their children's children stroll in gardens, debate in public places, or poke through the ashes of a wrecked civilization, they may not rise to call us blessed. But neither will they curse our memory because we permitted, through our silence, things to pass away as in a dream.

4

Reservation for Women in Parliament and State Assemblies

The Constitution 81st Amendment Bill introduced in 1996 incorporating reservation for women in the state and Union legislatures (lower houses) by providing an equal number of seats as has been provided at the local government level, the Women's Reservation Bill (WRB) has survived animated debate in and outside the Parliament. Moving in the trajectory of history through which the bill has passed gives an interesting insight into its main provisions, the perceptions and misperceptions notwithstanding the fact that its provisions by and large resemble the 73rd and 74th Constitutional Amendments. It is in consonance with the UN Resolution of reserving 30 per cent of seats for women in high political decision-making bodies and does not overstep the bounds of the Constitution. The proposed amendment has restricted reservation of 33.3 per cent of total elected seats for women keeping itself within the stipulation of the Supreme Court verdict though it is not in proportion to women's population in the country. (Balaji, 1965; Andhra Pradesh vs. Vijya Kumar).

Basically, the reservation provision for women owes its origin to two important factors: one international, i.e., the worldwide stress on inclusion of women in political decision-making, specifically the Beijing Platform of Action which categorically mentioned of educating women in civil, political and social rights emphasising on quota system, and the other internal, i.e., the organised independent movements of women in India since late 1970 not necessarily as addendum of other movements but independently as visible autonomous groups

projecting several problems facing women in the society, polity and the economy. These were the principal impetus underpinning enhancement of the numerical representation of women in high level policy-making structures to transform the traditional notions about gender role in the society, discrimination arising from such notions, injustice and violence. Indian women of the late 70s were diametrically changed human beings with immense capability to organise than their counterparts in the preceding period when quite a few elite women were involved in the freedom struggle or the Committee on Status of Women (CSW) was deliberating on women's issues. Notwithstanding the fact that opportunities for gender emancipation have been restricted to urban elite women, a new awakening has transformed the consciousness of women across the country boosting their confidence and demonstrating their abilities through involvement in several protest movements. Of course, most of the organisations were looking for government funding compromising their independent posture yet the public display of their resentment against several cases of injustice since the international women's decade had stirred the conscience of the policy-makers shaking their traditional notions of exclusion and trivialisation of women and their exploitation through vote bank politics. Though sporadic steps were taken through government intervention after the Third Five Year Plan incorporated schemes for the welfare of women, yet serious efforts were made to socially and economically empower women after 1975 precisely as a follow up of the world plan of action adopted in Mexico City. Political power sharing of course, was not supported as readily as the welfare measures and women were still debating on the notion of 'inferiority' tagged to their entry to the legislature through reservation. The Committee on the Status of Women therefore, recommended for all-women panchayats and in 1978 the Committee on Panchayat Raj Institutions recommended reservation of two seats for women in each panchayat. In the 80s and 90s women's issues had a focus on empowerment as reflected in the ninth plan document envisaging the creation of "an

enabling environment where women can freely exercise their rights both within and outside home as equal partners along with men" which is to be realised through the "National Policy for the Empowerment of Women (NPEW).

The NPEW (1988-2000) underscored empowering women through convergence of services, resources and infrastructure and outlined several priority areas, like economic empowerment, special support service, health, nutrition, prevention of atrocities and violence, natural resources and environment, media and advocacy and political participation of women by recommending 30 per cent of seats for women in all levels of legislation, *i.e.,* panchayats to Parliament." Its recommendations were widely supported and were incorporated in the Bill raising reservation to 33.3 per cent in urban and rural local government institutions which had an easy passage in the Lok Sabha in 1989 but was defeated in the Rajya Sabha. Later in 1992, the Bills were reintroduced by P.V. Narasimha Rao and upon their passage in the Parliament were incorporated as the 73rd and 74th amendments to the Constitution. Local government being state subject the states had to amend their G.P. Acts in consonance with the Central Act which, most of the states did making way for entry of about 75,000 women to represent the panchayats thereby "ushered, a social revolution" as "development issues will not ignore women neither can there be decision without their involvement".

This amendment had the persuasive influence in the demand for similar provision in the state and Union legislatures and was the immediate reason for the commitment of all political parties contesting in the 1996 general election to include reservation for women in their election manifesto. Even though political parties promised to sponsor one-third women contestants in the 1996 election, in actual practice this was not conceded, primarily because compromises on sharing political offices could be hardly made for the benefits of such office far outweigh any other benefit derived from any other source where women have been granted reservation. The failure of the political parties to adhere to their

commitments for reservation necessitated government intervention as the United Front government included the Reservation Bill in the common minimum programme and introduced it as the 81st Amendment Bill in 1996, proposing for 33 per cent reservation for women. There were as many opinions as the parties forming the United Front government; most important being the demand for reservation within the reserved categories. The Bill was referred to a JSC displaying the lack of political will to share with women the high level political decision-making process. In 1998, it was reintroduced as the 84th Amendment Bill by the BJP government but its passage was stalled in view of strong opposition on more or less similar grounds. Again it was introduced as 85th Amendment Bill in 1999 but lack of consensus pushed it back to its earlier position. Most interesting was its introduction on the very last day of the winter session of the Parliament in 2000 manifesting the lack of seriousness among the parliamentarians in their acquiescence on the Bill.

Resultantly, one important outcome of the opposition to the Bill was the determination of women members of the Parliament to unite against such opposition and speak in one voice in favour of reservation who perhaps realised that their electoral achievements have in no way impacted in overcoming the patriarchal notions surrounding the marginalisation of women in higher level decision-making structures. Women outside the portals of political power realised that idealistic considerations do not hold good specifically on issues relating to women, that women's aspirations to hold political offices is not possible in unreserved direct election as the prospect of winning is less and women as independents have still meager chances to successfully contest elections.

While the constitutionality of the Bill cannot be questioned, it has raised stormy debates particularly centering two major implications (due to overlapping nature, all the objections raised against it cannot be fully explained in a dichotomous categorisation) once the Bill becomes law. One, from the

structural context relating to the compositional changes in the lower houses by displacement of men in the legislature to the tune of about one-third as per its present strength with negatively perceived consequences like the perpetuation of family rule, domination of the upper castes, extent of representation of women's problems by the women representatives, fielding of candidates by political parties who had been sponsoring male candidates from the winning prospects, mobility and fund raising perspectives, etc. The existing political arrangement has been perceived to be changed to the detriment of the power elite as one-third reservation for women will facilitate realignment of forces pressing a perpetual tug of war between the traditional power holders and the new entrants. Besides the absence of a democratic political culture would eternise the kin factor and increase proxy control, rendering reservation for women meaningless and enhance the power of men without effecting a qualitative change in the Parliament or the state legislature which the present bill seeks to ensure. The fear that the composition of Parliament will be radically altered in favour of upper castes and upper classes is inherent in the demand for OBC quota within the reservation. On the whole the debates in the Parliament and outside focus mainly on: *(i)* opposition to the bill for reasons which camouflage patriarchal attitude and the loss *of status quo, (ii)* caste based support to the bill, and *(iii)* opposition to the caste based reservation.

The proponents of reservation focus on "redistribution, representation, integration, mobilisation, stimulation, fairness and development". Even those who doubt its outcome in reforming the traditional arrangement accept it as a precondition to reform, "one that will lead to feminisation of Parliament and make a difference in the quality of decision-making" and repose faith in women's capabilities in getting the laws implemented. The opponents view it as "diversion, misrepresentation, alienation, enervation, sedation, unfairness and stagnation". While some of them oppose reservation in principle and are scared of the possibilities of becoming a

permanent feature as has been the case with the SC and ST reservation others are opposed to women's reservation in particular for change in the *status quo,* proliferation of kin factor and proxy control.

Secondly, the difficulties in implementation brings into sharp focus the impracticability of the rotational system. The experience in panchayats has created more problems and raised questions about who will determine rotation? Whether it will precede every election? Which constituencies are to be rotated and when? What will be the yardstick for rotation? and so on. If the rotation of constituencies will be with each election then the frequency of election being very short over the past several years and such contingencies being not ruled out in future, the demarcation of constituencies will create more problems than solve any before and after each election. The rationale behind such provision is not to exclude men permanently from certain geographic areas which itself is a patriarchal perception less guided by justice for women (Singhvi, 1997). A more difficult problem inherent in this provision is women will have less contact with the people of a constituency which they represent, may be disinterested to develop the constituency as they will be withdrawn from it (unless it is to be represented by one of their family members). Winning in a new constituency will be far more difficult as women's resources are limited in comparison to men which ultimately will mean their unsuccessful electoral performance. The utilisation of MP fund will raise problems and women representatives may not be fair in discharging their responsibilities to the voters. A change of constituency every five years (and in contemporary scenario of political instability, possibly earlier than five years) "would snap that fundamental link between the electrorate and the elected and completely eliminate all incentive and interest in the development, nurturing and continued prosperity of the constituency which every representative must have and which is the very essence of representational democracy. It would make the very purpose of women's representation empty and devoid of substance".

The Issue of Other Backward Class

A major argument against the present provision of reservation is non-inclusion of reservation for OBC women grounded on the apprehension that the benefits of the provision will be appropriated by high castes which is the principal reason for stalling the passage of the Bill. Opposition to the Bill on caste and community issue is as much characterised by patriarchal mind set as it is by the perceptions arising from the radical transition of Indian society since the mid 70s when there was rise of militancy in every section of the society due to operational failure of the political system in ensuring a balanced economic development and evolving a culture of good governance unencumbered by corruption. The very question of national integrity was under attack and several regional groups emerged directly challenging the Indian nationhood. Their aspirations were overtaken by the regional political parties who intelligently exploited the aspirations of the masses for their electoral success. Precisely during this period "the political formations of the backward castes asserted with a voice of confidence which brought forward the transformations in the political arena and changed the caste composition of the Parliament."

A better comprehension of the demand for quota for OBC women will be possible neither in the perspective of the 73rd and 74th Amendments nor on the rise of the Dalit movement in the 70s but as a maturing process of the caste identities stretching over more than a century which moved in tandem with India's nationalist struggle. Though caste identities had a recognition through the Poona Pact "reservation for women was not accepted as the criterion for improving the lot of women rather it merged with the idealistic question of equality" (John, Mari E.). The communal award created separate electorate more or less to recognise the separate identities which demanded share in political power and the Dalit assertion had precisely taken shape during this period who could influence Gandhi in signing the Poona Pact (Omvedt, Gail). Their simmering discontent had a reflection in the

formative days of the Indian Constitution and a significant mileage was achieved through the provision of reservation for Scheduled Castes and Tribes who since then have become a major political and social force in the Indian democracy. The colonial government had to evolve means for accommodating these demands when it sought to implement the policy of gradual development of self-governing institutions which was reflected in the framing of the Indian Constitution. Coinciding with this period was the great awakening among all sections of Indian society including women. The issues of caste and community were resolved with equanimity by the colonial as well as the independent Governments of India but women's issues remained unresolved by both though the problem was in no way less than either caste or community.

Women in India were exhorted to involve in the nations' struggle for freedom in the early 20th Century precisely after the entry of Gandhi in the freedom movement but there was no special recognition of women's interests as Gandhi impressed upon nationalism to rise above sectarian interests because 'vivisection' of Indian society would be advantageous for the policy of divide and rule. But as much as Gandhi tried to unify the Indian nation under the rubric of Indian nationalism the communities either on religious, caste or language differences were attempting to assert their identity by forming distinct organisations. Thus, the Hindu Mahasabha was set up in 1920 which championed the cause of Hindu community thereby threatening the Muslims who perceived themselves as disadvantaged due to the denial of access to opportunities in employment provided by the colonial government. The dispute within the Congress, the formation of the Muslim League, the majority and minority questions and the division of the country were all the consequences of this separatist thinking among different sections of Indians who had asserted on the basis of distinct religious, cultural, casteist, and geographical identities. This was the time when throughout India caste consciousness was growing, Dalit movements were making their presence felt by demanding triple reservation, i.e., in education, employment and political

representation. Though the communal system of representation was denounced as vivisecting India, after Independence the Government of India acknowledged minority rights by making special provisions for them and the Constituent Assembly provided adequate safeguards to the minorities, backward and tribal people, depressed and other backward classes of society.

Apparently, 'Class consciousness' in India is not a new phenomenon as in 1874 the state of Mysore had granted reservation to Mysore Brahmins, Vokaligga, Lingayats, the latter two groups being more affluent and hence demanded a share in political power at par with the Brahmins. The First Backward Class Committee was set up in Mysore in 1928 and the Self Respect Movement in Madras was attacking Brahmanic dominance. Reservation as a policy was First introduced in the princely states of Mysore, Baroda and Kolhapur for promotion of education in the last decades of the 19th Century signaling that assertion of caste identity was moving in tandem with Indian nationalism who, in due course, penetrated decision-making structures by demanding reservation in royal employment particularly in Mysore where the Kannadiga Brahmins, Lingayats and Vokaligas gradually reduced the dominance of the Tamil Brahmins. In the national sphere reservation in the legislature was introduced for Muslims, Sikhs, Marathas, Europeans, Parsis, Anglo-Indians and Christians. The Poona Pact incorporated reservation of 148 seats for depressed classes in provincial legislatures to which elections were to be held in joint electorates. It further provided for reservation in administration by stating that "there shall be no disabilities attaching to anyone on the ground of his being a member of the depressed classes in regard to any election to local bodies or appointment to public services. Every endeavour shall be made to secure fair representation of the depressed classes in these respects subject to such educational qualifications as may be laid down for appointment to the public services. "But the depressed classes more precisely the Scheduled Castes were allowed 8.5 per cent reservation in Central services as well as other

educational facilities in 1942, on recommendation of viceroy to a memorandum submitted by Ambedkar as member of the Viceroy's Executive Council. After Independence the SC members were distressed because of opposition to the policy of reservation by eminent members but on the basis of Poona Pact provision was made for 10 per cent of seats for the SC and ST in the state and Union legislatures for 10 years ending in 1960. This has been extended several times and recently up to the year 2010 though reservation made under Article 335 read together with Article 46 has no time limit. The definition of Scheduled Castes initially included SC professing Hinduism and four castes among Sikhs namely Kabirpanthis, Ramdassias, Sikligars and Mazhabis. But in 1956 it included all Scheduled Castes professing Sikhism and in 1990 Scheduled Castes professing Buddhism were also included in the list.

Reservation as a principal mode of affirmative action is intended to give a share to the members of the society who have been denied such opportunities in the past but antagonised those sections of the society which had been traditionally privileged as per the caste and community hierarchies. This was evident from the famous Champakam Dorairajan case where the Supreme Court held that communal government order of the Madras Government fixing the proportion of students in each community that could be admitted to the state educational institutions ultravires under Article 29(2) which states that no citizen shall be denied admission into any educational institution maintained by or receiving aid from the state on grounds only of religion, race, caste or language and was not saved by the provisions of Article 16. But there was considerable protest in the northern states as a result of which the Constitution was amended for the first time and Clause 15(4) added which states that nothing in this article or in Clause (2) of Article 29 shall prevent the state from making any special provision for the advancement of any socially and educationally backward classes of citizens or for the Scheduled Castes and Scheduled Tribes. The judicial process has been used in our country recurrently to obstruct

the progress or to delay the implementation of reservation orders. Reservation was challenged in Mysore in 1962 on the ground that the list of backward classes were prepared only on the basis of caste which was unconstitutional. The judiciary has interpreted backwardness as related to caste but at the same time has held that it cannot be the sole dominant test. (Chitralekha *vs* State of Mysore, 1964) whereas in Jayashree *vs* State of Kerala the Supreme Court upheld the Kerala High Court decision that economic backwardness plays a part in social and educational backwardness. In the Thomas Case (State of Kerala *vs* N.H. Thomas, 1976) the Supreme Court upheld caste based reservation observing that the aim of the Constitution is to eliminate caste from the affairs of the state. The schedule which was prepared in 1935 for selection of castes had the connotation of depressed classes as termed by the British, backward as viewed in Mysore and Madras and untouchable which separated them from the upper and dominant castes was fixed as the criterion for determining the inclusive group in the ST category as there was no single criterion to determine the schedule. This listing has remained so till reservation was granted to the SCs by the Indian Constitution though of course, the connotation was debated and the residual of the SCs have now been enlisted in the OBC as per the recommendation of Bindheswari Prasad Mandal and revisions added to the list of castes included in the Mandal Commission thereafter to accommodate the demands of several groups who demanded their inclusion in the OBC category.

With this backdrop the question of casteist reservation within the quota of women's reservation is not an unexpected development which was further reinforced during the 80s and 90s, the period when women were asserting as autonomous entities and the caste configuration in the Parliament was changing with the entry of a significant number of backward class members mostly as party candidates. In 1996 the Parliament reflected this change when demands were raised by Dalit members for quotas for Dalit women which can be justified on the binary perceptions of the Dalit members,

one, threat to their *status quo* if the number of women will increase and two; the fear that reserved seats will be grabbed by the upper caste and upper class women which is not without reason as in the last five decades women's representation in the legislatures is by and large from these sections of the society.

The casteist perceptions veer round the assumptions that the Bill in its present form is an "upper caste ploy to stem the rising tide of lower caste men in politics." This is not altogether without basis because certain studies on the Panchayat Raj Institutions, where women represented two-third of the total seats reveal, that it is the power of the dominant castes which has been strengthened by women's reservation." But their demand should not be viewed as their compassion for Dalit women who suffer discrimination by the higher castes but by the Dalit parties themselves since in the allocation of party tickets to contest in elections they were no better than their higher caste counterparts in other parties. In the political movements like the Dalit Sangharsh Samiti of Karnataka, the Jharkahand Mukti Morcha and in regional political parties dalit women are not visible in the various levels of party offices. The feminists and upper castes have commonality in the rejection of quotas within quotas because 33 per cent of the seats in the Parliament will be filled by women radically changing the caste and class composition of the Parliament favouring the dominant group in the legislature. A latent factor in their posture is that women are acceptable to the ruling elite to counter the rise of OBCs because most of the women's organisations which support the Bill are funded by the government thereby restraining their autonomy to fight injustice.

Other Pertinent Issues

Besides the above an important implication of the proposed Bill is the predominance of political parties in sponsoring women candidates due to the reason that as independent candidates they have little chance to get through the cumbersome election process. There are procedural intricacies

for fighting as independents as these candidates are to be backed by 10 proposers whereas a party candidate has to be backed by one proposer. Besides an independent candidate contesting from two constituencies has two different symbols and has to campaign on two different symbols. These procedural complexities apart women candidates will have fewer chance of success unless backed by a party from the campaign and electoral strategies perspectives. The political parties have a very bad track record in fielding women candidates and therefore they are less likely to sponsor women. If under such circumstance women were compelled to fight as independents there is meager chance for their success in the election. But if they succeed, they will have a better bargain counter particularly in coalition governments or if any party does not get the required numerical majority to form the government to enter the Council of Ministers which may provide such women reasonable weightage in the decision-making process.

Secondly, 33 per cent reservation for women will certainly increase the number of women members, many more times than their present strength in the lower houses of Union and state legislatures but proponents of the Bill fear that this will limit their presence to one-third of the seats and eliminate women to contest from other constituencies. This fear is unwarranted as women are winning from certain constituencies in the absence of reservation for them. The same principle will apply to field themselves as candidates form the constituencies in which they were contesting. The real problem will emerge if they intrude in to the reserved constituencies or if the constituencies from which women are winning will be demarcated as reserved for women, then the actual reservation will shrink and few women will have the opportunity to enter the state and Union legislatures. In view of the present momentum of women's struggle for justice and if the same spirit persists, women will certainly raise a voice in the legislatures in evolving a solution to this problem.

Thirdly, the Bill provides for reservation only in the

lower house of the Union and state legislatures basing on the major arguments that reservation for SC and ST has been provided in these structures of the Union and state legislatures and the process of election to the Rajya Sabha is not as simple as that of the Lok Sabha which, however, is out of the fear of displacement of men from the upper houses rather than having any thing to do with the election process.

Fourthly, reservation for women has raised question of the interest that the member serves once she is elected to the legislature. A diffusion of interests and multiplicity of identities will certainly vivisect the already divisive trend of caste with gender. Other identities though predominant are not the creation of reservation. Unless an elected member rises above these considerations a democratic culture to govern will never emerge. In a representative democracy, however, the members oblige to the ideology of the party and the demands of the constituency from which one is elected. Other identities will defeat the very purpose of reservation.

Fifthly, there have been raised doubts about the impact women will leave to change the priorities and practices of political parties, its membership or leadership positions as the demands of the party would be dominant in guiding the performance of the women legislators rather than their conscience who would probably prefer to do so because of the adverse consequences of such action in building up their political career.

Reservation and Women

The debate centering reservation for women in the Parliament is supported by majority of the women members as well as feminists and activists but the perception of inferiority, which frustrated women's reservation in political decision-making structures during the struggle for freedom dominates some feminist writers and organisations. The negative perceptions are grounded on several factors characterising the political practices and the prevalent political culture as well as legacy of the national movement. In the

early 20th Century quite a few women were educated and the colonial government had initiated a spate of legislation amending the laws relating to the age at marriage, property and inheritance rights which helped women to overcome the barriers restraining their status in the family and participate in public activities. Their participation in socio-cultural activities along with their involvement in the struggle for freedom basically shaped the environment in which women operated later. The present women's movement as well as the types of responses that women had to the question of their reservation in political structures were influenced by several other factors linked to the modernisation of Indian society.

The politicisation of women occurred during the nationalist struggle when they showed keen interest in the moderate as well as radical activities in ending the colonial rule but it was the ethical question which predominated the involvement of women in their resistance to the colonial government and other activities to reform the society by harping on the Indian culture, its traditions and the religious perspectives. As politicisation and modernisation of women were synchronised with their participation in the freedom struggle, their education and emancipation were tied to the spiritual qualities of self-sacrifice, benevolence, devotion, and religiosity, basically on the Gandhian concept and reinforced by successive leaders including women. Though Gandhi could not restrain flurry of activities well underway to divide India on caste and community lines he had a persuasive influence on women to suppress their assertions if any, for political representation. This perspective among elite and lack of awareness among the large number of uneducated women shielded them from the influence of the feminist movement sweeping through the western world at that time.

But the dominant view that women were averse to reservation in the pre-Independence period is unfounded as the women's organisations like WIA were favourably disposed for 20 reservation in the new and enlarged legislatures through

proportional representation "by the newly elected members of council from a panel of names sent forward by the officially recognised associations of women". Pioneering women of the time like Sarojini Naidu had advocated for enfranchising women and this issue was strengthened by women's organisations like the Home Rule League, the Muslim League and the Indian National Congress. But she never argued for preferential treatment for women and converged with the Gandhian concept that women's task is the "spiritual reform of the world". Her views were grounded on non-admission of inferiority of women by endowing a political berth through reservation. Though Sarojini Naidu had not demanded reservation for women, Muthulakshmi Reddy as a nominated member of the Madras Legislative Assembly stated that "accounts of women's inferiority, their lack of economic independence, and inheritance rights, the need for marriage law reform, abolition of the devdasi system and so on required reservation to represent the women's point of view". AIWC, the most influential national women's organisation in the 30s to which Muthulakhshmi belonged, though initially supported reservation for women gradually withdrew such demand and reiterated "equality and no privileges". It was influenced by Gandhi who invoked the power of sacrifice of Indian women which mellowed down the voice of women for any special privileges through entry in legislature by reservation. The AIWC and the NCIW also did not represent for reservation for women before the Franchise Committee set up in 1932, reinforcing the colonial government's perception that "majority of Indian women were not ready". The women's organisations opposed many of its recommendations like wifehood qualification but agreed for restricting franchise to urban areas. This was because, they attached "equal importance to the quality as well as quantity of the women's vote" presuming that educated urban women voters could better exercise their franchise impressing upon the fact that "a more independent and well organised vote" was "important at the present juncture". The clamour for merit restricted public offices to few urban elite women who presumed to

have represented all women in the country as well as desperately attempted to contain communalism basing their argument on merit as the parameter for entry in to the legislature. Raj Kumari Amrit Kaur stated "we want to send our best women and our best men to the councils. Therefore, we do not want the canker of communalism amongst us. Once we are divided into sects and communities all will be lost." Aruna Asaf Ali argued "the legislatures must be filled with those who really feel that the country's interests stand above personal or communal considerations." Other Muslim women expressed that the good of one community does not mean that it will harm others. They apprehended exclusion of Muslim women under the joint electorates because of their comparative educational backwardness. But their views were not considered on the ground of creating "artificial hedges". Women's organisations posed to be above all communal considerations and minority voices were brushed aside "as numerically unimportant, since it had been decided that only the majority vote counted". Therefore, Indian women had lost an opportunity in the pre-independence period for political representation subsuming their aspirations in the overarching concept of unity neither did the colonial government consider women for preferential treatment for holding public offices though the expanded legislature and created 41 reserved seats for women which was allocated among different communities.

After enaction of Government of India Act 1935, in the first ever election held in 1937, 56 women entered the legislatures including five nominations. Women's organisations accommodated to the Gandhian view of no division on caste or community basis and did not raise the question of reservation for women, opposed any special privileges for them and held the view that reservation prevented women from contesting in general constituencies so that their intelligence and capacity would remain unquestioned. The reservation of seats for women in the legislature was rejected by the Committee on the Status of Women in 1974, more or less on similar grounds. The question of reservation of seats again surfaced in 90s as

new political formations of the Dalits like the BSP and SP emerged, Mandal report was accepted for providing reservation to the OBCs and the Congress government at the Centre incorporated in 73rd and 74th Amendments which included provision for 33 per cent of reservation for women similar to the provisions made in the Karnataka Panchayat Raj system.

When the 81st Constitutional Amendment was tabled for discussion in the Parliament in 1996, providing for reservation of 33 per cent for women in the Parliament and the legislatures, the caste and minority issues reflected the traditional controversies reverting to the early years of the 20th Century where women were mired in the question of caste and community differences. But the present problem of women is much more different and complex as women are subjected to physical and psychological tribulations in an inequitable sociopolitical order despite their progress in several fields unleashed by the development process. The women's movement of the 70s has sharply focused on these problems attracting the attention of the policy-makers but in the later part of the 20th Century it has been vociferous in its demand for empowerment including political empowerment as problems of women remain unresolved and a just social order is still out of their reach. Nevertheless, the opponents of reservation" take the cue from the pre-independence perception to this question which was concentrated on the 'inferiority' of women and argue that women's reservation will open up questions like whether women can be separate category over and above the social and educational backwardness characterising the Indian society? Are they a homogeneous group? Can their interests be separate from others in the social strata? and so on. The ruling elite apprehend that reservation for women will raise such demands from other groups and communities. Their arguments corroborate the posture of the CSWI which rejected reservation for women in the Union and state legislatures. Another important reason for their opposition is that reservation will raise question of the interest that the member serves once one is elected to legislature and it is feared that diffusion of interests and multiplicity of identities

will vivisect the already divisive trend of caste with gender. Unless an elected member rises above these considerations a democratic culture to govern will never emerge. The involvement of reserved seat legislators either of specific caste or gender, in matters of their identities, particularly when it conflicts with their dominant identities would have disastrous consequence in future.

As per postulation, reservation for women will facilitate the entry of elite women more easily than other women in view of the proliferation of their representation in the Parliament during the 50 years of India's independence. This fear is not unwarranted as lack of a democratic political culture has consumed the vitals of democratic governance in India. The predominance of the elites, the rich and powerful has turned all democratic institutions in to virtual competitive domains with no space for the veterans with proven credentials of social service, honesty and commitment. The privileged few who have joined their ranks from among oppressed sections of the society including women, quite often tend to internalise the well-established political practices and "among corrupt politicians there are many corrupt women".

Madhu Kishwar has a different argument against the reservation as in India male politician who "tries to bad mouth women in public or opposes moves in favour of women's equality is strongly disapproved of. Hence compared to many other parts of the world it is relatively easy to get legislation favouring women passed in India." But her perception has less relevance as contended by Menon that bad mouthing women by politicians or other high-ups may be disastrous but in employment, public places, court trials, the increasing violence against women, etc., does not hold that men's gesture has been disapproved. The passing of legislation relating to women might have other considerations like enhancing power, obtaining finance for a scheme, check population growth, get their support in election but not for fear of social disapproval. "Rape cases are used as political weapons for the ingress or egress of a government than having anything to do with the

victim or penalise the criminals. So far women have been perceived as the sole instruments of increasing population and, therefore, any legislation favouring abortion has more to do with as a birth control measure rather than allowing women to have right on their body. Therefore, the passing of a legislation camouflages wider implications which serve the interests of the power holders than actually ameliorating women's problems.

The why and how of passing a law is more important to study than what the law is on the surface. "The passing of apparently 'feminist' legislation has to be located also in the context of the compulsions of ruling elites in order to understand the complex dynamics involved.' Kishwar contends that the exclusion of women in Indian democracy is a Gandhian heritage which abnegates power as the appropriate area for women to contend for. Though her view has an element of truth, the idolisation of Indian women does not corroborate with the social practices centering women's subordination and oppression of women has increased beyond imagination with scant remedies from the instruments of state to match the mythical idolisation. Kishwar and the Shetkari Mahila Aghadi (SMA) have opposed the Bill on the ground that it will induct the female relatives of those in power" biwi beti brigade". The SMA in an open letter to the MPs has pointed out that this is "pushed by women in the creamy layer." Its appeal is grounded on the experience of reservation for women in the panchayats of Maharashtra where female relatives of the male leaders have occupied the reserved seats. Women's entry has in no way impacted on the performance of the panchayat neither has it checked corruption. SMA has suggested change in the election system by introducing three seat constituencies with each voter having three votes one of which for to woman.

Some of the women's groups support the quotas within quota for women but the leftists insist that the Bill be passed in the present form and then the quota system be incorporated. Quite a few Muslim feminist scholars have perceived the

system of quotas within quotas as an attempt to divide women into categories like Muslim and OBC that the quota system will segregate the Muslim women from the mainstream. This is also the argument of some women's organisations who support the Bill in its present form. Philips argues that the presence of women can be clearly "demarcated from that of race caste or religious identity—the belief that while these are politically produced categories, women preexist politics." The ECs proposal is apparently rational that all political parties should mutually agree to field women candidates in the election to Union and state legislatures failing which they will be derecognised by the Commission. Left parties have contended the Gill formula, as this will only give tickets to women to contest but not guarantee their victory in the election. Gill had in view the aborted attempts in Norway and Sweden where legislation for mandatory provision for all political parties to allow a minimum of 40 per cent to women on their electoral list was proposed which was compensated by the unilateral adoption by political parties to include women. Omvedt supports this view by stating that though this will not guarantee 33 per cent reservation it is a move "towards real empowerment and in a way that will bring about total welfare of society. She argues for proportional representation which will initiate a new kind of debate and the method will have to be evolved in the whole election process which will take time and in the meanwhile the WRB will be cold storaged only to be revived for the sake of debate. Mazumdar contends CSWIs recommendation for reservation of seats for women in panchayats instead of nomination was not tokenism but as an effective intervention and "for the health of Indian democracy"... "Without triple representation of women, in education, public employment and political representation women's position will not change because the thousands of years of social seclusion of the SCs has been redeemed by the triple reservation in education, employment and political representation so it will be for women." Citing from several sources she has argued for reservation for women for the simple reason that greater efforts can be made for

women's development through the involvement of women in the process of political decision-making.

Why Reservation Now?

Reservation for women was rejected in different fora before and after Independence as an ameliorative measure to improve the status of women as well as rectifying the imperfections in our democracy and it was viewed that development policies for women will generate conditions for their participation in high level politics like contesting in the elections which has been disproved in the last five decades. Since Independence, several policies have been implemented focusing women which served as the launch pad for their advancement in certain sectors but not in the political sphere. Political parties have women's wings as well as elaborate agenda for their development but are utterly miser in fielding women candidates neither have they recognised the ability of dedicated women by allowing their representation in the party offices. Many such women though have overcome familial patriarchy succumbed to party dictates which was more often than not subordinating to the dictates of male members of the party. The patriarchal norms guiding political parties have not provided women enough space to build their career in politics except for the kith and kin of the male members.

The relative invisibility of women in high level political offices is a mismatch of the extent, nature and level of participation of Indian women in politics outnumbering their counterparts in developed countries. They are no mere passive voters, turning out in large numbers narrowing the gap between their male counterparts but are active campaigners and contestants in national as well as state level elections with remarkably good performance as evidenced from their success in elections. Women have displayed their capability as independent voters, maturity in selection of candidates and awareness in their preferences. In the last one decade women's vote has been a decisive factor in electoral outcomes notwithstanding their familial and social subordination and educational deficiency. But compared to their population as

electors their participation in high level fora like contesting in election has never gone above five per cent and those who get elected is still smaller which is due to the complexities of contesting in a highly patriarchal social structure, reflected in the reluctance of political parties to field women candidates. Neither are women economically sound having resources for contesting in elections involving huge expenses or field themselves as independent candidates. In sum "there is no correlation between female population, their voting percentage and their numbers in the elected assemblies.

The Constitution of India empowers the State to "adopt measures of positive discrimination in favour of women to assist them to overcome cumulative socio-economic educational and political oppression faced for centuries". But in reality women are invisible in the national mainstream, they are harassed in the family, society, the work place, vindicating the absolute incompetence of the laws which have been enacted to protect women's rights and recognise their rights as human rights. An Inter-parliamentary Union Report in February 1997 revealed that women hold 7.2 per cent seats in the Lok Sabha, 7.8 per cent in the Rajy Sabha. Even as ministers they hold mostly unimportant posts like health, education, welfare, child development, etc. The gender specific allocation of jobs in offices and in manual labour is but an extension of the domestic role of women arising from a mindset which sans transformation in tandem with the amendments in law relating to women. Women's' representation in the Parliament or state legislative assemblies has never been more than 10 per cent despite the fact that they constitute 50 per cent of the total population. The fact that women in India are no way better in their social position than the social categories for whom reservation has been provided in the Union and state legislatures has never been seriously viewed. Therefore, in the Constituent Assembly reservation for women was defeated with an ideological presumption that the working of democracy in the normal course would ensure the representation of all sections of Indian society including women and reservation would underestimate the strength of

women to compete as equals. The CSWI considered this question but instead of reservation for women it recommended for establishment of statutory women's panchayats and election to the reserved posts though this provision only extended the earlier provision in some states of reserving one or two seats for women to be filled by nomination. But the inherent deficiencies of the policy making structures in representing women's interests, the operational imperfections of the implementing structures in ending gender discrimination, the atrocities on women and the increasing awareness among women about their life situations are some of the reasons that underscore reservation for women in legislature as essential. It is evident that triple reservation for the SC and ST categories has a tremendous impact on their all-round advancement over the last five decades and therefore, women's reservation is cardinal to link their participation as electors and their representation in the Parliament.

The reservation for women in local government institutions have provided important insight into conditions of possible transformation though in Maharashtra, Karnataka and Gujarat, entrenched power of the dominant caste and class groups has been strengthened by reservation. Most of the women are from political background and lacked in the capability to discharge their responsibilities due to child rearing and other domestic responsibilities. There is no reallocation of domestic functions in the families of the women panchayat members. But a study conducted by the author in Orissa reveals three different scenarios, one where women are taking the lead role, many of them are older in age, free from domestic responsibilities, are respected in their families and in the community and a large number of them are from non-political background. At the other extreme are panchayats where women are illiterate, poor, have been fielded by their male members, and irrespective of their age are not effective in their participation in panchayat affairs. In between are some panchayats where women though have come from political background have shown interest in the panchayat affairs but in most cases have not overcome male dominance. But they

have the courage to speak, ask questions about several important issues in the panchayat and *gram sabha* meetings despite the ire of the male members and traditional power holders. Therefore, it is naive to make a sweeping remark on the inability of women panchayat members because a small segment of aware and articulate women can influence the traditional perceptions guiding gender roles and encourage less interested women to participate in electoral competition. Other changes would gradually follow but this can be facilitated if reservation for women is effected from the panchayat to the Parliament.

REFERENCES

1. Abhishek Singhvi, *Seminar,* Vol. 457,1997 p. 28.
2. Mary E. John, "Alternative Modernities? Reservation and Women's Movement in the 20th Century India", *EPW,* October 28, 2000, p. 3823.
3. Gail Omvedt, *Dalits and the Democratic Revolution: Dr. Ambedkar and the Dalit movement in Colonial India,* Delhi, Oxford University Press.
4. Sumit Sarkar, *Modern India. 1885-1947,* Delhi, 1983, 1994; Macmilan.
5. Yogendra Yadav, "Electoral Politics in the Time of Change: India's third Electoral system 1989-99", *EPW,* August 21-28, pp. 2393-99.
6. Vasanth Kannabarian; and Kalpana Kannabarian, "From Social Action to Political Action—Women and 81st Amendment", *EPW,* February 1, 1997.
7. Nivedita Menon, "The Impossibility of Justice: Female Foeticide and the Feminist Discourse on Abortion", in Patricia Uberoi (ed.), *Social Reform, Sexuality and the State,* Delhi, Sage, 1996.
8. Madhu Kishwar, "Women and Politics, Beyond Quotas", *EPW,* October 26, 1996, Vasanth Kannabarian and Kalpana Kannabarian, *op. cit.*
9. Seema Alavi "Muslim Women Don't Need Reservation", *Times of India,* July 15, 1998, Seema Mustafa, "Forget Footing, Men Can't Even Stomach the Bill", *Asian Age,* July 18, 1998.
10. Shahid Faridi, "Left Criticises Gill Formula for Women's Reservation", *Asian Age,* April 25, 2000.

11. Anne Phlips, "Democracy and Difference: Some Problems for Feminist Theory in the Rights of Minority Cultures", Will Kymlicka (ed.), Oxford, Oxford University Press, 1995.
12. Omvedt, 2000, "Women and PR", *The Hindu,* September 12, 2000.
13. Malini Bhattacharya, *Seminar,* 1997.
14. This culture is rather difficult to evolve as successive elections in our country have experienced the inflow of kins in large numbers and even in parties led by women. The selection of candidates in the ensuing Assembly elections in Tamilnadu and West Bengal bear testimony to this.
15. Chandan Mitra, *The Pioneer,* April 14, 1999.

[Courtesy: Snehlata Pandey]

5

Women in Local Bodies

Unquestionably, it is proven fact that although distributive justice has been categorically underlined in all the development plans, the needs of women have not been adequately addressed. While, a majority of women in rural areas attend to domestic work and those who are engaged in free collection of goods (vegetables, roots, fish, firewood, cattle feed, etc.) and providing services (sewing, weaving, maintenance of kitchen gardens, orchards, poultry, etc.). The number of rural women in the age-group of 15-49 years engaged in domestic work is estimated at 43.8 million, and those engaged in free collection of goods and services is 26.6 million (Jain, S.P.). Although rural women constitute a large section of population of the country, their lives are still characterised by hardwork drudgery and without any basic amenities. They are trapped in the vicious circle of low income, ill-health, low nutrition, low productivity and low wages. As a result women were considered as target groups in the Community Development Programme (CDP).

Now on the front of political participation women won the right to vote as early as 1921 and have held high political offices, yet their participation in the elections has been disappointingly low. For instance, in 1984 election there were only 161 women among the 5493 candidates and Lok Sabha had only 42 members of the fair sex in a House of 545. However, their turnout at the polling booths have increased from 38.8 per cent in 1957 polls to 58 per cent in 1984 elections. The need of the hour, therefore, is to choose more women candidates and encourage them to participate actively in politics.

Now on the front of the Second, Third, Fourth and Fifth Five Year Plans programme for and participation of women did not receive any fresh impetus and continued on the earlier lines. But Rural Development programmes for women have only in recent decades recognised the crucial role of organisation and mobilisation as strategies for women's improvement and development. The programmes envisaged under community development had a strong component for women's development, social education, etc. But the emphasis was more on women's role in household activities rather than community participation.

In recognition to the importance of democratic institution at grass root level, the Panchayat (Village Council) at village level was established in 1961. The Panchayati Raj institutions were in fact, considered to be the most effective instruments for realising the goals of economic betterment and social justice for the least privileged. Participation of women, who constitute nearly half of the population, in Panchayati Raj institution has been considered essential for enabling them to participate effectively and independently in democratic and political processes and to influence decision-making. It has been recognised as a step towards equal society and a means of realising for women the development goals.

The introduction of 'Democratic Decentralisations' resulted in the establishment of Panchayat. But in most of the Panchayat Raj legislations enacted by different State Governments, women were to be coopted under special category. This did not result into the development of village leadership among women and their participation in the decision-making process. In this connection the Committee on the Status of Women in the Panchayati Raj Institutions has not been effective either in articulating women's needs, or in mobilising women for adequate participation. Taking note of this fact the Committee on Panchayati Raj Institutions recommended; (a) increasing representation of women in these institutions; (b) establishing a special committee of women Panchayat members and powers and funds to ensure that the decisions are made by women

themselves on priorities and choice in welfare and development programmes specifically for women and children; (c) provision of institutional finance and budget support for rural industrialisation projects for women, and (d) strengthening the constructive decision-making and managerial roles; (e) Mahila Mandals to ensure full access to development, resources and services.

The World Conference on Agrarian Reforms and Rural Development (WCARRD) had also recommended that Governments should "promote collective action and organisation by rural women to facilitate their participation in the full range of public services and to enhance their opportunities to participate in economic, political and social activities on an equal footing with men."

Thus it is obvious that local bodies at village level are required to play a meaningful role in promoting women's participation in development. Hence, it is increasingly felt that after four decades' experience what that performance of this institution is.

Uttar Pradesh (U.P.) being the largest state in terms of population in India has the maximum number of Gram Panchayats (72,826), Panchayat Samitis (876) and Zilla Parishad (56), followed by Maharashtra and Madhya Pradesh. Contrary to this, there are some States and Union Territories viz. Meghalaya, Nagaland and Lakshadweep, Mizoram, which do not have any Gram Panchayat at all.

As per 1980s counts, on an average, number of population and village in India come to 2,098 and 2.8 respectively. These two average were maximum in Kerala because of the densely populated state. And average number of Gram Panchayats per Panchayat Samiti and Panchayat Samitis per Zilla Parishad in India were 47.4 and 17.8 respectively.

Out of 2,12,248 Gram Panchayats only 506 (0.23 per cent) women Sarpanches were elected. The number of elected women members were very few (29.10%) as compared to

TABLE 1: STATE-WISE NUMBER OF PANCHAYATI RAJ BODIES (1979-80)

Sl. No.	***State/Union Territory***	***Gram Panchayat (Nos.)***	***Panchayat Samitis (Nos.)***	***Zilla Parishad (Nos.)***
(1)	*(2)*	*(3)*	*(4)*	*(5)*
1.	Andhra Pradesh	16,137	324	21
2.	Assam	714	—	20
3.	Bihar	11,378	578	8
4.	Gujarat	12,924	182	19
5.	Haryana	5,260	87	—
6.	Himachal Pradesh	2,355	69	1
7.	Jammu and Kashmir	1,482	—	—
8.	Karnataka	8,184	175	19
9.	Kerala	1,001	—	—
10.	Madhya Pradesh	16,233	459	—
11.	Maharashtra*	24,016	296	25
12.	Manipur	107	6	—
13.	Meghalaya	—	—	—
14.	Nagaland	—	—	—
15.	Orissa	3,832	314	—
16.	Punjab	10,610	118	12
17.	Rajasthan	7,292	236	26
18.	Sikkim	215	—	—
19.	Tamil Nadu	12,582	376	24
20.	Tripura	689	—	—
21.	Uttar Pradesh	72,826	876	56
22.	West Bengal	3,242	324	15
23.	Arunachal Pradesh	701	48	5
24.	A&N Islands	38	—	—
25.	Chandigarh*	21	1	1
26.	D&N Haveli	10	1	—
27.	Delhi	204	—	—
28.	Lakshadweep	—	—	—
29.	Goa, Daman and Diu	195	—	—
30.	Mizoram	—	—	—
31.	Pondicherry	—	11	—
	Total (All-India)	2,12,248	4,481	251

* Information relates to 1978-79.

Source: Rural Development Statistics, NIRD, Hyderabad, 1982.

TABLE 2: STATE-WISE COVERAGE OF PANCHAYATI RAJ INSTITUTIONS

Sl. No.	*State/Union Territory*	*Average Population/ Gram Panchayat*	*Average No. of Village Gram Panchayat*	*Average No. of Gram Panchayat/ Panchayat Samitis*	*Average No. of Panchayat Samiti/ Zilla Parishad*
(1)	*(2)*	*(3)*	*(4)*	*(5)*	*(6)*
1.	Andhra Pradesh	2,281	1.8	49.8	15.4
2.	Assam	18,007	29.1	—	—
3.	Bihar	4,458	6.9	19.8	18.6
4.	Gujarat	1,512	1.4	71.0	9.6
5.	Haryana	1,517	1.3	60.5	—
6.	Himachal Pradesh	1,367	7.2	34.1	—
7.	Jammu and Kashmir	2,604	4.4	—	—
8.	Karnataka	2,710	3.6	46.8	9.2
9.	Kerala	18,781	1.2	—	—
10.	Madhya Pradesh	2,132	4.7	35.4	—
11.	Maharashtra	1,445	1.6	81.1	11.8
12.	Manipur	5,607	4.8	17.8	—
13.	Orissa	5,245	13.5	12.2	—
14.	Punjab	1,254	1.2	89.9	9.9
15.	Rajasthan	2,910	4.9	30.9	9.1
16.	Sikkim	847	1.9	—	—
17.	Tamil Nadu	2,551	1.3	33.5	15.7
18.	Tripura	2,444	1.3	—	—
19.	Uttar Pradesh	1,043	1.6	83.1	15.6
20.	West Bengal	10,138	11.7	10.0	21.6
21.	A&N Islands	1,763	4.5	—	—
22.	Arunachal Pradesh	583	4.0	14.6	9.6
23.	Chandigarh	2,238	1.0	21.0	1.0
24.	D&N Haveli	7,400	7.2	10.0	—
25.	Delhi	2,941	1.3	—	—
26.	Goa, Daman and Diu	3,287	2.3	—	—
27.	Pondicherry	—	—	—	—
	All-India	***2,098***	***2.8***	***47.4***	***17.8***

Note: There is no Panchayati Raj set-up in Meghalaya, Nagaland, Lakshadweep and Mizoram.

Source: Same as for Table 1.

those of coopted (70.90%) in both the cases, Gram Panchayats as well as Panchayat Samitis. Further, if we have a look at the elected women members of Gram Panchayat to total number of Panchayats, it was only about one-fifth (19.41%). Again, in the Panchayat Samitis, a little more than one-fourth (25.35 per cent)), women members were coopted and only 13.27 per cent were elected.

However, the above statistics exhibit that women's participation in the Panchayati Raj is not upto the mark. It is felt that mere reservation will not solve the problem unless women members are given commensurate powers to function effectively. Panchayats should be given real autonomy and no subjected to excessive governmental controls. And then only women members of Panchayats will welcome the concept of Nayaya Panchayats.

TABLE 3: EXTENT OF WOMEN'S PARTICIPATION IN PANCHAYATI RAJ BODIES

Sl.No.	Items	Percentage
1.	Percentage of elected women members of Gram Panchayat	19.41 (29.10)*
2.	Percentage of coopted women members of Gram Panchayat to total number of Gram Panchayat.	47.29 (70.90)*
3.	Percentage of elected women members of Panchayat Samitis to total no. of Panchayat Samitis	13.27
4.	Percentage of coopted women members of Panchayat Samitis to total number of Panchayat Samitis	25.35
5.	Percentage of women Sarpanches to total number of Gram Panchayats	0.23

Note: Percentage of total, elected plus coopted.

Women as Leader

Women are considered an extremely pivotal point in the process of change in rural areas. The establishment of the Institution of Panchayat at village level in 1961 also provided

opportunities to women to participate in the decision-making process. Women's participation in these bodies was encouraged by coopting them as a special category. Women's participation in village-based institutions proved to be the most effective instrument in bringing about a change in their way of life in terms of economic well-being and adoption of new technology. Although these measures have not yielded the results to the desired extent, it cannot be denied that rural women have been exposed to the process of modernisation and avenues for interaction with the forces of social change.

While organising women's groups, an attempt was made on a country-wide basis to utilise these institutions to promote people's participation and as catalyst to social change. As these organisations were formed on democratic principles, the rural women tended to get community welfare affairs and participate in the development process by assuming leadership roles. Although the emerging village leadership, as has been found by a number of scholars, is confined to the upper castes/classes in village communities, the poor women also get the opportunity, and assume leadership roles, though to a limited extent, and get exposed to the process of modernisation and social change.

Participation of women in the village based on formal and non-formal organisations has thus, made significant changes in their social status as well as their position within the family. Further, mere participation of women in these organisations is a clear indicate of a change in the traditional norms which restricted free movements of a female member in society for social and political activities; women were expected to participate in such economic and social activities which were confined to the domestic spheres. Any deviation from this norm naturally resulted in an improvement in her position in the society. Participation of women in different organisations thus have two important connotations (i) it gives them a status in the society, and (ii) it permits contribution of women not only in rural development process but also for their own development. It also gives them an opportunity to

(a) work in groups on project of common interest, (b) associate with the on-going development programmes; (c) participate in the decision-making, process; (d) articulate women's needs; (e) leadership in the national development process.

The emerging women leadership in rural areas is to a large extent characterised by middle age, high literacy rate and income. However, in the light of the socio-economic features of the village leadership, it will be found that the characteristic features of women leadership in rural India are at variance in terms of age, education and occupation. As a result, the rural women have, in the first instance, been able to identify themselves as an important segment in the society. It has also helped in attracting the attention of the official functionaries to design and implement programmes for the benefit of women. This is evident from the fact that a number of specific programmes specifically meant for women beneficiaries in the field of education, health, employment, family welfare, vocational training have been designed and implemented in recent years.

Resultantly, rural women have also started showing considerable interest in organising joint economic ventures such as thrift societies dairy cooperatives, poultry and cattle farming, agricultural and allied activities, weaving and so on. The nature of these groups vary from place to place depending upon their pattern of work and availability of technical and financial assistance from outside. The change from home based action which has prevailed all along to collective action has made a significant change in the people's life style.

The introduction of women's organisations and the consequent emergence of women leadership at the grassroots level has brought about social changes in the rural women's life, in particular and village communities in general. These organisations have the necessary potential for bringing about more changes rapidly and if given proper opportunity and assistance these can provide further strides in the development of rural women.

Economic Motivation of Women

Development programmes of women should be addressed to the problems that concern rural women. Economic motivation is central to rural women's behaviour. Women need money not only to contribute to the family as a whole but also to save for emergencies when they and their families are in distress. Thus, when a women is urgently concerned with her family's economic and social security, she may not be interested in acquiring modern knowledge in nutrition or health practices or in literacy classes which, though related to her primary needs, are of secondary importance to her. However, once a certain amount of economic security has been achieved, rural women will be interested in other social changes desired for comprehensive development of the community and society. If national policy favours keeping rural women in economically productive work, then training and employment of rural women would be required for ensuring their effective participation.

The National Perspective Plan (1988-2000 A.D.) suggested the need for proper training for all women members of Panchayats and other bodies to enable them to exercise their authority adequately. A massive conscientisation programme for women in general needs to be taken up and modules designed for this purpose should adequately deal with social economic constraints which restrict their participation in political processes and institutional structure of democracy. Separate allocations are required to be made for this purpose. There is need to link women's development programmes with Panchayat and local functionaries for women's effective participation in development process.

Popular Participation

Popular participation has been conceptualised in relation to some form of political democracy and, of societal change and growth that term "development" suggests. More commonly in development literature it is examined from the point of view of government intervention in development, and in this respect, terms such as "mobilisation" and "coercion" have

been used to characterise the nature of the "participation", conversely, where "participation" emerges as a result of some kind of bottom-up process, it is characterised as being "authentic" and focusing on distribution.

In a recent debate, it is found that mere reservation will not solve the problem unless women members are given commensurate powers to function effectively. The need to link women's development programmes with Panchayat and local functionaries for effective participation of women in development was also highlighted. The formal reservation of women in Panchayati Raj structures through reservation of seats, election, etc., is not a sufficient condition for their effective participation unless and until it is supplemented by measures which help in resolving the socio-economic pressures inhibiting them. The same can be realised by mobilising women through awareness campaign and inter-personal communication by implementing the scheme which help them attaining economic independence and by enhancing educational facilities at very proximity.

Now to conclude, the condition of women crucially depends on the extent of economic independence and it has been observed that Indian women are lagging behind in this sphere. The long term trend in economic participation of women indicates an overall decline in percentage of workers to total female population. Here, there is one aspect which need to be considered from a policy point of view, that there is a need to replace the traditional value system, which is based on an inequality of sexes where the females play a subordinate role, with a more egalitarian system. Even if there is no absolute equality between the sexes, there is need to bring about a betterment in the women's quality of life.

The strategy is to tackle the issue on three main fronts—education, employment and health. It is observed that in most of the programmes women as a group have been neglected. Hence, it is suggested that Panchayati Raj institutions can act as a link between the service agencies at the higher levels and women's group.

Certainly, Panchayati Raj has many achievements to its credit, the more important of which may be identified here. Politically its inception has become democratic seed-drilling in the Indian soil, making an average citizen more conscious of his rights than before. Administratively, it bridged the gulf between the bureaucratic elite and the people. Socially, it generated a new leadership which was young having a modern and pre-social outlook. Finally, viewed from the developmental angle, it helped rural people to cultivate a developmental angle.

As far as women's participation in the Panchayati Raj is concerned, it is not up to the mark. It is observed that mere reservation will not solve the problem unless women members are given commensurate powers to function effectively.

REFERENCES

1. Asoka Mehta Committee Report.
2. Government of India (1988), *National Perspective Plan for Woman 1988-2000 A.D.,* Report of the Core Group set-up by the Department of Woman and Child Development, Ministry of Human Resource Development, Govt. of India, p. 3.
3. Govt. of India (1978), *Report of the Committee on Panchayati Raj Institutions,* Min. of Agriculture and Irrigation, Deptt. of Rural Development, New Delhi.
4. Jain S.P. and Reddy V.K. (1981), *Rural Organisations: An Evaluation,* NIRD, Hyderabad.
5. Jain, S.P. (1983). 'Leadership Among Rural Women', *Social Change,* Sept. 1983, Vol. 13, No. 3, pp. 9-10.
6. Jain, S.P. (1985), 'Rural Development in India through Last Decades', Background paper presented in an International *'Seminar on Women and Development,* 13-16 February, p. 1.
7. Lieten, G.K. (1988), 'Panchayat Leaders in a West Bengal District', *Economic and Political Weekly,* Vol. XXIII, No. 40, October 1, p. 2069.
8. Oakley, Peter and Marsden, David (1984), *Approaches to Participation in Rural Development,* ILO Geneva, p. 18.
9. Pearse A. & Stiefel M. (1979), *Inquiry into Participation—A Research Approach* (Geneva, UNRISD), Pearse and Stiefel

discuss this understanding participation in terms of a "process of incorporation."

10. Prakash Rao E.V. (1987), 'Operational Dynamics of Panchayati Raj', *Kurukshetra,* Vol. XXXV, No. 9, June, p. 15.
11. Sirsikar, V.M. (1970), *The Rural Elite in a Development Society,* Orient Longman's, New Delhi, p. 189.
12. Tahrunnessa Abdullah (1981). 'Women's participation in rural development; a Bangladesh pilot project', in ILO edited book, *Women in Rural Development—Critical Issues,* ILO Geneva, p. 36.

6

Decision-Making and Political Participation

As is mandatory, it is the fundamental right of every citizen to contribute to the decision-making process. It is, in fact, the citizen's duty as well and is based on the presumption that each member has adequate means and conditions to achieve a full realisation of his or her personality as an entity in society. While from a feminist perspective, an analysis of women's participation in political processes has questioned the narrow definition of political participation as accepted by the mainstream of political scientists and policy-makers. The New Delhi Document on Women in Development (1985) recognised that despite the rapid growth of informal political activity by women, their role in the formal political structure had virtually remained unchanged. This recognition has resulted in a serious debate on the concepts and indicators for political participation. As a consequence of the debate appropriate indicators of political participation and fresh strategies have to be evolved, not only for formal political activities but also for full involvement and participation in non-formal mass action.

Suprisingly, there had hardly been any mention of this subject in the National Plan of Action for Women drawn up in 1976. Perhaps for the Government of India and the U.N. at that time, the issues of health, education and employment had a higher priority than political participation. However, subsequent national documents prepared at the time of the Nairobi Conference of 1985, the Non-Aligned Meet (NAM) of the same year and the Forward Looking Strategies after

Nairobi Conference, have recognised the importance of this theme and raised issues related to the nature of political participation of women, the problems faced therein and the strategies to be evolved.

Now it is most appropriate, to attempt a definition of political participation which is broader than the one covering women's participation only in the electoral and administrative processes. It includes the gamut of voluntary activities with a bearing on the political processes, including voting. support of political groups, communication with legislators, dissemination of political views and opinions among the electorate, and other related activities. Besides social relationships, there are spheres of power-relationships which are generated and institutionalised by being used to encourage, control or move people's behaviour, attitudes and beliefs in specified directions. Political participation can be considered to include an involvement in any form of organised activity that affects, or seeks to affect, these power relationships. It refers broadly also to "activities by those not formally empowered to make decisions, these activities being mainly intended to influence the attitudes and behaviour of those who have powers for decision-making." In fact, protests and demonstrations against those in power also form part of political participation. Women's participation has covered a range of activities including movements, protests and support meetings on all issues connected.

An analysis of the above terms, with particular reference to the participation of women, indicates that there has only been a limited application, mainly because of various dubious considerations of social, economic and political variables. Broadbased political participation of women is severely limited due to a nexus of traditional factors, these are the domination of Indian politics by considerations of caste, class, religion, feudal and family status etc., all of which are parochial essentially patriorchal forces that work in favour of men against women. Consequently, women are still left on the periphery of the political process, and political participation

remains elusive to most of them, inspite of their voting and election, and also capture of some seats of power and influence. As amply brought out by various scholars, the most crucial problem in any attempt to measure women's political participation simply by studying official or organisational membership and voting, is the finding that much of the Third World politics occurs outside conventional political institutions. Hence, political participation seeks also to re-organise the lives of members of human society, and ensure that the participation by women is not underestimated by being branded 'nonpolitical' and women's concerns treated as 'social' in nature. No doubt, Gender equality is a prerequisite for effective participation of women in strengthening the institutional structure of democracy. Women have been marginalised because of several socio-economic constraints. The number of women in leadership positions at the local, village, district and national level is still not commensurate with their numbers in society.

Political Participation of Women: A Review

In India, limited adult franchise was granted to women in 1937. Since then, women have been participating in political processes, as voters, as candidates contesting the elections, involved in deliberations both in the State Assemblies and Parliament and also through holding public office at different levels and in the judiciary where women perform watchdog roles in the protection of sanctioned rights.

To a great, extent, women's participation in formal elections is dependent on the mobilisation efforts of the political parties general awareness among the community of the importance of exercising franchise, and the overall political culture. No serious efforts appears to have been made to mobilise women as a political pressure group by any political party. Caste, personality and families of candidates appear to be more important to voters than party ideology or affiliations. Factors like education, religion, class and tradition also seem to affect women's participation.

One great difficulty with the Indian political scene is that it is impossible to generalise about the inter-relationship between any single factor and political behaviour. Patterns of political behaviour from different regions show different relationships, influenced as they are by inter-related factors like the social status of women, their economic position, the cultural norms, and above all, the regional outlook towards women's participation in the wider society. Then again, there are some situations which are conspicuous by obvious contradictions. Kerala, which has a record of rapid growth in women's political mobilisation and women's literacy, also has a record of electing very few women members to the legislature. Voting as an indication of political participation for women in India, has its own strength and weakness. Voting has a tremendous impact for equalising and mobilising women. Yet, it has to be noted that voting requires the least initiative and internal motivation. Very often the woman citizen treats the day of voting as a welcome break from her dull and tiring routine and does not appear to have a notion of why she should vote for a particular contestant.

Coming to women as candidates, the number of women contestants in parliamentary elections has not increased significantly over the years. Political parties seem uniformly reluctant to field women candidates. The high cost of electioneering is another deterrent to most women candidates. Because of these factors there is an increasing tendency among women to contest elections as independent candidates. Inspite of this, the present Parliament has the largest number of women members ever since Independence.

The proportion of seats won by women to the Lok Sabha stands in 1988 at 46 seats out of a house of 537 seats. The Rajya Sabha has 28 women in a house of 245 seats. There has been a greater representation of women in the Rajya Sabha by nomination. The pattern is not very different at the State level.

The All India total stands at 44 women elected out of 241 women contestants, as against 1486 men out of 8415 male

contestants. For instance, in Orissa in 1980, for the House of 147 members, 10 contestants were women of whom only 5 were elected. In 1980 in Tamil Nadu, 5 out of 17 women candidates won. An indepth study of women at grassroots level politics reflects a similar trend. Interviews with 143 women members of Panchayat Samitis and Zilla Parishads in Maharashtra reveal that the women of upper castes, wives of big landowners and politically influential persons, tend to pre-dominate in the positions reserved for women in local bodies.

Inspite of the general dismal picture of women's role in Indian democracy, there has been a rise in the number of women in key positions of power. For many years, India had a women Prime Minister at the helm of affairs. At present, there are eight women Ministers/ Ministers of State in the Cabinet. At present there is no women Chief Minister but, there is one women Governor. In the Administrative machinery also, there is an increased representation of women. In the Indian Administrative Service, there are currently 339 women out of a total of 4548. There are six women Vice-Chancellors in the country. The All India Services employ 994 women out of a total of 16, 987 officers (5.8%). The Indian Forest Service has only 10 women officers (0.6%), and the I.P.S. 21 women officers (0.9%). Stereotyping of jobs still exists and women in positions of power have not been able to influence macro level policy decisions on women.

The concept of participatory development, the importance of intermediaries e.g. voluntary action groups and educational institutions were recognised as important instruments to achieve the developmental goals for women. Participatory development through group organisations has been successfully attempted in several innovative projects carried out by women's organisations. The contribution of the, voluntary organisations has been considered as particularly significant in demonstrating the effectiveness of participatory development as a process of empowering women, to articulate their needs, to take part in decision-making and in following their own vision. In this

regard, the participation of women in the Panchayati Raj institutions, which were considered to be the most effective instruments for realising the goals of economic betterment and social justice for the least privileged, was felt essential. The CSWI report suggested the establishment of all-women panchayats at village level, with autonomy and resources of their own for the management and administration of welfare and development programmes for women and children, as a transitional measure to break through the traditional attitudes that inhibit most women in articulating their problems or participating actively in the local bodies. The empowered committee, while examining the recommendations, suggested that the sub-committee, while examining the subjects relating to management and administration of programmes for women and children should have the power of panchayat with earmarked funds.

Participation of women in Panchayati Raj institutions has been recognised as a step towards equality. The Committee on the Panchayati Raj institutions, 1978 recommended the reservation of two seats for women in panchayats and to co-opt women in case they did not come through elections. It also suggested that a Committee of women be set up within panchayats to operate specific programmes for women and children. The co-option of two women members in panchayats, has not brought any perceptible impact on women's participation in the Panchayati Raj bodies. Co-option is done only in letter and not in the spirit of getting the women involved in panchayat activities. The participation of women in panchayats as it is today hardly gives any scope for women members to participate effectively and independently in democratic and political processes or to influence decision-making.

Performance of Women Legislators

Contrary to the normal expectation that women members in Parliament as well as the State Legislatures take little part in the proceedings and remain silent spectators, they have been very active and are found to take a lively part in the debates. Apart from subjects of direct relevance to them

like welfare, child development, removal of dowry and social malpractices, educations and health, centre-state regions, security, food and civil supplies and other specialised and sensitive subjects have drawn the attention of many members. There are numerous instances during the years of their participation in debates and in helping to move resolutions for legislative measures and bills. On their part, they have been feeling that the media coverage is inadequate for them as it is generally focussed on men. Women have also taken part in, and in some cases initiated, calling attention notices and adjournment motions, in the Parliament and in State Assemblies, and made a mark with significant and well-articulated contributions.

Women MPs have participated actively in the debates on dowry and influenced the government to make changes in the existing dowry laws. They have also given useful suggestions such as having a National Commission on Women, having women judges on family courts and special courts for hearing cases of dowry heaths. On various occasions, they have raised questions regarding the common civil code, immoral traffic in women, dowry deaths and rape cases.

Political Parties and Women

Besides participation in the general elections/ contesting elections is a very important dimension of participation is through the political party. As far as political parties are concerned, although at election time declarations are made of granting 15-20 per cent seats to women, no party has been able to achieve the target. In fact many studies have shown that before the women's decade, political parties were not even stressing on women's issues, in their campaigns or is mobilising rallies. In the last decade all political parties have shown great interest in women's problems as a result of various developments but primarily due to the pressure of women's groups. Parties in their manifestos promise to women all opportunities for increased participation in social, economic and political life. Yet, the record of most of the parties is poor so far as women are concerned. Though exact figures are not

available, it can be safely presumed that membership of women in parties does not exceed 10 to 12 per cent of their total membership. Parties hardly make a sincere attempt to reach out to women or to put them in positions of authority. To take the example of Congress (I), Mrs. Indira Gandhi was the only woman President of the Congress Party in the post-independence period. However more recently in the year 2005 the same party is being presided over by Mrs. Sonia Gandhi (daughter-in-law of late Indira Gandhi). Though she had stated that "women have a special role to play in the party and in the shaping of a new society," yet women have not really been able to make their presence felt at the decision-making levels. There have been a few illustrations of women placed in decision-making positions as in the Congress Centenary Celeberation Committee or in the Nehru Birth Centenary Committee. In a few State Congress Committees, women have been Presidents and at the AICC level, it has been a practice to have at least one women as the General Secretary. To protest against this continued neglect, the State convenors of the women's front at their meeting convened in January 1985, passed a resolution requesting the Congress President to issue instructions to include women as state convenors in the state election coordination committees and to allot at least one Assembly seat in each parliamentary constituency to women. A number of political parties have strong women's wings spread all over the country, but advocate revival of traditional values, encourage fundamentalism, eulogise mythological women characters and generate communal sentiments.

In sum, it would not be correct to state that the women's decade has forced all political parties to be alert to women's problems. The major contention of the left parties that women's problems will get solved once a classless society is established, still continues. However, under the pressure of women members, at least the inclusion of women's issues in their manifestos has been feasible. Yet, access to significant decision-making positions in political parties continues to elude women. Today, very few women hold crucial positions. In

fact, one of the main reasons for the growth of autonomous women's groups is the disillusionment that arises, owing to a consideration of women by some political parties as peripheral elements, inspite of their involvement in day-to-day political work. This is not a problem on the Indian scene only, but is a global issue.

Trade Union Organisation and Women

Participation of women in trade unions has been a topic which has acquired significance during the last two or three decades. Studies have shown that though it might be difficult to participate in day-to-day activities of the trade unions, women have provided very great strength during crisis periods, such as strikes. A recent study on the more than a year long textile strike of Bombay in 1982 proved that without the support of both women textile workers and the wives of male textile workers, the leaders would have found it difficult to continue.

Unfortunately, the prevalence of partriarchy prevents men colleagues from accepting women's crucial role. In a recent conference on the problems of working women and their participation in trade unions, a scholar noted: "Today after more than a decade of our struggle we find to our satisfaction that the questions and problems of working women and women in general are being discussed widely in our country by various organisations, individuals, press and also by the Government. The question is also being highlighted in international forums." Despite these efforts, many trade unions in the country are yet to pay adequate attention to women's issues and joint efforts have to be made to make a common cause to fight for the demands of working women. The scholar has also documented a number of struggles of women workers from different states indicating the militancy and tenacity of women who were involved in struggles of Adivasis, contract workers, women coal miners, plantation workers, etc.

A recent report also gives the picture of the women membership in the CITU and the proportion of women office

bearers in some of the States. Of course, the picture is very dismal. The total membership has been around 10 per cent in 1986, and an infinitesimal proportion as office bearers.

The issues which concern women most such as equal wages, non provision of maternity benefits and child care facilities, retrenchment of women workers in the wake of Equal Remuneration Act, have not been taken up seriously by trade unions. The studies on national trade unions suggest that there are instances where they expressed their concern regarding these issues by passing resolutions and holding consultation but there is hardly any evidence that trade unions agitated or called a strike to meet these demands nor have their journals taken cognizance of these minor efforts. In this context, it has been even suggested that a separate women's cell or a union for women would ensure more participation of women. It was also strongly felt that one of the major tasks is to orient the male leaders to remove their gender bias and incorporate more and more women in the decision-making bodies.

An analysis of the problems of women working in the unorganised sector throws light on the sexist attitude of mainstream trade unions. It is well-known that women constitute a majority of the unorganised labour force. The working conditions in this sector are abyssmal. There is no security jobs, no fair wages, no facilities and no rights to demand for the improvement of their situation etc. It goes to the credit of grassroots level organisations such as the WWF and SEWA and the researchers who have highlighted the problems of these women, that attempts are now being made to create some kind of structure to ventilate their problems. In the absence of support from the official trade unions, the women workers turning to some of the women's organisations for pressing their problems is a very striking trend.

Informal Participation of Women

The history of women's large-scale participation in the nationalist movement is well-known and in fact, one can go

back to 1905 when women freedom fighters showed immense courage in fighting the British rulers. Of course, more strikingly, mass participation of women was recognised during the Civil Disobedience Movement in 1930 and also during the Quit India Movement of 1942, when thousands of women courted arrest. Some women participated in the revolutionary movement as couriers distributing literature, risking police repression, imprisonment and even capital punishment. Similarly, in the Tebhaga Movement for land reform, which took place during 1946-51 in Bengal, it has been reported that women participated at all levels. There was a Nari Bahini (Women's Volunteer Force) which would help guard villages at night. Studies have recorded many stories of women's courage, militant spirit and innovation during these struggles. Investigations into the role of women in the Telangana and Naxalite movements subsequently have revealed that women not only gave shelter to the revolutionaries and served as liaison among various groups but also took leading part in direct political action.

One of the most significant events which dramatically brought to the forefront women's issues in the last decades has been the re-opening of the Mathura rape case in the Supreme Court which triggered off a women's protest movement. A series of rallies, campaigns, morchas, dharnas and demonstrations were held to protest against rape, wife beating, dowry deaths, molestation of women, media distortions, foeticide and other issues.

Thus the record of women's participation in political processes other than the formal has bene quite creditable. Of course, while women have been visible in mass movements, group upsurges and protest struggles, their presence is not felt in structured decision-making institutional settings. Even in the structures where women's participation is substantial, they have not been given positions of power. However, it can be stated that protests made by women activists and scholars have resulted in their role in the grass roots level movements being recognised.

Burning Issues

The incorporation of Equality for Women as No. 12 in the Twenty Point Programme of development enunciated in 1986, and certain special schemes like Legal Literacy Programmes, Awareness Generation Programmes, Prevention of Atrocities Against Women are evidences of conscious attempts made by the Government to empower women to handle complex situations. The setting of the National Expert Committee on Women Prisoners and the National Commission on Self-Employed Women are significant steps in the right direction. The most formidable hurdle in the programmes and policies of the Government has been non-implementation or very limited imlementation of these measures. Before recommendations to remedy the situation are suggested, it would be useful to have a brief discussion on why women's participation in political affairs is limited.

As mentioned in the Non-Aligned Document, "understanding of obstacles to women's effective participation in political life has generally been clouded by various assumptions regarding women's behavioural pattern, their "backward consciousness, " lack of interest in public issues, or biological differences in their mental make up. An assessment of the situation at the end of Decade with all the shortfalls in reliable data suggests that, while the visibility of women in the political and developmental process has increased because of greater efforts to obtain first-hand information, the search has also helped to identify powerful, sometimes hidden forces, of resistance that obstruct the march towards the goals of the Decade."

On the question of peace, since women are one of the most vulnerable groups in a region effected by armed conflicts, special attention has to be drawn to the need to eliminate obstacles to the maintenance of peace. Women's equal role in decision-making with respect to peace and related issues should be seen as their basic right and as such should be enhanced and encouraged at all levels. Women should be able to participate actively in decision-making processes related

to the promotion of regional, national and international peace and cooperation. Nonetheless, it should not imply that women's ability to support causes is restricted only to pacifist issues.

One of the arguments for non-participation has been that the women will-fully place themselves in marginal positions towards matters "political." The crucial problem is that women find themselves being judged and judging themselves by two standards. One standard is of feminity, of the private world which regards them as nurturant, passive, emotional, home oriented and subordinate to men. The other standard is that of their modern role which is the standard of the public world which expects women to be rational, active, achievement oriented, ambitions and competitive. Women in such a situation have two options. Either they follow the rules of the game of politics and are called unfeminine or act in politics guided by the standards of feminity and are seen as peculiar. A very strong reason explaining women's limited participation has been the theory of women's "backward consciousness." However, it has been seen that in non-formal mass movements, women responded with great enthusiasm and responsibility on crucial themes. Whether it is a movement against foreign government under Mahatama Gandhi's leadership or it is a protest against vested interests in economic or political spheres or confronting the oppressive landlord or contractor, women have not hesitated; they have made sacrifices and suffered repression along with men.

The observations that women when elected do not participate in the debates or women elect those candidates whom their men wish to support, have been proved wrong with more and more research findings. Women do raise relevant issues on a wide range of subjects, and studies on voting behaviour suggest that the secret ballot system helps considerably in exercising individual preference, though these findings/revelations are underplayed by policy-makers and political scientists due to gender biases.

Subordination of women in society acts as a structural constraint to their participation in political activities. Owing

to the gender-based division of labour in the family, women have to bear the full responsibility of household chores. It is the women's duty to bring fuel, fodder and water and to cook. They have to look after the rearing and education of children besides socialising. These constraints operate more or less for all classes and communities of women.

Another significant deterrent factor is that of the political culture which prevails today. Not only have the political processes become complicated but many decisions are made behind the scenes. It has also become very expensive and difficult for women, who have little control over resources. Further, the atmosphere of growing violence. character-assassination and unscrupulous struggles for power, have been a serious deterent to women's participation in an effective manner.

In mass movements which are issue-oriented and aim at achieving concrete objectives, women are able to participate, leave the chores of the house to someone and suffer the hardships and privations of political confrontations. But when an activity requires routine, continuous work which is often complicated to follow, women find it difficult to participate due to lack of supportive structures.

If women have to become integrated fully into political life, cultural change is necessary. In the past few centuries, the world has been divided into the separate spheres of the public and private. While women are no longer restricted to "private" activities related only to their families, their outside activities are "privatised" by men and society at large. Another pre-requisite for women to be active participants in decision-making activities, is the provision of facilities, like education, training, information and above all, economic security.

In conclusion, it may be said that during the Womens' Decade, there has been some achievement in making women visible in the political sphere. There has been more positive action on the part of the government to integrate women in the decision-making process. It appears that the operation of larger politico-economic forces generate a political culture

that women find difficult to get involved in. Women through the Constitution have been allowed to enter politics but there is a vast difference between allowing and integrating. As a scholar puts it "Toleration is not an active principle, it is a passive one. It places a premium on the elimination of tangible barriers but makes no commitment to a positive value of inclusion and membership. Political liberation of women, therefore, would mean that women would be seen not as deviants or even as welcome strangers." In short, women's real active political participation will necessitate changes both in value and in the social structure.

It is an establisheed fact that education of citizens not only builds up knowledge and information but also helps the citizen understand the complexities of the political process. It is, therefore, recommended that the programme of free universal education upto the age of 14 should be vigorously implemented. Further, serious attention needs to be paid to the content of education. The courses of studies and the text books should inculcate values of gender equality, self-respect, courage, independence etc., which would help develop the personalities of women.

Men and women in positions of power should be sensitised to women's issues.

Government should effectively secure participation of women in decision-making processes at National, State and local levels. This would imply use of special measures for recruitment of women candidates:

- A more effective step would be to declare a certain percentage of constituencies in the lower tier of panchayati raj as exclusively womens constituencies and all executive positions in a certain number of territorial jurisdictions reserved for women candidates.
- The Planning Commission and all ministries and government departments must have a Women's Cell.
- 50 per cent of all grassroots functionaries must be women. To facilitate its implementation, relaxation of minimum

educational qualifications is needed, which can be supplemented by short training curses for women.

— More women need to be inducted in ministries at the centre and in state governments and they must be allowed to function in areas suitable to their capacities and not be restricted to 'soft' sectors.

— All government delegations to international meetings must include at least one or more women members.

— Wherever a Committee or Commission is set up by Government for any purpose, 30 per cent of its representation must be of women.

— The Union and all State level Public Service Commissions must have women representatives.

— The Planning Commission and State Planning Boards must have adequate representation of women.

— Reservation should be made of 30 per cent seats at panchayat to zilla parishad level and local municipal bodies for women. Wherever possible, higher representation of dalits/tribals, women of weaker sections should be ensured.

— 30 per cent of executive heads of all bodies from village panchayat to district level and a certain percentage of chief executives of panchayati raj bodies at lower, middle and higher levels must be reserved for women.

All women members of panchayats and other executive bodies must be trained and empowered to exercise their authority. Both men and women members must be sensitised to women's issues. A committee should be formed to look into the training needs of women panchayat members and to help in designing modules separate allocations may be make for this purpose. Particular attention must be paid to the development of interprersonal communication skills amongst the trainees/community leaders.

Concerted efforts are needed to elicit participation of women through establishing links between the elected representatives and the development functionaries as being experimented in Rajasthan through the Women's Development

Programmes (WDP). The whole experiment is based on a decentralised administrative structure. Plans of action should be formulated through frequent meetings and discussions. Further the prime need is to see that the representatives have to be made answerable to the electorate. WDPs in other States must also be linked with panchayat/local functionaries for more effective participation of women in development.

One of the greatest hurdles in contesting elections is the exhorbitant expenditure. This factor not only makes it difficult for women, who have very limited independent resources to participate, but completely eliminates women in the poverty sector from entering the arena. This situation leads to prominence of upper castes, upper classes, urban women in the political sphere. To counteract this inequitous situation, serious steps must be taken to reduce election expenditure. Further, enormous amounts needed for election, lead to corruption and various nefarious practices. If steps are taken to decentralise the political machinery, then unnecessary expenditure in reaching out to a very large electorate could be avoided.

A major step needed to facilitate women's participation both in formal and informal political processes is provision of support services. In all kinds of public participation as well as in seeking opportunities for self-development, the primary responsibilities of women for looking after home and children always come in the way. Unless arrangements are made for child care and other domestic responsibilities, sustained participation of women in the public sphere is not possible without the integration of men in the private sphere. This not only means that men share the familial responsibilities but a new value needs to be given to this joint sharing both in public and private spheres which would ultimately lead to a better quality of life.

In a democracy, political parties have a very significant role to play. The parties should take such measures which would facilitate participation of women. All political parties must be urged to ensure that at least 30 per cent of the

candidates fielded for election are women till such time as women can stake their claim to nomination as equals. It should be examined if the Election Commission can be empowered to enforce this.

It is the bounded duty of political parties to provide political education to the people. They should organise study circles in which not only political understanding of the complex situations is provided, but controversial issues having implications on gender relations is also analysed.

Women members of the political groups should be vigilant about their rights and contributions. Whenever sexist attitudes are exhibited or sex discrimination is practised, women members should build up solidarity and oppose such practices. They should also press for implementing whatever has been promised to women; whether the question is of allocation of seats or of providing a creche or taking a stand in Parliament.

In generating a participatory political system, the role of voluntary organisations or non-governmental organisations is very crucial. There is evidence that when NGOs are active and play the role of pressure groups, the representatives also become alert. Through raising the awareness of the community, NGOs can help in fielding candidates who are responsible to the people. They can focus the attention of the people on crucial issues facing women and elect members who understand those issues and are working towards it. Organisations and Grassroots women's groups have in fact effectively drawn the attention of the government to atrocities perpetrated on women, to custodial rape, to harassments for dowry, to plight of the women in the unorganised sector, and so on. NGOs can also provide training for future women leaders. They can organise legal literacy programmes and study circles for political education as well as develop participatory methods of working, and thus serve as a practical training centre for effective political participation by women. They should not adopt a beneficiary or 'welfare' approach while working with their target groups. Even if a few NGOs play their role

adequately and with courage, a new climate of commitment and responsibility could be generated.

NGOs should work as pressure groups or political action groups to press for the fulfilment of promises. They should also provide support to the elected women representatives, when they are presenting women's cases in the deliberative bodies. In short, there should be a very strong link between women representatives and those organisations working with the community.

Media should play a productive role in enhancing women's participation. It should give wider coverage to various activities and measures taken by women, and should highlight the problems of women. In order to project women's issues and achievements, perhaps mainstream media may not be adequate and, therefore, it is necessary to develop an alternate media system that could portray women's struggles and experiences, help generate values which encourage gender equality and justice, and build up a positive image of women participating in public life.

7

Political Dynamics of Women: A Case Study

Kerala is a 'model' state of India having unique distinctions. Kerala has the best and ideal physical quality of life index with 100 per cent literacy, high educational standards, low infant mortality, better sex ratio, besides other qualities and living standards. The successful enactment of land reforms gave a better sense of equality and social justice. The increasing level in the marriage age of both men and women in another positive aspect in this line. However, there are socio-economic problems even today like gross unemployment, unproductive returns from education, competition among communities, impact of personal laws in which religion may have a major say, unproductive use of Gulf Money etc. The absence of an industrial climate, preference of the job-seekers for service sector jobs, investment in real estates like palatial buildings, increasing standard of living are some of the negative aspects in this society and its economy.

Kerala was rather different in the beginning of the nintheenth century than we get now. The society was uneven, hierarchical. Tamil Brahminical system dominated with limited avenues for the natives to develop. There were evil systems like caste oppression, religious discrimination particularly in Travancore. The practice of untouchability was rampant. Besides, women in all religions and castes were living in a lower position unlike men. Some of the earlier writings about the plight of women and their urge for protest were found in the earlier novels like 'Indulekha'. Actually the urge for social reform came within these castes and communities in

different periods. But the first mass agitation for political freedom, democratic rights, social justice and struggle against religious and caste discrimination were found in the 'Malayali Memorial' which occurred on 11 January, 1891. The Memorial also pointed out the fact that literacy level in 1891 among women was only 0.46 per cent while among men it was 11.08 per cent. The predominance of Tamil Brahmins in Travancore administration had been brought under severe public criticism since local people had no avenues to develop by getting an employment from this peculiar situation.

The evil effects of matriarchal family system among Nayars, Ezhavas (to some extent), the practice of the typical 'marriages' among the younger male members of the Namboodiris with Nayar women, the practice of untouchability system among Hindu castes, the near monopoly of land ownership with Namboodiris, the extreme form of feudal order and the like had created deep schisms in social development. Gender justice was beyond comprehension during those days. The pattern of matriarchal joint family system originally had some virtues since it gave the women property rights and equality with men and this assured them some independence. Noted political leader of Kerala late C. Achutha Menon had pointed out that the whole system subsequently degenerated into a tyrannical regime of the *Karanavan* of the *tharawad* (head of the matriarchial joint family). In practice, the marriage relationships were weak in matriarchial family. Although we get a picture of a degenerated society the most vulnerable position was that of the women itself.

The traditional marital institution prevalent in Nayar community of Kerala was in its effect crippling the social development of women. The ordeal she had to undergo owing to the existence of polygamy and the loose type of relationship existing in the traditional society caused serious problems. Kathleen Cough's social anthropological study of the Nayars (1959) in the former kingdoms of Calicut, Walluvanad and Cochin gives a very detailed account of the system, which existed during those ancient periods. While the various Acts

in the twentieth Century led to the individual partition that broke the family or 'tarawad' system, the new regulations definitely benefit the Nayar women in general much more than she was liberated from the unethical practices of the past. The impact of land reforms also had its influence as new style of occupation, modern forms of social relationships, and mobility came in to being. However, as the disintegration of matrilineal system takes place, there are problems too. Chie Nakane (1963) argues that the present Nayar still lives in the matrilineal atmosphere. The author raises the question "how long does it take the Nayar to become free from a matrilineal ideology, the shadow of the tarawad life?" However, the author's predictions are not true today since nuclear family system among the Nayars has almost come to stay. Further, there is a general improvement in the position of the Nayar women which has been achieved through education, employment and married life without any of the influence of traditional taboos of the matrilineal system.

Among the Namboodiris, the reforms were aimed at the right of every male member to marry in his own caste, abolition of polygamy, widow remarriage, education of girls and the rights to individual family property. Similarly Christian missionaries inspired an agitation against the uncivilised practice of the Nadar women keeping their breasts uncovered (in olden days, women belonging to lower castes could not cover their breasts). The missionaries while converting them to Christianity encouraged the Nadar women to cover their breasts with blouses and ultimately succeeded in bringing an order from the king, permitting Nadar women to cover their breasts against the opposition from the upper castes.

The lead for social reforms among the Hindus came within each community but was spread over different periods. The social arm if Namboodiris was formed in 1908, known since then as the "Namboodiri Yoga Shema Sabha". The Ezhavas formed the Sree Narayana Dharma Paripalana Yogam (SNDP) in 1903, the Nairs formed the Nair Service Society (NSS) in 1914 and the Harijans formed the Sadhu Jana

Paripalana Yogam in 1907. As a result of these and with the increasing awareness there was the need for bringing legislations for effecting the reforms into practice.

The first Nayar Act, 1088 ME (1913) brought some changes in the laws of inheritance and family management for those following the 'Marumakkathayam' law of succession. Here, the partition patterns was modified to female or Tavashi Partition' and not on individual partition of the Nair Tarawads. The second Nayar Act (1925 A.D.) brought individual partition of the family property. The Act deprived the nephew of all the claim to the property of uncles and made polygamy illegal. The Nayar Act was followed by reforms in other Hindu Communities like the Izava Act (Ezhavas), the Nanjanad Vellala Act, and the Travancore Kshatriya Act. "The Izava Act was a codification of the laws relating to marriage, succession, family management and partition among the Izavas. This Act also imposed legal prohibition in the matter of polygamy. While the progress of social ideas in Marumakkathayam communities like the Nayars, the Vellalas and the Ezhavas had been recongnised in the proper Acts, no such enactment has been made yet for the Kshatriyas. As a result the natural development of that community had been retarded, but the Kshatriya Act (Act VII of 1932 AD) rectified this anomaly.

The social reform movements in Kerala had also addressed the problems of women since uplift of women was crucial in the development of the society. But these were of different nature since each community had its own separate laws, rules of conduct and rituals. The growth of SNDP Yogam: the NSS and the like highlighted the growing awareness for social development among the members of these communities. Again, the development of Christianity is another aspect. The Church played a unifying part in the life of the average Christians especially in regard to marriage, worship and rites. The economic progress of the community belonging to different groups is of special significance. The hardworking character of the people urged them to migrate to different

parts of the State, to other states and even to foreign countries for employment and sustaining opportunities. They have settled down in Malabar region since 1920s, hitherto a separate part of Malayalam speaking areas until 1956. They made the land fertile, cultivated new crops, braving climate, wild animals and finally achieved economic progress. Similarly they resorted to trade, business and industry where they faced little competition, professions like teaching, nursing also had good prospects. In fact, there is a higher percentage of women from Kerala settled down in America who are engaged in the profession of nursing. Sociologists argue that this phenomenon of ethic occupational concentration deserves a special study.

Paradoxically, there are problems among the Christian women of Kerala. The famous Mary Roy's case resulted in the annulment of the Christian Succession Act by the Supreme Court in 1986. The practice among most Christian groups is that, woman will be given her share in the form of dowry at the time of marriage (Earlier the Travancore-Christian Succession Act and Cochin Christian Succession Act provided only 1/4 and 1/4 of the share for women, respectively. Naturally this deprives them of equal share when the men are getting their share from the family later. While the traditional system in a patriarchial setup had its merits, it also brought unexpected issues as well. The ongoing debate about the delay in effecting the Supreme Court judgement retrospectively-also raises question about the neglect of the Christian women in the community. However, considering the education, professional skill, teaching, health care, willingness for migration and the like it cannot be said that Christian women face severe problems compared to their counterparts of other religious groups. Moreover, the reform movements within the factions of the Christianity are so up to date and possess even an exposure to international patterns as well. The social development of Christianity in Kerala during this century and particularly of their women folk has to be appreciated.

But this has been modern development as the traditional pattern of matrilin (which had some positive aspects) benefited

the Nayar women for sometime. Jeffrey cities the instances of 34 per cent of female literacy existing among the Nayar women which was more than that of the Syrian Christian. Again, before 1981, the female literacy among Nayars was 6.9 per cent in contrast to that of 2.9 per cent among Syrian Christians (who later advanced so much). The patriarchy among Syrian Christians in the past, child marriage, property descendance through men and the like put the Syrian Christian women at a disadvantage. "The controversial passage of the Travancore Christian Succession Act in 1916, and its Cochin counterpart in 1921, illustrated the male dominance of the Syrian Christian family. But old practices changed soon. For the Christian women, the political advantages lay in what could be gleaned from European protestant practices—female education and careers (which could bring income, status) and the political careers like Mary Poonen Luckose.

One thing is very certain from the analysis of the problem. There has been uneven levels of development among the different sections of the society which in the long run influenced the other communities as well. The arrival of democracy, integration of Travancore and Cochin in 1949, the reorganization of the State with the integration of Malabar (and the loss of Kanyakumari areas in South of Trivandrum) together created the new socio-political atmosphere. Illiteracy was substantially reduced, education expanded and the challenge of employment made them more conscious of learning skills and acquiring technique and general education levels. The growth of radical ideas, election of the Communist Party to power in 1957 the initiatives for land reforms and the subsequent changes are also significant. In this socio-historical context, the development of women and their involvement in social affairs become so natural and essential. This can be considered a total transformation over a period of one hundred years at least. Today educated and employed women enjoy significant status in the society. This urge is found among the younger elements and is a positive trend indeed.

Jeffrey argues that in the modern Kerala, women unlike

in the past, are not contained, but in a position to reach out to a public political process. Hence, he attributes to the new process of the growth of public politics and the fluctuation of women's roles unfolded and interacting together in the 1970's, the development of the 'Kerala model'. However, he admits that the recruitment to political leadership and political process had not been impressive. Again,' the women are prone to social divisions of Kerala and the fragmented women organizations are unable to lead women to political process. It may not be difficult to locate the women organizations at the structural level but their sphere to influence is very limited. Among political parties, the Congress had launched the Congress Women's Front (later known as All Indian Mahila Congress). The Front has much to raise the social awareness of women through its programmes and political activities. But, in the earlier periods its effective dynamism is limited to a few major political issues and policy choices. The CPI(M) has launched the All India Democratic Women's Association. Smt. Sarojini Balanandan was the President and Smt. T. Devi was the General Secretary of the Association in Kerala.

The major argument here is that the political parties in Kerala have not attracted the women yet to actively involve them in political process, although they are very conscious of garnering votes from them during elections. The proportional advantage of women in Kerala over men in population, their high literacy and skills, competition to get employment and the likes have not been actually matched by a similar recruitment in public affairs. The political leadership of all the parties is in fact male dominated. Although there is no such thing as oppression or alienation, women's involvement in party politics leadership and recruitment is not effective. The role of women in politics is largely limited to student politics at college levels, women worker's organizations at the organized sectors, eco-politics and few other areas. Women have been organized at non-party levels also to fight their causes. Similarly, their leadership in common cause Gandhian organizations, environmental issues etc., is also noted. All

these however, cannot be considered effective channels for political leadership.

With the available figures, the following is a discussion about the involvement of women in politics during the are independence period. A subsequent debate on their political involvement in the post-independence period is also attempted here. The dawn of independence increased their chances of development and shifting roles in articulation. However, political participation of women did not increase substantially especially on the level of leadership. To substantiate this, data regarding women representation in the various legislatures (pre and post-Kerala State formation) have been provided. The data from 1920's have been collected from the document released by the Secretariat of the Kerala Legislature (1990). The average woman representation in the (1956-94 period has been really marginal 3.51 per cent only. Even in 1987 Assembly Elections, there were only twentysix candidates in the fray of whom eight were elected (which is a record) in a House of 141 members.

TABLE 1: HISTORY OF WOMEN REPRESENTATION IN TRAVANCORE: 1888-1947

Sl. No.	*Name of the assembly*	*Total strength*	*Elected*	*Nominated*	*Women representatives*	*%age*
1.	Travancore Legislative Council	50	28	22	2	4.00
2.	Sree Mulam Popular Assembly (1904-32)	99	NA	NA	5	5.05
3.	Sree Mulam Assembly (1933-47)	72	48	24	3	4.16
4.	Sree Chitra State Council (1933-47)	37	22	15	3	8.11

The history of women representation in legislative politics from 1888 to 1956 very clearly substantiates their limited representation. In fact, the Travancore State, has been credited to have had its first legislature in 1888. Again, the credit of

the first lady member of any legislature in India goes to Kerala when Dr. (Mrs.) Mary Poonnen Lukose was nominated to the first Travancore Legislative Council in 1922-23. Similarly, numerous others were nominated in the subsequent periods in Travancore and Cochin States. Prominent among them include Elizabeth Kuruvilla. Anna Chandy, Mary Alexander, T.V. Narayani Walsaiam Rose, Gnanasikhamoney Hepzibah, I. Narayani Amma, Thressaimma Korah. C.D. Ponnamma, Annie Tliayyil, Meenakshi, N. Menon, Mrs. K.M.R Menon, Accamma Cheriyan, Annie Mascarene, Kuttimalu Amma, Ranganayaki Ammal, P. Thankamma, Thottakkat Madhavi Amma, Mrs. G. Pavithran, Paravathi Nenminimangalarn, Mrs. Swans, Miss G.M.D'suza, Meenakshykutty Amma, Joshua Anni, Thankamma W. Menon, Miss. Anni Joseph, K. Dakshayani Velayudhan and Mrs. T. Francis. This "list comprises mainly of nominated or coopted members. Representation of Pulaya Caste was given for the first time in 1945-48 periods.

TABLE 2: HISTORY OF WOMEN REPRESENTATION IN COCHIN: 1925-1949

Sl. No.	*Name of the assembly*	*Total strength*	*Elected*	*Nominated*	*Women representatives*	*%age*
1.	Cochin Legislative Council (1925-38)	54	36	18	8	14.18
2.	Cochin Legislative Council (1945-48)	58	38	20	5	8.62
3.	Cochin Legislative Assembly (1948-49)	58	53	5	2	3.45

Mrs. Kuttimalu Amma held the distinction of being elected to Madras Legislature from Malabar both in 1937 and 1946. The prominent leaders in Travancore-Cochin State were Accamma Cheriyan, Anni Mascaren. K. R. Gown Amma, Kusumom Joseph, Devaki Gopidas, Elias (Mary Antony), Thankamma Menon. T.C. Leek Devi Amma and others. Mrs. Leela Damodara Menon was active in the politics of the

Malabar region of Madras State until 1956 and later in Kerala Politics.

TABLE 3: HISTORY OF WOMEN REPRESENTATION FROM MALABAR IN LEGISLATIVE ASSEMBLY

Sl. No.	*Name of the Assembly*	*Total strength*	*Elected*	*Nominated*	*Women representatives*	*%age*
1.	Madras Legislative Assembly 1937	NA	NA	NA	1	—
2.	Madras Legislative Assembly 1946	NA	NA	NA	1	—

TABLE 4: HISTORY OF WOMEN REPRESENTATION IN TRAVANCORE-LEGISLATURE ASSEMBLY AND TRAVANCORE-COCHIN LEGISLATIVE ASSEMBLY: 1948-56

Sl. No.	*Name of the Assembly*	*Total strength*	*Elected*	*Nominated*	*Women representatives*	*%age*
1.	Travancore-Cochin Legislative Assembly (1948-49)	120	120	—	4	3.33
3.	Travancore-Cochin Legislative Assembly (1949-52)	178	178	—	6	3.37
3.	Travancore-Cochin Legislative Assembly (1952-53)	109	109	—	1	0.92
4.	Travancore-Cochin Legislative Assembly (1954-56)	118	118	—	2	1.69

Source: Compiled from Secretariat of the Kerala Legislature. *Hundred Years of Legislation in Kerala: 1888-1988.* Trivandrum. 1990.

Miss Anni Joseph and Dr. (Mrs.) T. Francis were elected to Cochin Legislative Assembly during 1948-49. During the same period there were four women members elected in the Travancore Legislative Assembly,—Accamma Cherian, Annie Mascarene, Devaki Gopidas and Elias (Mary Antony). There were six women members elected in the Travancore - Cochin Legislative Assembly (1949-52). Accamma Cheriyan, Anni

Joseph. Anni Mascarene, Devaki Gopidas, Dr. (Mrs.) T. Francis, and Thankamma. N.Menon. However, there was only one female member elected in the Travancore-Cochin Legislative Assembly (1952-53). K.R Gowri Amma. In the next Assembly (1954-56) there were only two elected members from the women set,—K.R. Gowri Amma and T.C. Leela Devi. The first elections to the State Assembly were held in 1957. This was soon after the State Reorganization in 1956 which created the Kerala State on the 1st November 1956.

TABLE 5: WOMEN LEGISLATORS IN KERALA ASSEMBLY: 1957-1994

Assembly	*Year*	*Total strength in the House*	*Women legislators*	*% of representation*
I	1957-59	127	6	4.72
II	1960-64	127	7	5.51
III	1967-69	134	1**	0.75
IV	1970-77	134	2	1.43
V	1977-79	141	1	0.71
VI	1980-82	141	5***	3.55
VII	1982-87	141	5	3.55
VIII	1987-91	141	8	5.67
IX	1991-94 (Continues)	141	8	5.67

Source: Compiled from Secretariat of the Kerala Legislature. *Hundred Years of Legislature Bodies in Kerala: 1888-1988.* Trivandrum, 1990, pp. 1031-1052.

** In 1965 the Assembly election was above since no Party or Coalition could form a government.

*** Including Mrs. Raichel Sunny Panaveli who was elected in a bye-election held in 1986 due to the death of her husband who was the sitting member, Mr. Sunny Panavely.

It is more or less like the pro independence position, although a slight revision is there. The highest representation for women was found in the Eighth and Nineth Assembly by Second Assembly. It has been observed that the major and medium parties of Kerala have not offered more seats for women although women enjoy a proportional advantage in the State's population. In fact, the first priority for any party

in an election is winning the seats, and hence their preference goes for the most probable candidate in that particular constituency. Since the political mobilisation of women in the organizational politics of the parties is actually weak, the women do not constitute any strong pressure group within the political parties. Consequently, their voice is limited during the process of bargaining, choice of candidate selection in party committees, and issuing Party tickets. However, this does not mean that the parties are nor interested in their causes. Not does it mean that there are no women leaders in these parties.

TABLE 6: IDENTIFYING WOMEN LEGISLATORS IN KERALA ASSEMBLY: 1957-94

S.No.	*Women Legislators*	*Party Name*	
I. First Kerala Legislative Assembly: 1957-59			
	1. Aysh Bai. K.O.	CPI	(elected Deputy Speaker during 6 May 1957-31 May 1959)
	2. Rosamma Punnoose		
	3. K.R. Gowri	CPI	
	4. Sarada Krishaan	CPI	
	5. Kusumom Joseph	CPI	
	6. Leela Damodara Menon	Congress Congress	
II. Second Kerala Legislative Assembly: 1960-64			
	1. Nafeesath Beevi, A.	Congress	(elected Deputy Speaker during 15 March 1960 9 September 1964)
	2. Leela Damodara Menon	Congress	
	3. K, R Saraswathy Amma	Congress	
	4. Kusurnam Joseph	Congress	
	5. Sarada Krishnan. O. T.	CPI	
	6. Aysha Bai. K. O.	CPI	
	7. K. R. Gowri Amma	CPI	
III. Third Kerala Legislative Assembly: 1967-69			
	1. K. R Gowri Amma	CPI (M)	

contd...

S.No. Women Legislators	Party Name	
IV. Fourth Kerala Legislative Assembly: 1970-77		
1. Ponnamma Jacob	Kerala Congress	
2. K. R Gowri Amma	CPI (M)	
V. Fifth Kerala Legislative Assembly: 1977-79		
1. Bhargavi Thankappan	CPI	
VI. Sixth Kerala Legislative Assembly: 1980-82		
1. Bhargavi Thankappan	CPI	
2. K.R Gowri Amma	CPI (M)	
3. P. Devootty	CPI (M)	
4. M. Kamalam	Janatha Party	
5. K.R. Saraswathy Amma	Kerala Congress	
VII. Seventh Kerala Legislative Assembly: 1982-87		
1. M. Kamalani	Congress	
2. K. R. Gowri Amma	CPI (M)	
3. P. Devootty	CPI (M)	
4. Bhargavi Thankappan	CPI	
5. Raichel Sunny Panaveli	Kerala Congress	(elected in the year 1986: bye-election)
VIII. Eighth Kerala Legislative Assembly: 1987-91		
1. Bhargavi Thankappan	CPI	(elected Deputy Speaker during 2 April 1987-25 June 1991).
2. K. R. Gowri Amma	CPI (M)	
3. Prof. Nabeesa Ummal	CPI	
4. Mary Kutty Amma. J.	CPI (M)	
5. Rosamma Punnoose	CPI (M)	
6. M T. Padma	Congress	
7. Rosamma Chacko	Congress	
8. Leela Damcdara Menon	Congress	
IX. Ninth Kerala Legislative Assembly: 1991-1994		
1. Rosamma Chacko	Congress	
2. Shobhana George	Congress	
3. K.C. Rosakutty	Congress	

S.No.	*Women Legislators*	*Party Name*
4.	Alphonsa Georte	Congress
5.	M.T. Padma	Congress
6.	K.R. Gowri Amma	Independent
7.	N.C. Radha	CPI (M)
8.	Prof. Meenkashi Thampan	CPI

* Data regarding serial numbers I-VIII compiled from Secretariat of Kerala Legislature. "Doyens of Past and Present". *Hundred years of Legislative Bodies in Kerala:* 1888-1989. Centenary Souvenir. Trivandrum, 1990, pp. 18-37A, p. 676.

** Ninth Kerala Legislative Assembly. Secretariat of Kerala Legislature Party Wise list. Trivandrum. January 20, 1994, pp. 1 -6.

Identifying Ministers

Very few number of women legislators had the distinction to represent the cabinet in Kerala Politics. Consequently the chances of women leaders to become Ministers are also limited. Altogether only four of them were appointed as Ministers during the period 1948-94. From the congress Party Annie Mascarene, M. Kamalam and M.T. padma served as Ministers in different periods with the former getting a small stint in the Travancore-Cochin State (see Table 7). The undivided Communist Party of India as well as the CPI (M) gave deserving accommodation to K.R. Gowri Amma in the Cabinet as Minister in all the four Governments it led. But she was unfortunate enough to miss the much coveted. Chief Ministership in 1987 when it was said that the LDF came to power by projecting K.R. Gowri Amma as the Potential Chief Minister. On the other hand, it may be noted that the three women legislators who became Ministers in the Congress led Governments could not hold very important portfolios.

There were three occasions when women legislators were elected to the position of Deputy Speakership in the Kerala legislature, in 1957-'59, 1960-64 and 1987-'91, (see Table 6). The Undivided CPI set the pattern and it was followed by the Congress in the next Government. Later, in 1987, Bhargavi Thankappan from CPI was also elected Deputy Speaker in the Eighth Assembly of Kerala.

TABLE 7: IDENTIFYING MINISTERS: 1948-94

Sl. No.	Name	Portfolio
1.	Annie Mascarene (Congress)	Minister for Health and Power from 5-7-1949 to 3-1-1950)
2.	Gowri Amma	Minister for Land Revenue and Excise, from (Communist Parry of India) 5-4-1957 to 31-7-59.
	—do— CPI (M)	Minister for Revenue. Food and Civil Supplies, from 6-3-1967 to 1-11-1969.
	—do— CPI (M)	Minister for Agriculture and Social Welfare, from 25-1-1980 to 20-10-1981.
	—do— CPI (M)	Minister for Industries and Social Welfare, from 2-4-1987 to 25-6-1991.
3.	M. Kamalam (Congress)	Minister for Co-operation from 24-5-1982 to 25-3-1987.
4.	M. T. Padma (Congress)	Minister for Rural Development from 27-6-1991 to-date.

Source: Secretariat of the Kerala Legislature, *op. cit.*, pp. 678-687.

The erstwhile Travancore-State had the unique distinction of having an aristocratic lady as the Regent when Her Higher Maharani Sethu Lakshmi Bhai took up the administration leadership of the State during 1924-31 since the young Manaraja was a minor. But that was a solitary exception as the subsequent key positions in the politics and administration of Travancore, Cochin and Kerala, since 1948, went to men.

Women Political Leaders of Kerala

The conventional attitude of society limiting women's role in public affairs, the male domination in the party ranks and leadership, the challenges of leadership recruitment in Party politics have no doubt constrained the scope of generating a galaxy of women political leaders, in Kerala the role of women in national movement and social reform movement had also been less compared to men. Probably women themselves have to be freed from the traditional moorings of society. The modern parties which revamp their machinery

have given sufficient scope for the recruitment of new blood to the organization particularly from the youth, workers, white collar employees, depressed classes and the like. However, in spite of the parties, involvement in launching and spear-heading some women's organizations of political and voluntary characters, a mass recruitment to politics has actually not taken place. Jeffrey (1993) argues that while women in Kerala are literate, cultured. politically conscious, qualified and deserving to reach civil service positions, there is a general tendency in society for not bringing them to public affairs. He had identified -some of the prominent women leaders whose political career was not very successful in the ultimate analysis. This list included leaders like Accamma Cheriyan, K.R. Gowri and others.

Here, it can be noted that we can see that there is definitely an increasing pride of place for women in Kerala society owing to the development of several factors. However, Politics seems to be a different arena altogether for the ladies. Again, there had not been any successful attempt in developing a powerful feminist movement in society. Yet, Kerala was able to produce a few women leaders, who had sincerely involved themselves in political activities. They served in party organizations, besides trying their luck to get elected to legislative bodies as well. However, in the pre-independence period, most of the women leaders who became legislators got their position primarily owing to the policy of nomination adopted by the rulers of Travancore, Cochin States and the Madras Presidency.

In fact, the freedom movement and the struggle for responsible government attracted a set of women leaders mostly from the middle class to involve themselves in politics. Within this group, a section of them were graduated to party politics and electoral game in the post-independence period while a great many others went into oblivion owing to retirement or for some unknown reasons. In the post-independent period, some of the parties, especially the undivided CPI and the Congress Party, attracted able and promising women leaders

to join politics through student and youth organizations of their parties. But the tempo of the women leadership gradually receded in the midst of family life and other situations. There are several reasons for this—for instance there is actually no proper atmosphere for the increased recruitment of women in Kerala politics. Again the lead for encouraging women should come from women themselves which is also lacking since there is no recurring pattern of women recruitment to party politics. The problems of expenditure, fear of scandals and the like are other reasons. It is true that reservation of seats for women in Panchayati Raj Institutions has created a good opportunity but this is a new trend altogether. Actually women have a crucial role in major aspects of policy making but this is not accepted by the tradition of Politics. The following discussion is a round up of the selected list of women leaders belonging to various parties in the history of Kerala's Politics.

Smt. T. Narayani Amma

She was a nominated member in the Sri Mulam Assembly for fifteen years (1933-47) and this period also witnessed the emergence of rapid demands for social changes. She was also a champion of the rights of women and highlighted their problems. She had presented "Travancore Anti-Dowry Bill" on January 27, 1940 in the Sri Mulam Assembly. She stressed the problems of dowry system that was creating havoc to women and also noted the poor economic conditions of the people in Travancore compared to other states and provinces. The lead taken by her had its influence, later in Cochin also. On February 21, 1948 V.R. Krishnan Ezhuthasan moved. The Cochin Women's Fundamental Right to Property' Bill.

Smt. Annie Thayyil

She was a freedom fighter, author of 78 books to her credit, editor of a Women's magazine, legislator, and prominent figure in the ranks of Congress leaders from Cochin. She served in the Cochin Legislative Council during 1945-47 and was an elected member of Travancore-Cochin Legislative Assembly during 1948-51.

Mrs. Mary Poonnen Lukose (1888-1976)

Mrs. Lukose has the distinction of being the first lady member of any Legislature in India when she was nominated in the first Travancore Legislative Council in 1922-23. She was a medical practitioner and was elevated to the Durbar Physician in 1924, at a time when only 15 per cent of the Travancore women were literate (more than seven times the all India proportion). Her contemporaries in her B.A. education included State Congress leaders like Pattom Thanu Pillai and T.M. Varghese. Mrs. Luckose was continuously nominated in the Assemblies of various periods till 1944.

Smt. Accamma Cheriyan (1909-1982)

A legendary leader from the ranks of women in the State Congress of Travancore, she was in the forefront of the struggle for responsible Government. She had spent two and a half years in jail. Her spirited leadership against the autocratic regime of Diwan Sir C.P. Ramaswamy lyer and the famous Kaudiar Palace March of 1938 is still fresh in the memory of the older generation in Travancore. Her political career, unfortunately, was not very successful. Originally she was a teacher and later headmistress by profession. She was elected unopposed to the Travancore Legislative Assembly in 1948 and elected to the Travancore-Cochin Legislative Assembly in 1949-51. She soon estranged herself from the Congress and resigned from the Party for its opportunistic policies. In the 1952 elections, the Congress did not field even a single women candidate and according to the Party leaders, women's proper place is in the kitchen. Although married to a State Congress activist, V.V. Varkey, she agreed to run as an independent candidate backed by opposition parties in Travancore-Cochin. Accamma Cheriyan lost the race but got polled 43 per cent of the total votes in her favour. She temporarily retired from politics but again joined Congress in 1967. She contested again but as a Congress Party candidate in elections in the year 1967 and failed again miserably, probably owing to the Anti-Congress wave that swept the Kerala Assembly elections. She is retired from politics since then. Analysing

the problems, allegations, bad taste campaigns she had to face in her career. Jeffrey notes that "her career exemplified the price Kerala women would pay if they strayed from areas of life deemed fitting and respectable". He argues that the experiences of Accamma Cheriyan rather deter Kerala women from public politics than encourage them.

Annie Mascarene

She was an advocate by profession but was attracted to the State Congress activity during the freedom struggle. She had the distinction of being elected to the Constituent Assembly in 1949 from Travancore. In 1948 she was elected to the Travancore Legislative Assembly. She also served as the Minister for Health and Power in Travancore-Cochin State during 1949-50. In the first General Elections she was elected to the Lok Sabha and served as such for five years from 1952-57.

Smt. Anna Chandy

She has the double distinction of being the first lady lawyer of the whole of Kerala (1931-32) and the first woman High Court Judge in the country. She was a nominated member in the Sri Mulam Popular Assembly and later in the Travancore Legislative Council. She was also the Editor of "Srimathi', the only women's weekly-newspaper in the whole of the country, edited by a lady. Smt. Anna Chandy moved a resolution in December 1934 at the All India Women's Conference in Trivandrum calling for the establishment of birth control clinics throughout India. The resolution was moved at a time when conservatism was widespread against these ideas. The proposal was a progressive one and was supported by Mrs. Lakshmi N. Menon, who later became Deputy Minister for External Affairs in Government of India.

Smt. Kuttymalu Amma (1905-85)

A leading figure in the freedom struggle from Malabar. Smt. Kuttymalu Amma had involved in a variety of professional activities. She was elected to the Madras Legislative Assembly

in 1337 and in 1946. She was a social worker, women activist and was deeply interested in journalism. She served as the Editor of the Popular Malayalam daily 'Mathrubhoomi' for a long period.

Mrs. Usha Krishna Kumar

She was the General Secretary of All India Mahila Congress and recipient of Mahila Siromani Award (presented by Mother Teressa) in 1992. She was conferred International Women's Award by the NRI Institute, Delhi in 1992 and nominated for Gaurav Puraskar Award. She entered active politics in 1981 from Kerala and is still being involved in various political assignments both in Kerala and outside. She was the secretary of Kerala Pradesh Mahila Congress, Vice-President of All India Women's Conference and Joint Secretary of All India Mahila Congress. She had campaigned in elections, served as an observer for Congress Party in various States. Widely travelled in Europe, Asia and former USSR Usha Krishna Kumar is also involved in various socio-cultural activities. She is the wife of S. Krishna Kumar, former Minister of State for Defence. In the November 1993 Assembly elections, she contested as the Congress candidate from R.K. Puram Constituency, New Delhi but lost by a narrow margin. Her political involvement has basically two broad dimensions—one as activist of Congress Party and two as champion of the cause of empowerment of women in India.

Smt. K.R. Gowri Amma

A towering personality in Kerala politics, K. R. Gowri Amma was born in a well-to-do family of Ezhava Community in Travancore. However, the majority of the members of the Ezhava Community during that period were in backward position. She was attracted to Communism in 1348 while studying law. The period was also marked by tensions and problems owing to the revolutionary role of the party then. Braving the police arrests and traditional scepticism about Communism, Gowri Amma was soon accepted as the leader of the working class. Since 1952, she won all the elections

from Alappuzha district in 1952, 1954, 1957, 1960. 1965, 1967, 1970, 1980. 1982, 1987, and 1991. except in 1977 elections. In the Third Assembly (1967-69) she was a lone female member in the House. Mrs. Gowri Amma was made a senior Cabinet Minister in all the undivided CPI and CPI(M) led Governments (see Table 7). She occupied positions in the Party up to the rank of State Secretariat. Again, she also served as the President of the Communist Party-led women's association in Kerala. Married to T.V. Thomas, a CPI Leader , but she had to lead an estranged family life, after the CPI split in 1964. Her commitment to the Party and to society was solid. As a Revenue Minister in the first Communist Government (1957-59) she was responsible for initiating the Land Reforms in Kerala.

In the midst of the tightly contested 1987 Polls, the CPI(M) also projected her as the future Chief Minister. However, this did not materialize. The party later stated that it had never projected Gowri Amma as the potential Chief Minister for 1987 Polls. Ironically, in 1994, Gowri Amma was formally removed from the primary membership of the Party after a series of rifts and ego clashes with the party leadership. The issue become a great media event at the national level also. She had made up her mind to launch an organization for the protection of democracy and to fight for the cause of the weaker sections of society rather than preferring a retirement from politics altogether. Jeffrey earlier argued that, "Gowri's career highlights the limitations of women in Kerala. Though schooling for girls and salaried jobs for women are desirable, participation in public politics is not. A women who goes outside the regulated routine of home and office becomes the target of gossip". However, Gowri Amma does not subscribe to this view. Jeffrey further quoted her view that "Kerala has had strong women movements from the working sections and not in the form of feminist intellectuals.

Smt. Rosamma Punnoose

The sister of the former State Congress leader Accamma

Cheriyan, Rosamma married the Communist leader P.T. Punnoose and has been a CPI activist throughout. She was elected to the Kerala Assembly in 1987. She also served as the Chairman of the Plantation Corporation and State Housing Board.

Smt. Leela Damodara Menon

She was one of the founding leaders of the Congress Women's Front in Kerala. She served in the Madras University Senate in 1950 and Kerala University in 1964. Married to A. Damodara Menon, a Congress leader, Smt Leela Damodara Menon has been active in the Congress Party and its fora. She was elected to Kerala Assembly in 1957, 1960 and in 1987. During 1947-80 she was elected to Rajya shabha from Kerala. Currently, she is the President of the State Mahila Congress.

Smt. Bhargavi Thankappan

She was elected to Lok Sabha from Adoor (Reserved } Constituency in 1971 and served till 1977. She was elected to Kerala Assembly in 1977, 1980, 1982 and in 1987 consecutively. In the Fifth Kerala Assembly (1977-79), she was the lone female member in the House. Bhargavi Thankappan was elected the Deputy Speaker of the Eighth Kerala Assembly (1987-91), the third female member to hold the post in Kerala.

Smt. M.Kamalam

She has been an active worker of the Congress party from Malabar. After the split in the party in 1969, she moved initially with Congress(O) which later merged with Janata Party. The Janata Parry suffered rifts and for a short while she was in the Democratic Janata Party which formally merged with Congress(I) in 1982. She was elected to Kerala Legislative Assembly twice, in 1980, and 1982. During 1982-87 period she served as Minister for Cooperation. She is active in the Congress Party and its fora. However, she lost the 1937 and 1991 elections. Recently she has organized a unit for propagating Gandhian ideals in society.

Smt. Susheela Gopalan

She has been an active worker and leader in the undivided Communist Party and the CPI(M) since 1964. She had organized the coir workers and poor peasants, besides championing the cause of women. Smt. Susheela Gopalan is the wife of the legendary leader of the CPI (M), Sri A.K. Gopalan. She was elected to Lok Sabha twice in 1967 and 1991.

Smt. M.T. Padma

She was Minister for Fisheries and Rural Development in Kerala. Besides, she is working as the General Secretary of the State Mahila Congress. She began her political career in 1968 through Kerala Students Union and became active from 1972. Later, she worked in District Congress Committee and Pradesh Congress Committee of the party. She is holding Master's Degree in Science and Bachelor's Degree in Education and Law. Smt. Padma is of the opinion that through organization such as Mahila Congress, she will be able to create awareness about women's welfare programmes and propagate Governmental activities in the field. Regarding the limits to women's involvement in political activity, she identified the following problems:

(i) the social set-up creates not only hindrances but also cultural constraints,

(ii) creating self confidence on the part of the women is very essential for political activity,

(iii) recognition from the family is important and usually it is possible for the married women to acquire that societal recognition,

(iv) again, there is no income for the women political leaders while they hold party positions.

This is quite opposite to an employed girl who receive monthly salary. A party functionary has economic constraints. Hence, there is no value for women political leaders who had no income from politics unlike an employed girl. She is of the firm belief that the reservation for women in Panchayati Raj Institutions will certainly increase political participation of

women. Hence these provisions are essential in the beginning stages.

Conclusion

In fact, the general position of women in Kerala has improved considerably during 20th century. The land reforms also helped in bringing a better position to the women. The replacement of the joint family system with nuclear family also helped the changes in this direction. Again, women also played a prominent role in the freedom struggle. Political consciousness and general awareness of the Kerala women can be considered as high. They are educated and highly politically conscious. However, most of the women in Kerala aspire for jobs that bring them status, financial independence and courage in daily life situations. Even those who are not interested in jobs prefer to be educated. In general women are considered to be capable of leading a successful family life. However, this status of women is also due to the general development of the society through various factors. Today, we can find women in middle and high level salaried jobs as senior civil servants, as teachers in Universities, Colleges. Schools and in professions such as nursing. The State also has a lady I.P.S. Officer. The leadership provided by Smt. Gugathakumari, Smt. Lakshmi N. Menon and Smt. Madhavikutty and others in environment and cultural literary fields are also well appreciated in the society. But, unfortunately, this type of women's general involvement and growth in public position is not matched in politics, which is also a public activity. In electoral politics, there role is actually limited. Data presented in Tables 1 to 6 highlights only a marginal growth in women's representation in legislative bodies even after Liberal politics and democratic participation got well entrenched in the State.

While women's political participation in elections is increasing, this is again not matched by effective women organizations that can influence the community, in toto. There are not many women leaders in the higher ranks of political parties at the State or local level. This is a general

situation present among all the parties. Commenting on this Mrs. Usha Krishna Kumar the All India Mahila Congress leader, opined that there exists considerable scope to involve women on issues affecting the society. This includes economic issues, women and child welfare, promoting women entrepreneurs, involving them in Khadi and Village industries and the like. The women have to be mobilised starting from lower level to higher levels. For achieving this women from good family background should come forward. The male dominance in political processes is a reality today in Kerala. In spite of the women representation and leadership in the middle and lower ranks of political parties and its auxiliary wings and statutory representation acquired in , the civic bodies, the limitation of women leadership unfortunately has come to stay in Kerala politics.

REFERENCES

1. Annamma Thomas and T.M. Thomas , *Kerala Immigrants in America: A Sociological Study of St. Thomas Christians,* Simons Printers, Cochin. 1984. pp.109-110.
2. C. Achuta Menon, "Renaissance Movement in Kerala" cited in C. Achuta Menon Foundation, *For an Indian Model: Essays in Homage to C. Achuta Menon.* Trivandrum, 1993, pp. 53-54.
3. Chie Nakane (1963), "The Nayar Family in a Disintegrating Matrilineal system in Yogesh Atul, (Ed.) 1993, *op.cit.,* p. 303.
4. G. Gopakumar, *Congress Party and State Politics,* Deep and Deep Publications, New Delhi, 1984, pp. 258-260.
5. Interview with Mrs. Usha Krishna Kumar, General Secretary of Mahila Congress at New Delhi, on 8 February, 1994.
6. Interview with Mrs. Usha Krishna Kumar, General Secretary, Mahila Congress at New Delhi on 8 February. 1994.
7. Interview with Smt. M.T. Padma, Minister for Fisheries and Rural Development at Trivandrum, on 27 February, 1994.
8. M.J. Joseph, "Gendered Justice," Economic and *Political Weekly.* Vol. XXVIII, No.50, Dec. 11, 1993, p. 2711.
9. Robin Jeffrey, *Politics, Women and Well-being: How Kerala Became a Model.* Oxford University Press, Oxford, 1993, pp. 94-98

10. S.E. Kathleen Gough (1959), "The Nayars and the Definition of Marriage" in Yogesh Atul (Ed) *Understanding Indian Society,* Har Anand Publications, Delhi, 1993.
11. Secretariat of Kerala Legislative, *Hundred Years of Legislative Bodies in Kerala: 1888-1958,* Trivandrum, 1993, pp. 104-105.

8

Women in Politics

> "Besides the practical knowledge which defeat offers, there are important personality profits to be taken. Defeat strips away false values and makes you realise what you really want. It stops you from chasing butterflies and puts you to work digging gold."
>
> —*William Moulton Morston*

I

Politics and governance are the field which are dominated by men all through the ages everywhere. Though we find instances like Cleopatra, Queen Elizabeth, Queen Victoria, Rani Laxmibai, Chand Bibi, and more recently or Margeret Thatcher, Sirimavo Bhandarnaike, Indira Gandhi, Benazir Bhutto etc. heading the Government of their respective nations/states. It is worthwhile here to be noted that most of the women leaders occupied the position by virtue of their belonging to either royal families or to elite and aristocratic class by way of inheritance of sort.

Are there differences in the access of men and women to authority and political power? Do men enjoy greater influence in the elaboration and application of political decision than women? Are there basic differences in the political status of women in the different states within India, in cities of different sizes, in different castes, classes and communities? Specifically, what about urban versus rural women?

Many general questions are also there on the degree and

patterns of political involvement and behaviour among women: How far do women exercise their recognised political rights and prerogatives? Do all women exercise them equally? Or, are there differences amongst them as to their interest and involvement in political affairs? What part that women play at each level of political participation? What role, do they play in elections, campaign activities, electioneering and in direct political action? What is their role at higher levels, that is, in legislatures and executive positions? What is the influence of demographic and social factors on their political involvement and behaviour? Are there differences in their political involvement and behaviour by age, education and social status? Or, do these differences arise from their psychological and personality make-up? How far do urbanisation, intellectual atmosphere of the family and role beliefs directly influence their political participation and behaviour? In what ways do attitudes of men affect the degree of political involvement and participation among women? Are men willing to accept women on equal terms? Or, do they feel that women should be admitted to political offices only in exceptional circumstances and then only within strictly defined limits? What are the policies of the different political parties with respect to the involvement of women in political affairs? What factors enter in their selection for elective and executive positions?

Other general questions focus on what women do in politics: What influence does their participation in public life have on the political policies of the political parties and the bias of their propaganda? Do women concentrate on specialised matters, such as health, education, motherhood, family welfare and housing, etc., that is, on all matters which are considered to be a special interest to women? Or, do they have more broad-based interests in politics? And is any short or long-term shift taking place in their political concerns? All these and many other questions should be asked and they lead to an immensely complex analysis.

Very scanty reliable information is available, however,

to help answer these questions. However, if an attempt is made it would consist largely of commonsense generalisations. Anyone, who is foolish enough to agree to discuss the question "What is the position of Indian women in the field of politics?" must, therefore, focus of a few elements—and hope for the best.

It seems apparent that women differ considerably among themselves as to their political involvement and patterns of political participation. Some women vote like their husbands or join the ranks of those who with complete responsibility ignore politics entirely. Because of the nature of sex roles and authority structure in the family, they find it almost natural to follow the male 'authority figure' when they go to the polls. Others participate in politics on their own but concede to male pressures. Still others realise the significance and value of their political prerogatives and use them quite independently.

Again, the structural position of a woman discourages both political participation and political independence. Political scientists are of opinion that a high degree of political participation, depends at least in part, on the presence of group pressures emphasising the importance of the ballot, and the absence of cross pressures discouraging political independence. In the case of women, each variable works against their participation in public life. A woman finds little encouragement to participate in politics. Unless she has a supportive husband or father, it is just as easy for her not to go to the polls. Moreover, the whole idea of women's place contradicts the idea of female political independence which is hard to gain. When women participate in politics, they respond to public affairs as individuals rather than as members of a special interest with a distinctive set of interests. This has special significance for those who argue that women should form a front of their own, independent of other political parties, and express their disinterested opinion and fight for issues of vital concern to them. It would suggest that the idea that women should organise along sex lines, nominate women,

urge special legislation and vote en masse, represents utopia. Women differ in emotions, ideals, and prejudices just as much as men do after all they too are human beings.

Again, there are several alternate courses through which a woman gets to higher forms of political participation. She can get to it via the widow inheritance, or as a stand-in candidate or through a complex network of social and patronage links. Whatever the avenue of her entry into politics, she has to depend on the favours of male party officials for her political promotion.

Most women in top legislative positions either accommodate or depend on male leaders for whatever influence they might exert. Lacking a strong power base of their own, it is often hard for them to build their own independent spheres of influence. Moreover, the fact that most women remain in office for brief periods, would entail that there would be little opportunity for them to build influence. It is only in exceptional circumstances, that a woman has an opportunity to build her own sphere of political influence. Male political leaders like to appoint those women to political posts who they think share their point of view about political matters or who would be amenable to their political influence without hampering their hallow.

When elected to party or legislative positions, they find it difficult to concentrate on issues that are of special concern to women. While they may continue an interest in health, education and welfare, their pattern of participation is quite varied. This fact supports recent findings that the political behaviour of men and women is quite similar at higher echelons.

Mostly, there is a keen competition of available elective and executive positions and success in this competition depends on a large variety of pulls and pressures. A woman as woman stands little chance of success in this tug of war. She must mobilise other pulls and pressures if she wants to succeed.

From the above propositions it is obvious that women are, by and large, characterised by a passive political orientation. It seems clear that the sources of passive and dependent political orientation among women are rooted within the social structure itself. In tradition and practice, the Indian social structure provides an elaborate and segregated network of roles for each sex, with little interaction or exchange between them. This division of labour, in most cases, has led to division of authority as well.

Now, the idea that the two sexes should fulfil different roles and responsibilities is buttressed by institutions such as the family, and transmitted from generation to generation through the socialisation process. Males continue to be raised in a way that encourages a participatory life-style, females in a way that contributes to withdrawal, and attitudes and behaviour reinforce each other. Consequently, with few models of 'independent' women to emulate, only a small percentage of women are willing to risk failure in the female world of marriage and motherhood in order to prove their worth in the male world of politics in simple natural course.

It seems quite clear that the real obstacle to equality in the political sphere lies in the division of domains between men and women; and the legal provisions have not substantially altered this. Women enjoy the right to vote and to be elected to decision-making positions, but these legal provisions are of little help. Nor would they mean much as long as the structure of relationships between the sexes continues to reinforce the idea that the man should be dominant in action toward the world outside the family and the woman should accept his leadership passively. Only a substantial upheaval that undermines the structural basis for traditional views of male and female roles would modify the existing assymetry in the political status of men and women.

The recent Inter-Parliamentary Union conference, held in New Delhi, gave the campaign for 33% reservation for women in the Indian Parliament and State legislatures a much-needed shot in the arm. Former Prime Minister H.D.

Deve Gowda's statement at the conference promising necessary measures to achieve equal partnership between men and women in society was seen by Indian delegates as an indication of the Government's commitment in this regard. However, recent moves in the direction of reducing the quota to 15% are suggestive of agreement on the principle of reservation but not on the quota itself.

The conference, which was attended by 240 delegates from 78 countries, focussed on the theme of "Towards Partnership between Men and Women in Politics." The conference had its share of rhetoric, declarations of political commitment and Communist-bashing, the last coming from the representatives of some of the "new democracies" in Europe. The supporters of reservation for women in the legislatures outnumbered those who felt that women's induction should be voluntary and start from the top. The final consensus was that establishment of quotas for women's political participation is "legitimate and practical." It was also felt that women need to be established in the political party systems as well—in the membership and hierarchies of political parties, and with respect to the candidates chosen by them to contest elections.

The deliberations showed a consonance of views and experiences between delegates from the Indian subcontinent and Africa. The Zambian delegate, Gladys Mutukwa, said that affirmative action had drastically increased the number of women in Parliament and other bodies in Uganda, South Africa and Mozambique. The African delegates suggested that the mechanism of affirmative action be applied at all levels of political life, especially in political parties. They were unanimous that an increase in the existing 30% reservation (in Zambia, Mozambique, Botswana, Uganda, South Africa, Namibia and Kenya) was necessary and that parity in membership could be attempted later. They also wanted the abolition of discriminating customary laws in their countries.

George Anastasspoulos, vice-president of the European

Parliament, raised the crucial issue of women's presence in the labour force as a pre-requisite for their political participation. "The route for greater participation has been the strengthening of women's status," he said. "Women, at least in the European Union, are today full participants in the labour market."

An Austrian delegate, Irene Preudenschuss-Reichl, citing a referendum held in her country, said that the imbalance in sharing paid and unpaid work is "critically linked with women's under-representation in political life." Namibian President Sam Nujoma said that the lack of facilities for mothers to take care of their children at the workplace impeded women's participation in public life.

Statistics of women's representation in Parliament revealed a dismal picture, the exception being the Nordic countries, where it ranged between 30-50%. Sweden is at the top with 40%. In Germany, Argentina and South Africa women's representation was between 25 and 29%.

Speaking of Sweden's experience, Viola Furubjelke, parliamentarian and president of the Standing Committee on Foreign Affairs, told *Frontline* that every political party in her country had women's organisations, which demanded in the 1970s that seats be reserved for women in Parliament. Measures such as the provision of centres for child care, homes for the parents of political activists as well as free meals for their children at school strengthened that demand. Sweden is probably the only country where Parliament has a child-care centre. "It is a fulltime job for us," Furubjelke said. Nearly 50% of ministers in the government are women. Women have been given important portfolios such as Labour, Social Affairs and Justice.

The percentage of women in the Canadian Parliament is 19%. Shiela Finestone, a Canadian MP, said that it was mandatory for all political parties to have equal representation from both sexes. All committees, boards of directors and even the election commission had to have an equal number of men and women on them. While there was no specific reservation

for women in Parliament, the Federal government saw to it that minority and disadvantaged groups (women, handicapped and indigenous peoples) were adequately covered under the laws on equity with respect to employment and remuneration.

Cyprus presents a different picture. Androula Vassiliou, the Foreign Affairs Minister of Cyprus, lamented that although 89% of women in her country were university graduates, their political role was not taken seriously. Vassiliou, who is an advocate of reservation, told *Frontline* that there was no Ministry to look after women's affairs. There is a permanent agency, however, established by the previous socialist government, that deals with women's rights. "When we fought elections, journalists wrote more about what we were wearing and than on the issues we raised," she said.

A striking feature of the current European situation is that that there has been a significant decline in women's parliamentary participation in the former socialist countries. In a somewhat debatable explanation of this phenomenon, Polish delegate Jerzy Wiatr said that it reflected a rejection of Communist politics, which, according to him, was based on the "enforced mass participation of men and women." He said that while women constituted one-third of the membership of the Communist parties that were in power men had a near-monopoly of key positions of power.

Alena Svobodova, MP from the Czech Republic and member of the Communist Party of Bohemia and Moravia, explained the decline in women's participation in different terms. She told *Frontline* that specific socio-economic conditions were responsible for the low level of women's participation in politics. "In the period between 1948 and 1989, the conditions for universal participation of women were gradually developed." Women's employment increased, women gained significant positions in many professions, participated in research and, overall, improved their educational status. There were laws that guaranteed a three-month period of maternity leave for working women, that ensured that their children and other family members were taken care of when they fell ill, that

created part-time jobs, and so on Creches, kindergartens, after-school centres, hostels and youth clubs for school and pre-school children were in abundance and ensure a woman's right to participate satisfactorily in the labour market.

After the fall of the Socialist government and the subsequent split of Czechoslovakia, socio-economic conditions worsened. "Of the 3% unemployed in the Czech republic, 62% are women," she said. The government shut down many nursery schools and kindergartens. As a result, women were forced to stay at home and look after their children. Although the new government offered better opportunities for education and a wide range of fields of study and opened new vistas for private business, services necessary for making household work easier became very expensive. The cost of health care, housing and transportation went up. "The legislative protection of women's rights has been narrowed, especially in the area of work," said Svobodova. The Labour Code was violated in many areas. Minimum wages were denied and there was an unwillingness to employ women in part-time jobs.

"Women do not demand their rights any more for fear of losing their jobs," Svobodova said. Old notions such as "a woman belongs in the kitchen" are now propagated, and a loss of interest in public activities and economic dependence on the husbands has become the norm. "This has affected the political and economic participation of women," Svobodova said. The level of women's political participation was not commensurate with their level of education. "Regrettably, women and family issues are not the priorities of the government of the Czech Republic." She said that there was no executive or legislative body that enforced women's rights. A bill introduced by the opposition to establish a parliamentary committee for women's rights was voted down in Parliament.

The delegate from Estonia, which was part of the Soviet Union and which is now led by the Reform Party, blamed the period of transition the country had been going through since the 1990s for the low level of political participation by women. While admitting that a weak women's movement

was also responsible for the low numbers, Valve Kirsipuu, an MP, said that the earlier system only ensured "formal participation of women." The former Union of Soviet Socialist Republics had reserved 42% seats for women in the Duma but it was more like the will of the administration, she told *Frontline*. The women's movement in Estonia was not political unlike the one in the former USSR. "You cannot force women into politics if they do not want it," said Kirsipuu.

Antoneta Deda, an Albanian MP from the ruling Democratic Party, said that the number of women MPs in her country had gone up from 8 in 1994 to 21 in 1996. "The 20 women MPs in the Democratic Party are highly educated," Deda told *Frontline*. Though over 40% of the MPs during the Communist era were women, "they were mainly tractorists, milkmaids and farmers... you know, the dictatorship of the proleteriat... but a milkmaid cannot be an MP; may be in one case but not in others," she said. To become an MP, a woman needed "ability, organisation, debating skills, publicity and party loyalty," said Deda who was all for quotas but very clear about where the representation would come from.

Geeta Mukherjee, parliamentarian and one of India's representative at the conference, disagreed with the views of the Polish, Albanian and Estonian delegates that political participation was forced on women in the former Socialist bloc countries. Women in these countries had a history of political activity and it was not easy for them to opt for the domain of the household. According to her, it is the absence of social security measures that have forced women to go back to their families. "Women want their families but that is not the only thing they want."

In Greece, 6% of the members of Parliament are women. Minas Stavrakakis, MP from the ruling socialist party, said that the party's constitution provided for women's participation at all levels of political organisation. There was 20% representation for women in the Polit Bureau, the Central Committee and the sub-committees of the party.

The overall focus of the conference was on changing attitudes; in this context the conference also declared the need for "nothing less than a new social contract in which men and women work in equality and complementarity." The integration of women in the political process at all levels of political life is essential for the democratisation of politics. The conference characterised quotas as a necessary evil to be applied on a temporary basis in order to address "the current dramatic imbalance between men and women." The conference declaration also stated that quotas "should be abolished once the desired effect has been achieved." Although little commitment was sought from governments and Parliaments, the IPU recommended that parties should have quotas for women within their structures and put up women candidates for at least one-third of the seats they contested in elections. In political campaigns, one-third of campaign resources should be allocated to women.

On the question of quotas, Geeta Mukherjee said: "For us, there is no other way out. We hoped that the percentage of women would increase in Parliament and State Legislatures but that did not happen. It is now the political duty of the state to ensure such participation." Mukherjee said that Bangladesh, Nepal and Sri Lanka hoped to emulate India once the 81st Constitutional Amendment Bill was passed. The resolutions of the conference might just become platitudes because the Bill on women's reservation has not found a place in the list of bills to be tabled in Parliament in the current budget session.

Thus it can be safely inferred that women politicians are guided by their patrons in their everyday functions. Hardly they have frank say or independent decision-making. This, a long journey is yet there to realise the drams devised for.

II

In terms of etymology, Political participation can be considered to include an involvement in any form of organised activity that affects, or seeks to affect these power relationships. It

refers broadly also be "activities by those not formally empowered to make decisions, these activities being mainly intended to influence the attitudes and behaviour of those who have powers for decision-making." In fact, protests and demonstrations against those in power also form part of political participation. Women's participation has covered a range of activities including movements, protests and support meetings on all issues connected with labour, dowry, rape, domestic violence, price-rise, food adulteration and deforestation, as also movements for the promotion of peace.

But however, with particular reference to women's participation in India has only been limited application, mainly because of various dubious considerations of social economic and political variables. Broadly political participation of women is severely limited due to a nexus of traditional factors, these are the domination of Indian politics by considerations of caste, class, religion, feudal and family status etc., all of which are parochial essentially patriarchal forces that work in favour of men against women. Consequently, women are still left on the periphery of the political process, and political participation remains elusive to most of them, inspite of their voting and election and also capture of some seats of power and influence.

The most crucial problem in any attempt to measure women's political participation simply by studying official or organisational membership and voting, is the finding that much of the Third World Politics occurs outside conventional political institutions. Hence, political participation seeks also to re-organize the lives of members of human society and ensure that the participation by women is not underestimated by being branded 'non-political and women's concerns treated. as 'social' in nature.

There are several socio-economic constraints by which women have been marginalised. The number of women in leadership positions at the local, village, district and rational level is still not commensurate with their numbers in society. In India, limited adult franchise was granted to women in

1937. Since then, women have been participating in political processes, a voters, as candidates contesting the elections, involved in deliberations both in the State Assemblies and Parliament and also through holding public office at different levels and in the judiciary.

Women and Voting Behaviour

Voting is the basic activity by which the citizen get assimilated in the political process. Women's participation in formal elections is to a great extent dependent on the mobilisation efforts of the political parties, general awareness among the community of the importance of exercising franchise, and the overall political culture.

Looking back to the past history of the women's political participation we find that no serious efforts appears to have been made to mobilise women as a political pressure group by any political party. Caste, personality and families of candidates appear to be more important to voters than party ideology or affiliations. Some other factors like education, religion, class and tradition also seen to affect women's participation. However, voting as an indication of political participation for women in India, has its own strength and weakness. Voting has a tremendous impact for equalising and mobilising women. Yet, it has to be noted that voting requires the least initiative and internal motivation. Very often the woman citizen treats the day of voting as a welcome break from the dull and tiring routine and does not appear to have a motion of why she should note for a particular candidate. However, over the years, the number of women contestants in parliamentary elections has not increased. Political parties seem uniformly reluctant to field women candidates. The high cost of electioneering is another deterrent to most women candidates. Because of these factors there is an increasing tendency among women to contest elections as independent candidates.

The proportion of seats won by women to the Lok Sabha stands in 1988 at 46 seats out of house of 537 seats. The

Rajya Sabha has 28 women in a house of 245 seats. There has been a greater representation of women in Rajya Sabha by nomination. The pattern is not very different at State level. The all India total stands at 44 women elected out of 241 women contestants, as against 1486 men out of 8415 male contestants. For instance, in Orissa in 1980, for the House of 147 members, 10 contestants were women of whom only 5 were elected. In 1980 in Tamil Nadu, 5 out of 17 women candidates won. An in-depth study of women at grassroots level politics reflects a similar trend. However, the redeeming factor is that women in rural areas are capable of progressive thinking and have the potential for valuable social participation if a conscious effort is made to secure their involvement.

Women in 9th Lok Sabha (1989)

Much water has flown through Ganges since the Ninth Lok Sabha. However it is perlinent here to present the women's position in the 9th Lok Sabha. Luck apparently ran at for the majority of women who tried their electoral fortunes for the ninth Lok Sabha as only 28 of the approximately 150 women candidates in the fray have been returned. This poor presence of women in the House of 525 at the moment gives a clear indication that the new Lok Sabha is lacking much of the colour and glamour of the previous one which had 43 members of the fair sex, most of them on the treasury benches. The women parliamentarians, however, constituted less than eight per cent of the Lok Sabha's total strength. This percentage has dropped to about five in the just constituted ninth Lok Sabha.

Of the 28 women members, almost half are the new faces. It is a mere coincidence that the member of women returned this time is just the same as it was in 1967 as well as 1980. This number dropped to 21 in 1971 and declined further to 19 in 1977. It went up to 28 in 1980 and swelled to 43 in 1984. Significantly, the majority of the women returned to the Lok Sabha in 1984 belonged to the Congress Party but this time the case was reverse.

TABLE 1: NO. OF CANDIDATES CONSITUTION ELECTED TO THE STATE LEGISLATIVE ASSEMBLIES BY SEX IN STATES/UT FROM 1978-83

Sl. No.	State / Union Territory	1978				1979-80				1982-83			
		Contested		Elected		Contested		Elected		Contested		Elected	
		M	F	M	F	M	F	M	F	M	F	M	F
1.	Andhra Pradesh	1491	47	284	10	—	—	—	—	1647	73	282	12
2.	Assam	917	21	125	1	—	—	—	—	448	3	108	1
3.	Bihar	—	—	—	—	2925	77	312	12	—	—	—	—
4.	Gujarat	—	—	—	—	950	24	178	5	—	—	—	—
5.	Haryana	—	—	—	—	—	—	—	—	1068	27	83	7
6.	Himachal Pradesh	—	—	—	—	—	—	—	—	432	3	65	8
7.	Jammu and Kashmir	—	—	—	—	—	—	—	—	515	7	75	—
8.	Karnataka	1137	28	245	9	—	—	—	—	1977	98	777	2
9.	Kerala	—	—	—	—	587	132	235	5	682	17	136	9
10.	Madhya Pradesh	—	—	—	—	1950	50	302	18	—	—	—	—
11.	Maharashtra	1777	42	280	8	1488	49	269	19	—	—	—	—
12.	Manipur	—	—	—	—	394	7	60	—	—	—	—	—
13.	Meghalaya	255	7	59	1	—	—	—	—	309	8	60	—
14.	Nagaland	—	—	—	—	—	—	—	—	244	1	60	—
15.	Orissa	—	—	—	—	720	10	142	5	—	—	—	—

16. Punjab	—	—	—	—	703	19	111	6	—	—	—	—
17. Rajasthan	—	—	—	—	1375	31	190	10	—	—	—	—
18. Sikkim	—	—	—	—	233	11	32	—	—	—	—	—
19. Tamil Nadu	—	—	—	—	1012	17	229	5	—	—	—	—
20. Tripura	—	—	—	—	—	—	—	—	119	11	56	4
21. Uttar Pradesh	—	—	—	—	4525	94	401	24	—	—	—	—
22. West Bengal	—	—	—	—	—	—	—	—	1179	26	287	7
23. Andaman and Nicobar Islands	—	—	—	—	—	—	—	—	—	—	—	—
24. Arunachal Pradesh	84	2	30	—	93	2	29	1	—	—	—	—
25. Chandigarh	—	—	—	—	—	—	—	—	—	—	—	—
26. Dadra & Nagar Haveli	—	—	—	—	—	—	—	—	—	—	—	—
27. Delhi	—	—	—	—	—	—	—	—	379	12	52	4
28. Goa, Daman & Diu	—	—	—	—	174	3	30	—	—	—	—	—
29. Lakshadweep	—	—	—	—	—	—	—	—	—	—	—	—
30. Mizoram	153	1	29	1	147	3	29	1	—	—	—	—
31. Pondicherry	—	—	—	—	128	4	29	1	—	—	—	—

M: Male. F: Female.

Source: Election Commission of India, New Delhi.

Encouraged by the spectacular success of its women nominees in 1984 the Congress-I decided to field 53 women candidates this time but unfortunately most of them could not withstand the anti- Congress (I) wave that swept the northern region and fall at the hustings. Of the 53 women put up by the Congress (I), only 15 got elected, representing a success rate of 28 per cent. The BJP which put up to women candidates had a better showing with five of them being returned. The performance of the Janta Dal and the other parties including the leftists has not been any better with two women each entering the Lok Sabha under the banner of the JD, CPI (M) and Akali Dal (Mann group). The CPI and the BSP have one each.

The scenario, therefore, is that of the 28 women in the House, 26 is adorning the opposition benches while two of them on the treasury side. Of the 12 women nominated by the Congress (I) in Uttar Pradesh only three were elected. However, the high profile women MPs have been rejected by the electorate. Among these defeated were also the close relatives of politicians in power. Bihar returned two women this time against nine in 1984. Of the 10 women fielded by the Congress (I) in State only one emerged victorious. The other member is Janata Dal's Andhra Pradesh improved its tally returning all the five Congress(I) women nominees, similarly Punjab improved its tally by returning three women Madhya Pradesh also returned three women. Tamil Nadu also retained its tally by returning -both of the Congress(I) MPs. West Bangal which had sent five women to the Lok Sabha in 1984 has returned just two this time. Surprisingly, no women candidate has been returned from Orissa, Gujarat, Haryana, Himachal Pradesh, Jammu and Kashmir, Delhi, Arunachal Pradesh, Sikkim, Tripura, Meghalaya and Nagaland.

As far as political parties are concerned, although at election time declarations are made of granting 15-20 per cent seats to women, no party has been able to achieve the target. In many studies have shown that before the women's decade, political parties were not men stressing on women's

issues, in their campaigns or mobilising rallies. In the east decade all political parties have shown great interest in women's problems as a result of various developments but primarily due to the pressure of women's groups. Parries in their manifestos promise to women all opportunities for increased participation in social, economic and political life. Yet, the record of most of the parties is poor so far as women are concerned.

However, a number of political parties have strong women's wings spread all over the country, but advocate revival of traditional values, encourage fundamentalism, ecologies mythological women characters and generate communal sentiments. Some others struggle around issues such as economic demands, world peace, atrocities against women, secularism, national integration, price-rise etc.

Women's participation in trade unions has been a topic which has acquired significance during the last two or three decades. Studies have shown that though it right be difficult to participate in day to day activities of the trade unions, women have provided very great strength during crisis periods, such as strikes. A distressing fact is that the prevalence of patrierchy prevents men colleagues from accepting women's crucial role.

Today after more than a decade of our-struggle we find to our satisfaction that the question and problems of working women and women in general are being discussed widely in our country by various organisations, individuals, press and also by the Government. The question is also being highlighted in international forums. Despite these efforts, many trade unions in the country are yet to pay adequate attention to women's issues and joint efforts have to be made to make a common cause to fight for the demands of working women. A recent report also gives the picture of the women membership in the CITU and the proportion of women office bearers in some of the States. The total membership has been around 10 per cent in 1986, and an infinitesimal proportion as office bearers.

It is well-known that women constitute a majority of the unorganised labour force. The working conditions in this sector are abyssmal. There is no security of jobs, no fair wages, no facilities and no rights to demand for the improvement of their situation etc. It goes to the credit of grass roots level organisations such as the WWF and SEWA and the researchers who have highlighted the problems of these women.

Informal Participation

Remarkably mass participation of women was noticed and recognised during Civil Disobedience Movement in 1930 and also during the Quit India Movement in 1942, when thousands of women courted arrest. Women from various castes, communities and regions have participated voluntarily and together, to raise their voice on important issues. More recently rural struggles in Bihar, Himachal Pradesh, Marathwada region and five Tamil Nadu districts centre on various issues ranging from expropriation and redistribution of the land of a Bodhgaya Mahant in Bihar the politics of liquor licensing and Government water supply in Himachal Pradesh, to struggle for canal water and public lands by untouchable poor peasants in drought prone Marathwada, and struggle for self-respect, employment and justice among Tamil Nadu landless labourers. Such participation makes women politically conscious.

The famous Chipko Movement (movement for saving trees in the forest) initiated in 1972-74 is an example of the powerful impact that women's initiative can have on the power brokers, contractors and family members. Thus the record of women's participation in political processes other than the formal has been quite creditable. Of course, while women have been visible in mass movements, group upsurges and protest struggles, their presence is not felt in structured decision-making institutional settings. Even in the structures where women's participation is substantial, they have not been given positions of power. Patterns of political behaviour from different regions of India show different relationships, influenced as they are by interrelated factors like the social

status of women, their economic position, the cultural norms, and above all the region outlook towards women's participation in the wider society. Than again there are some situations which are conspicuous by obvious contradictions Kerala, which has a record to rapid growth in women's political mobilisation and women's literacy, also has a record of electing very few women members to the Legislature. In contrast, Uttar Pradesh, with its general low profile of women's political participation, has persistently elected a large number of women to the Legislature. The major contention of the left parties that women's problems will get solved once a classes society is established, still continues. However, under the pressure of women members, at least the inclusion of women's issues in their manifestos has been feasible. Yet, access to significant decision-making positions in political parties continues to elude women.

REFERENCES

1. Jean Bethke Elshtain (1981), *Public Man, Private Woman—Women in Social and Political Thought,* Martin Robertson, Oxford.
2. Govt. of India (1988), *National Perspective Plan for Women—1988-2000 AD,* Min of HRD, Deptt. of Women and Child Development, p. 153.
3. Special Correspondent (1989): 'Women Found the Going Tough', *Hindu,* Dec. 7, 1989, p. 6.

9

Communism and Women

Very recently, CPI(M) has inducted Mrs. Vrinda Karat in Polit Bureau. It is said she is the first woman to be elevated to Polit Bureau. This news is really welcome step and optimistic.

Here in the present chapter we are reproducing erudite outlook interpreting relations of women with Communist Party of India in West Bengal. Since West Bengal and Kerala are the only two states in India where Communists remained at the helm of affairs, it is befiting to present women's role under Communist patter of governance.

Ronald Tiersky says, "The essence of Stalinist communism" is its monolithic internal politics, and Stalinism is the attempt to make all politics into internal politics." Like the CPI(M), the Bengali Hindu family is organised along strictly hierarchical lines: the men who occupy its highest rungs exercise the most power. Yet the family, like the party, mystifies such inequality and projects itself as a solidaristic unit whose members share identical interests. Democratic centralist principles in the home fortify the CPI(M) in the world, at the cost of perpetuating sexual inequality. If the CPI(M) in West Bengal now accepts women's subordination within the family, the communist movement has not always done so. As sectarian as it might have been in its early stage, the CPI was far more willing than the CPI(M) is today to challenge "bourgeois practices" that sometimes included traditional relations. Though communist leadership has always been from the *bhadralok,* its identification with middle-class interests and commitment to electoral success have grown simultaneously.

Bengali women the political sources of quiescence are rooted in the CPI(M)'s democratic centralist principles of organisation, electoral preoccupations, and class reductionist ideology. Obviously, certain facets of West Bengal's economic and social structure strengthen the CPI(M)'s approach. Women's primary and often exclusive identities as wives and mothers—the product in turn of both economic and social influences—cannot be disassociated from the CPI(M)'s tendency to neglect women's political interests, under-represent them in the party and the government, and project their maternal roles onto the public arena. The more difficult question is whether the CPI(M) can escape these socioeconomic influences.

Tacit acceptance of female seclusion, which as noted earlier has its roots in upper-caste traditions, benefits the CPI(M) in several ways: it accords with the CPI(M)'s attempt to create a cross-class coalition in which middle-class interests will predominate. The stability of women's roles as wives and mothers reassures those who fear radical change and demonstrates the CPI(M)'s sympathy for traditional practices.

Bengali Communism

Given the formidable barriers they had to overcome, communist women were more audacious in the 1940s than they are today. Moreover, they clearly struggled harder to resolve contradictions between their public and private roles. However, the bleaker reality is that the CPI never seriously challenged sexual inequality, cultivated female leadership, or addressed the problems of poor rural women.

The account that followed is based on reminiscence of the first generation of Bengali communist women. Virtually all of those who were interviewed spoke of the risk and romance entailed in becoming a CPI member between 1939 and 1942. Most of the young women who joined the CPI during this period were from wealthy, conservative families. Many had been active in the so-called terrorist movement, a violent, anti-imperialist struggle in the first two decades of the twentieth century. To recount agonies of Bani Dasgupta,

who joined the CPI Student Federation in 1939 is most appropriate.

> It is difficult to describe my sense of excitement when some students told me about the Communist party. You see my father was from a big *zamindar* [landlord] family. I used to hear labourers screaming with pain when they were beaten for being lazy and dishonest.... Here was a party which would put an end to such injustice. I began to attend the student meetings. When my relatives found out they locked me in my room at night. When they realised that they could not stop me, they drove me out of the house—beat me with shoes—because they said I was an insult to the family.

Dasgupta arrived in Kolkatta in 1941 with a letter of introduction to party leaders and the two rupees (approximately a nickel) she had left after paying her train fare. Like many other young, middle-class women who had left their homes to work for the party in Kolkatta, she moved into a communally organised home that was headed by Manikuntala Sen, the senior-most woman in the CPI at the time. The fifteen men and women who shared the house lived in an extremely egalitarian fashion, sharing meagre incomes and ample household responsibilities. Dasgupta recalled that often they could not afford to eat for several days at a time. At the suggestion of CPI comrades she gave up graduate studies to work as a full-time party member for a monthly salary of twenty rupees (about seventy-five cents). The first generation of Bengali communist women did not question the party's neglect of gender issues. Having taken the radical step of severing ties with their parents, they sought camaraderie and protection from male comrades. Many were financially dependent on the party. But the more important explanation for their silence was that they considered the CPI the major font of opposition to women's oppression.

Usually, Communist men and women attempted to organise their personal lives in an emancipated fashion. Breaking with traditional practice, they rejected arranged marriages, lavish weddings, and the dowry and often married across

religious and caste lines. In some areas where the communist movement was strong party members consecrated marriages with an exchange of garland rather than through religious ceremonies. In striking contrast with their present stance, communist men tended to marry women who were full-time political activists. Although these women were primarily responsible for housework and child care, their husbands encouraged their political activism.

The CPI seems to have increasingly-absorbed dominant cultural values once it became incorporated into the formal political arena. In Gita Mukherjee's view, from the 1950s the CPI undermined the autonomy of mass organisations among women and other groups by relying upon them for electoral mobilisation. More broadly, in West Bengal as in numerous other contexts, women's activism tended to be confined to periods of political crisis. In the absence of revolutionary upheaval, women were not compelled to perform men's jobs in fields, factories, or battlegrounds. But even in its heyday, the CPI was ill-equipped to challenge gender inequality, particularly among poor rural women. There was a deep cultural abyss between urban, educated, upper-class communist leaders and the rural poor. The rift was compounded by the CPI's alienation from indigenous cultural traditions, in part because of its close links with the Soviet Union.

The Mahila Atma Raksha Samiti (MARS)

During 1944-48, the communist movement was closely identified with a renaissance in Bengali theatre, film and literature. After the government legalised the CPI in 1942, it created a number of mass organisations, including the Mahila Atma Raksha Samiti (MARS). Although only 112 women attended its first meeting in 1942, its membership had risen to 43,500 by its second annual meeting two years later.

MARS's first major contribution was to rehabilitate poor rural and urban women during the tragic Bengal famine in 1943. It created orphanages formed soup kitchens, opened first-aid centers, and organised demonstrations against

hoarders and black marketeers. Manikuntaila Sen described MARS as having been especially active in relief work because women were the worst victims of the famine. MARS's other major commitment was to antifascist organising in response to the threat of a Japanese invasion of India and Germany's attack on the Soviet Union. At this time the CPI's declaration that the "imperialist war" had become a "people's war" was doubly ironic: the CPI's refusal to challenge British imperialism alienated it from the Congress-led nationalist movement, which was mobilising peasant men and women on an unprecedented scale. Moreover, opposition to Nazi Germany had little meaning to poor rural women. Because of its reluctance to criticise the Allies, the CPI did not even expose British complicity in creating the famine.

Comparatively, with the Union of Italian Women and other European women's organisations that grew out of the Resistance, MARS derived much less political capital from its antifascist work. In part this was because Indian women were less affected than Italian women by fascism. In Italy, not only were the communist and socialist parties outlawed; but fascist legislation forced women out of schools, the work place, and political life. Thus, as Judith Hellman argues for Italy, the antifascist struggle became synonymous with a struggle for the restoration and expansion of women's roles.

Though, currently some CPI members like Bani Dasgupta criticise the CPI's war-time stance. But Kanak Mukherjee, an old-time communist who subsequently became a member of the CPI(M) Central Committee, adamantly defends the CPI's position: "You cannot judge the correctness of a party line by whether the people are behind you. Otherwise we would always be running after the people."

Coming to Tebhaga (two third) movement in Bengal initiated under the aegis of Bengal Provincial Kisan Sabha, a Communists' peasant outfit, most account of the Tebhaga Movement (1946-48) indicate that peasant women demostrated extraordinary militance, particularly in later phases of the movement, as government repression increased. Women formed

nari bahinis, fighting troops, which confronted landlords, encircled the police, and forcibly harvested the paddy. They played an especially important role in organising communication by transmitting messages between activists, hiding cadre who had gone underground, and sounding alarms when police were approaching. Women's activism in the Tebhaga movement provides an excellent illustration of the dual significance of socioeconomic and political influences. While, local women leaders mainly comprised those who had escaped the strictures of seclusion: *adivasis,* Rajbansis (low castes), and widows. An excellent example is Bimala Maji, who overcame the restrictions her in-laws imposed on her after her husband's death and became the leading female activist in Midnapur district. Maji reported that many women became conscious of their own interests through attempts to protect their families. They demanded income from the labour they had performed; some of them also spontaneously protested sexual harassment by landlords and even by their own husbands.

Simultaneously, stress must also be accorded to the political forces that permitted women's fleeting but significant activism. MARS played a relatively minor role in the Tebhaga Movement, largely because of its urban, middle-class composition and its distance from poor rural women. However, in the early stages of Tebhaga the CPI was in its radical phase and did not discourage women's spontaneous protest. After the fall of 1947, when the CPI appealed to peasants to reject direct action and rely upon legal channels, women's militancy subsided. By the early 1950s, MARS's reliance on the CPI inhibited recognition of the transcendent nature of women's oppression across class, caste, and party lines. The government repression was not confined to the CPI but also directed at its mass organisations. Thus, although MARS was often led by noncommunist women and included members with diverse political affiliations, it was forced to go underground when the government declared the CPI illegal as a result of its decision to pursue an insurrectionary path; MARS subsequently became small and isolated.

Similarly, for years communist women participated in the Congress Party-affiliated All-India Women's Conference (AIWC), which comprised a broad cross-section of women. Vidhya Munshi described it as an important national forum in which communists could disseminate their ideas, make contacts with otherwise inaccessible women, and influence relevant legislation. Thus they could fight in parliament for the passage of the Hindu Code Bill, which gave women legal rights to divorce, remarry, and inherit property.

In consonance with CPI policy, which called for revolutionary opposition to the Nehru government, MARS worked underground between 1947 and 1951. During this period it encountered a great deal of opposition. Police shot and killed four communist women at a demonstration in Kolkatta in April 1949; numerous women were killed in the districts throughout this period.

The Formation of the PBGMS

After the CPI emerged from its sectarian phase, women formed the National Federation of Indian Women (NFIW) in 1954. Vidhya Munshi reported that communist men initially opposed the creation of the NFIW for they feared that it would divide and weaken the party. Women overcame their resistance: the NFIW became affiliated to the erstwhile Soviet-based Women's International Democratic Federation, which by no means espoused independent feminist goals. MARS, which was reconstituted as the Paschim Bangla Mahila Samiti (PBMS) in 1953, became the most vocal constituent of the NFIW in West Bengal. The NFIW poured its energies into constructive activities and establishing contacts with communist-bloc women's organisations. It explicitly refrained from organising agitational movements among the rural poor.

The rifts within the communist movement proved more damaging yet to communist women's organising efforts. Although dissident Communist party members formed the CPI(M) in April 1964, women members of the two parties worked jointly in the PBMS until 1971. Relation between

them became estranged as a result of the downfall of the CPI(M)-led United Front Government in 1971 (here it is to be noted that currently again the UPA government at the centre is backed by the Leftists) and attendant strains between its constituents. The PBMS remained affiliated with the CPI, whereas the Paschim Bangla Ganatahtrik Mahila Samiti (PBGMS) was established as a separate organisation, linked to the CPI(M).

The PBGMS, which came into existence as a result of split, was more sectarian than its predecessor. The contrasts between the two communist women's organisations became particularly marked after the Left Front government was elected in 1977. The CPI was not an offshoot of the Left Front coalition at this time; it had been severely discredited because it had supported the Congress party's national Emergency declaration in 1975. Its marginalisation from the formal political arena freed the CPI-affiliated PBMS, unlike the official PBGMS, to join feminist groups in struggles against suppression and atrocities against women.

PBGMS influence on the CPI(M) further declined during the Left Front government's tenure in office. The CPI(M) increasingly used the PBGMS as a vehicle for securing electoral support and discouraged the PBGMS from organising agitational movements. Again, the CPI(M) became less responsive to women, who now constituted only one part of a large and heterogeneous constituency. In short, added to the CPI(M)'s earlier economic reductionism was its growing political reductionism: its tendency to narrow the scope of confrontational activities because of electoral imperatives.

Women under the Left Front Government

If the undivided Communist party created a counter-community for a small group of urban, middle-class women in the 1940s, the CPI(M) has replicated its efforts, this time for rural women in the 1980s. Indeed, one of its major achievements is to have imparted feelings of dignity to poor rural women. This intangible gain is apparent at government

rallies in Kolkatta. The women who arrive in party-sponsored buses from the surrounding villages clearly attend these demonstrations for their entertainment value. But equally unmistakable is their sense of solidarity, efficacy, and pride that "their" government is in office. Their sentiments grow out of political context that is relatively free from police repression, cast and "communal" conflict, and violence against women. For example, in contrast to north India states in which the incidence of dowry deaths is high and rising, in West Bengal the Left Front government has helped contain their escalation by appointing dowry prohibition officers in all the districts. It is also committed to hiring women police officers to investigate cases of dowry-related harassment and murder. The Left Front government has achieved several small but significant improvements in the condition's of rural women. It has expanded the scope of the West Bengal Social Welfare Advisory Board (SWAB), which is financed and staffed jointly by state and central governments. SWAB activities include social work, rehabilitation programmes, and vocational training. The board also sponsors thirty-four women and child welfare programmes that organise non-formal education, nutrition classes, nursery schools, and craft centers in the villages. SWAB has formed village committees, each of which includes a female *panchayat* member and a director of programmes for rural women. With central government assistance, the West Bengal government has recently provided poor rural women loans to promote income-generating projects. It has provided women with opportunities for employment in small-scale and cottage industries, particularly in handloom cloth production. It has increased pensions for widows from thirty to sixty rupees a month. The Legal Aid Department provides free legal services to widows, prostitutes, and destitute women.

In the sphere of education, the Left Front government provides free tuition to the twelfth grade, textbooks to the fifth grade, and, on an experimental basis, midday meals. According to Kanti Biswas, minister of education, since 1977 the government has opened twelve thousand schools and

appointed forty-six thousand teachers; it has increased the proportion of school-age children attending school from 69 per cent to 96 per cent. As a result, literacy rates increased from 34 per cent to 40 per cent between 1971 and 1981.

Resolutions from recent party congresses reveal an increased commitment to women's political participation. At its eleventh congress in 1982, for example, the CPI(M) identified women's struggles as "not just a struggle for social reform but an integral part of the Indian people's struggle, for democracy and socialism." The same congress passed, a, resolution that stated that membership in the All-India Democratic Women's Association, the national women's organisation that is affiliated with CPI(M), would be open to nonparty members. Within West Bengal, the Left Front government nominated sixteen women to contest the Legislative Assembly elections in 1987; fourteen were elected, twelve on the CPI(M) ticket and two from other leftist parties.

Overall, however, when compared with the efforts of autonomous women's organisations and socialist governments elsewhere, the CPI(M) has scarcely attempted to restructure women's economic, political, and social roles.

Ironically, the CPI(M) has been insufficiently Marxist in ignoring the links between women's sexual inequality. Thus it has not questioned women's limited inheritance rights under Hindu law and in Bengali social custom. Moreover, it has redistributed land only to household heads, who are generally male. Thus, its most striking failure with respect to women is its major achievement with respect to men: tenancy reforms.

Shortly after the government had initiated "Operation Barga," an independent women's organisation, the Center for Women's Development Studies (CWDS), organised a workshop for rural women in Bankura district. At this meeting, a landless *adivasi* woman said, 'Babu, it is all well and good to give *puttas* [land titles] to our husbands. But if they leave us, we become landless again." A participant in the workshop,

D. Bandhopadhyaya, land reforms secretary to the West Bengal government at the time, persuaded the central government to include the principle of joint *puttas* in the seventh five-year plan. New Delhi left the initiative for implementing this proposal to state governments. Yet by early 1988, the West Bengal government was registering only the names of households heads on land records.

Resistance to joint *puttas* clearly reflects men's fear of women's economic independence. But given the fact that *adivasis* and *dalits,* who are less prejudiced, are the major recipients of land titles, the more significant obstacles must be sought elsewhere. Despite Bandhopadhyaya's encouragement, the PBGMS did not mobilise peasant women around this critical issue. Ironically, even top-ranking PBGMS members often opposed joint land titles. Kanak Mukherjee commented, "If we give *puttas* in women's names, next children will be demanding land in their names. And what will happen if the couple separates? The land will become even more fragmented."

By bestowing land titles on household heads, the CPI(M) exacerbates economic disparities between men and women and buttresses male domination. Since Hindu women can neither remarry nor easily return to their natal families, women whose husbands abandon them are rendered impoverished. The problem is compounded by the government's failure to significantly increase credit facilities and employment opportunities for women. Nor has the PBGMS demanded that women should be recognised as sharecroppers in their own right, although such a designation is legally permissible. Although women toil alongside their husbands on leased land at a range of cultivation tasks, Shyamali Gupta, the PBGMS secretary, argued that people would reject the notion that women work as hard as men.

One frightening manifestation and consequence of the Left Front government's tendency to ignore women in pursuing land reform is female malnutrition. A survey of two West Bengal villages by Amartya Sen and Sunil Sengupta reveals

that, ironically, girls suffered more severe malnutrition in Kuchli village, which had experienced land reform, than in Sahajapur village, which hadn't. Yet boys' nutritional level was much better in Kuchli than Sahajapur village. Severe female malnutrition could have been curtailed by direct nutritional intervention in the form of supplemental feedings to boys and girls alike. Such a programme among *adivasis* in Sahajapur not only improved children's nutritional level but also significantly reduced the sex bias.

Bengali women's dependence is compounded by their inability to secure loans for cultivation and self-employment. The Left Front government has neither provided women with credit facilities nor helped them secure central government loans. In 1984 and 1985 only 5 per cent of the beneficiaries of Indian Rural Development Programme (IRDP) loans were women. Although the proportion of female beneficiaries increased to 10.4 percent in 1985-86 and 14.4 per cent in 1986-87, it still fell far short of the stipulation of the central government that 30 per cent of the beneficiaries should be women. Far from setting a precedent among India's twenty-two states. West Bengal was one of the ten states whose performance was, poorest in providing IRDP loans for women. The dearth of female beneficiaries must be attributed in part to the *panchayats'* failure to execute central government directive. According to Prasad Rai, director of *panchayats,* banks have also resisted providing women loans for self-employment, a core component of the IRDP package, fcr fear that women are apt to default. Yet Asim Dasgupta informed me that repayment rates for women were much better than for men.

Inspite of the widespread whin that the key to women's emancipation lies in their incorporation into social production, the PBGMS has not seriously attempted to the pressure group for increasing employment opportunities for women or to improve their working conditions. It has not challenged the displacement of women in industry as a result of closure, nor in agriculture as a result of mechanisation. Simultaneously,

it failed to vocalise the issue of bringing female agricultural labourers under the purview of labour legislation. Nor has it experimented with intermediary technology that could increase their productivity and relieve them of work load. They only achievement of the government worth record in this sphere is the attainment of equal wages for male and female agricultural labourers in West Bengal that too in fragmental way.

That women can greatly profit from employment in nontraditional jobs is evident from the experience of *adivasi* women in eastern Bankura district. Few employment opportunities were available to men or women in this, drought-prone arid area during most of the year. Women's cooperatives were responsible for all stages of the production and marketing process: manufacturing the items, managing the accounts, and communication with distributors in Kolkata.

Similarly, women have been invisible and confined to narrow, sex-linked roles in the political realm. There were only two women in the previous Left Front government (1982-87), both low-ranking ministers responsible for "soft" portfolios: a minister of Relief and Social Welfare and a minister of state for Education. In a later government, only one of thirty-two cabinet ministers was a woman: Chaya Bera, who heads Relief, one of the weakest ministries in the government. Given the unprecedented number of women who were elected to the Legislative Assembly in 1987, women's underrepresentation in the cabinet is deplorable.

The Left Front government has not created a women's ministry. Manjari Gupta, the president of the All-India Democratic Women's Association, the national women's organisation affiliated with the CPI(M), opposed "artificially separating the problems of women and of men." Other PBGMS members believed that the Social Welfare Ministry could adequately address women's issues. Yet a quick review of Social Welfare programmes reveals that few address the fundamental sodoeconomic needs of the vast majority of women; most attend tot women, under extreme duress, such,

as vagrants, widows, and prostitutes. Moreover, programmes are generally devised and funded by the center and poorly implementated by the state government in poor way.

Antipathy to women's political representation is evident from the fact that a large proportion of women who serve on the *panchayats* are nominated rather than elected. In the 1978 elections, for example, 47,527 members were elected to West Bengal's 3,242 *gram panchayats;* a total of 97 women were elected and 5,803 women were nominated. Shyamali Gupta admitted that local party cadre often openly opposed women's candidacy.

Two consequences of the CPI(M)'s failure to sponsor women candidates are especially noteworthy. It perpetuates the electorate's prejudice against women's participation in public life. It also contributes to timidity: the women who are appointed to the *panchayats* have not gained the sense of efficacy that is associated, with political contestation.

The WB government's State Planning Board has introduced further decentralisation reforms. Although including women in the newly formed committees at the district, subdivisional, and block levels would seem an important aspect of ensuring wider representation.

Further, few women are included among the upper echelons of CPI(M) leadership. At the national level, one woman Mrs. Vrinda Karat is in the Polit Bureau while some other are in the national level, and only four women on central committee—Kanak Mukherjee, Godavari Parulekar, Ahilya Rangnekar and Sarla Maheswari. Five of the ninety-seven members of West Bengal's State Committee are women: Nirupuma Chatterjee, Aarti Dasgupta, Shyamali Gupta, Rekha Goswami, and Kanak Mukherjee. A few of the district committees include women but they generally constitute only two or three of up to forty members.

Although the women who occupy political office need not automatically represent women's interests, female representatives visibly manifest women's identities as social

actors. Moreover, if CPI(M) male and female leaders hold similar views, peasant men and women do not. Thus, even the most subjugated women, Mahishyas in Tamluk, expressed grievances at women's limited life chances. Nor should culturally relativist perspectives be employed to deny inequality. That Bengali women eat less nutritious and smaller quantities of food than their husbands may be customary but is also unjust.

The CPI(M) has accepted as natural the prevailing sexual division of labour in both private and public spheres, and thus perpetuated women's sex-linked roles. For example, the government has sacrificed both the quality and the scope of girls' education.

In reality, this can be admitted that the CPI(M) has failed to question women's subordination in the family, as manifested through the taboos surrounding divorce, widow remarriage, and women's infertility. No concerted efforts are made to educate rural women about the everyday forms of sexual inequality they experience and perpetuate: restrictions on their physical mobility, feeding their families before they eat, and their exclusion from major religious rites. Nor has the PBGMS devoted much attention to violence against women. It has ignored newspaper reports of families who have performed sex-selection tests in order to abort the female fetus. The fact that women are primarily responsible for housework and child care has seriously constrained their political activism. Shyamali Gupta noted that women displayed low levels of political consciousness because they had little time to devote to reading, study groups, and party activity.

The CPI(M) leadership's theoretical justification for the party's passivity is the familiar reference to Engels: women cannot be emancipated until socialism is achieved, at which point their liberation is assured. It also justifies inaction by appealing to another Marxist tenet: the notion of class conflict as the motor force of history. Aarti Dasgupta, the most prominent female leader in the CPI(M) affiliated CITU argued: "As trade unionists we work for the labouring class as a

whole and do not make invidious distinctions between men and women; to do so would be wrong and anti-Marxist." The CPI(M) opposes reserved seats and special quotas for women, *dalits,* and *adivasis.* Shambunath Mandi, the minister for scheduled castes and tribes and an *adivasi* himself, argued that it would be preferable to reorganise the quota system on a class basis. "As long as there is no legal baron women's participation, there is no question that they will come up in political life and there is no need for reservation," Kanak Mukherjee argued. Yet, as the Congress government at one stage recognised in instituting the system of reserved seats, meritocratic principles do not govern competition for positions in education and employment. Nor, as we have seen earlier, is the Left Front government's own composition free of gender bias. Not surprisingly, the Left Front government has failed to fill its reservation quotas.

More significant than the CPI(M)'s economic reductionism is its political reductionism. As the CPI(M) has become increasingly committed to the exercise of power, its relationship to women has become highly instrumental: women should be seen, particularly on election day, but not heard! Electoral considerations also contribute to women's invisibility in the formal political arena. When asked why the CPI(M) did not nominate more female candidates, several party members responded that women were less likely than men to be elected. Those women who are appointed to political office often project women's nurturing roles to avoid alienating the electroate.

Contrary to the common assumption that Marxists oppose the family, in West Bengal as in the erstwhile Soviet Union, China, and Italy, communist parties have strengthened familial loyalties to their own advantage. Judith Stacey argues that the Chinese Communist Party made concessions to patriarchal morality in order to facilitate acceptance of its mass-politics line. By recognising the class status of families rather than individuals, it prevented women from realising the direct benefits of land redistribution. Judith Hellman argues that

the Italian Communist Party presented the family as a key element in the reconstruction of postwar Italian society and was loath to intervene in its members' "private lives." Similarly, the CPI(M) fears male opposition if women were to acquire independent land holdings. Given an environment charged with religious conflict, it fears being voted out of office if it were to propose far-reaching reforms of the religious laws that govern the family.

The PBGMS's dependence on the CPI(M) greatly magnifies inequalities between the two organisations. A very large proportion of PBGMS activists are married to men who are active in the CPI(M) and generally outrank their wives. Once again we observe the interplay of democratic centralism in the home and the world: PBGMS members are unlikely to challenge the CPI(M), since doing so would require them to question the superiority of both male party members and their own husbands. Furthermore, interviews revealed that the most talented women could devote the least time to women's issues because they were preoccupied with party and government responsibilities. Chaya Bera, minister of Relief, described herself as responsible for her department as a whole, not for women's particular concerns. Kanak Mukherjee's presidency of the PBGMS has become virtually an honorific position since she became a member of parliament.

The PBGMS in turn reproduces democratic centralist principles when organising poor rural women. Through close consultation with party officials, PBGMS leaders in Calcutta generally decide which issues to raise throughout the state. They then convey directives to the district level women's organisations, which in turn convene meetings at the block and village levels. Nando Rani Daal, president of the PBGMS for Midnapur district, reported that the major demands of demonstrations between 1980 and 1985 included greater state autonomy vis-a-vis the center, higher prices for agricultural produce, equal wages, reduced inflation, and global peace. With few exceptions, rural women thus have

little opportunity to organise around the problems they confront in their daily lives.

Democratic centralist principles further buttress female seclusion. For example, women can generally become politically active in the CPI(M) only with their husbands' consent. Thus, virtually all the husbands of the married women who were CPI(M) members or supporters were involved in party activity themselves. But even then, politically active women are suspect in the public eye. Chaya Bera noted, "A serious disadvantage for women is that they can be maligned and gossiped about more easily than men. When I was contesting the election. this time [1987] Congress (I) made up a lot of unspeakable, slanderous stories about me. People like to believe such stories about women."

The CPI(M) is hardly in a position to create greater public acceptance for women when it upholds their tradiational roles in both the party and the family. CPI(M) members often tolerate glaring contradictions between their public and private lives. For example, while publicly denouncing the dowry system, many party members participate in it. The PBGMS has not challenged the dowry system through political education and mobilisation.

One explanation for the CPI(M)'s sexism may be its adaptation Bengali social values. Because Hindus consider women the repositories of tradition, the CPI(M) can demonstrate its indigenous character by upholding female seclusion and subordination. Numerous CPI(M) leaders took great pains to dissociate themselves from feminism which they believed was a Western import. The CPI(M)'s domestication of Marxism has protected it from a widespread criticism of the pro-Soviet CPI: that it is alien. The cost entailed in this approach is the CPI(M)'s acceptance of "indigenous inequality."

The PBGMS projects an image of womanhood that is based on upper-caste, upper-class norms. Its assumption that women are economically dependent socially secluded, and politically inactive is reflected in its emphasis ore home-

based income generation projects and sex-finked constructive activities. This urban elite ideal ignores the greater, independence of women from lower castes and classes in the rural areas. Given their need to engage in wage labour, many female agricultural labourers who were interviewed had little time for what they considered recreational activities. Thus, the communists' conservative views of gender roles are closely linked to their conservatism with respect to class. Conversely, CITU is weakened by its underrepresentation of women. CITU restricts itself to the organised sector of the economy in which male workers predominate. But workers in the informal sector, in which women are concentrated, especially need trade union support, for wages are abysmally low, working conditions are wretched, and they are excluded from the purview of labour legislation. Moreover, in neglecting to organise in the informal sector, CITU weakens its own potential for expansion and fails to tap incipient militance among exploited workers.

The CPI(M)'s response to *adivasi* struggles is reminiscent of its approach to autonomous women's movements. It has opposed the Jharkhand movement's demand for a separate state for the *adivasis* who inhabit Midnapur, Bankura, and Purulia districts. It has similarly opposed the Gurkha National Liberation Front (GNLF) demand for regional autonomy for Darjeeling's Nepalese inhabitants. It has ignored these ethnic movements, termed them divisive, and failed to recognise their legitimate demands. Ironically, given its commitments to Marxist ideology, it has overlooked the material bases of ethnci conflict. The CPI(M) has also failed to appreciate and achieve proportional political repesentation of *adivasis* (as of women) in state and local office.

Summing Up

The CPI(M)'s achievements with respect to the rural poor as a whole mask growing inequalities within the family as male household heads alone have gained landownership, credit facilities, and agricultural technology. The PBGMS perpetuates the sexual division of labour within the home

and the world by confining its demands to incremental, sex-typed reforms and accepting its subordinate role within the communist movement; The CPI(M)'s preoccupation with electoral success and its democratic centralist principales have been especially damaging for women. But the influence between party strategy and female subordination is not unidirectional. The CPI(M)'s obliviousness to gender inequality and sex-typing of women's roles narrows its approach to class inequality and contributes to its overall conservatism.

In its defense, the Left Front government is constitutionally prohibited from legislating certain reforms that could improve women's conditions. Most notably it has no control over the entire gamut of laws governing the family. Moreover, the fact that the disjunction between the home and the world is so great in Bengali Hindu society might suggest that the CPI(M) simply caters to public opinion, when for example it projects women's maternal roles onto the public arena. Evidence for the culturally bound character of the CPI(M) women's organisation in West Bengal is the greater militance of its sister organisation, the Janvadi Manila Samiti, in New Delhi. Similarly, the PBGMS can scarcely be held responsible for its *bhadramahila* composition when the entire Bengali communist movement owes its existence to the *bhadralok*.

However, there is'not simply one monolithic, internally consistent cultural paradigm in West Bengal. Women's freedom increases as one moves down the caste and class hierarchies. Thus, instead of imbibing *bhadralok* values, which are heavily laden with upper-caste snobbery, disdain for manual labour, and male chauvinism, the CPI(M) and PBGMS could appropriate the sexually egalitarian traditions of *dalits* and *adivasis*.

10

Women Uprising During the Freedom Struggle

The movement for national freedom had its roots in growing frustrations, humiliations and injustices of an alien administration. The differences of caste, the prevalence of untouchability, discriminations based on sex, were reinforced by the indifference of government towards social reform.

The national movement in India did not begin with the idea that India should be liberated from the clutches of British control and domination. The early 19th century social reform and educational programmes initiated by Raja Rammohun Roy, Ishwarchandra Vidyasagar, and the Brahmo Samaj dealt with definite social evils. The transformation of the movement for social reform to the demand for political independence, took some decades. It was given an economic base and content by Dr. Dadabhai Naoroji in his classical study "Poverty and Un-British Rule in India," which highlighted how Britain was responsible for India's poverty and economic backwardness.

The freedom movement did not even begin with the founding of the Indian National Congress in 1885, which in its early years was something like an annual get-together of the affluent elite and the educated. While they were concerned for the welfare of the country, their activities were restricted to demands for small concessions; and they sought through well-phrased and polite resolutions the redress of grievances and pleaded for greater participation of Indians in the services and administration. It was left to Gandhiji to wean the

country from the gospel of violence. He gave ethical and moral content to an otherwise purely political struggle by repeatedly emphasising the importance of means. This called for harmony and tolerance, passive resistance and non-cooperation with injustice and evil, and elimination of violence and hatred.

Practically, in the beginning, women's participation in the national movementwas insignificant, but in helping with social reform their sympathy was expressed in deeds rather than in words. This is not to be wondered at, as women were still in the thraldom of ignorance and tradition-bound and till they were educated and freed they could contribute but little towards national freedom. It is not surprising that one of our early revolutionaries—Bhikhaji Cama—had to work outside India, against immense odds to build public opinion in favour of India's political independence.

Sarojini Naidu was the first Indian woman to enter into active politics and live to see India attain freedom. She fulfilled the many concepts of political leadership in India. Hailing from a family of scholars, daughter of a great scientist, a brilliant student, educated at Cambridge, a well-known poet, married outside her caste to an eminent doctor she became leader in her own right. The entry of a woman of such eminence into active politics was not only a great asset to the Congress but a real inspiration to the hesitant womanhood of India. The fact that she left home, husband and children to identify herself with the movement for freedom had a tremendous impact on women in determining their future participation in the national movement.

In the early decades of twentieth century women still lived protected lives. Despite that instance are there of many women like Vidyagouri Nilkanth and Sharadaben Mehta and Begum Hamid Ali of Gujarat, Sarala Devi Choudharani, Sarala Ray, Lady Abala Bose in Bengal, the Begum Mother of Bhopal and hosts of others, some known all over India and others respected in their own states like Sister Subbalakshmi and Dr. Muthulakshmi Reddy of Madras, and many others,

were actively associated with educational and social work. Their concerted interest in the welfare of women has brought about a silent revolution and a good deal of the services have come to the women of India through the unrecorded effort of these great women. Without their work and sacrifice political freedom by itself would not have been so effective.

The levels of women's involvement in the national movement depended largely on the methods of policies followed by the National Congress. Sati was abolished, widow remarriage was legalised and the Special Marriage Act was passed to legalise marriages contracted outside the pale of established religions. With the establishment of the Presidency colleges and universities, higher education came within the reach of women also. Early attempts of women to go for higher education and professional courses did not receive much encouragement.

Again coming to the field of political struggle, few women were associated with the National Congress, initially. They attended the sessions as wives and visitors. It was so till Mrs. Naidu strode in as a distinguished participant. The first woman to be elected president of INC was Annie Besant in 1917. Eight years later in 1925 Sarojini Naidu became its second woman president. They did not have any woman to secured them till Indira Gandhi was elected president in 1959-60, and more recently Sonia Gandhi. Participation of women in policy-making political bodies has been limited. Whatever participation there was at the lower levels it was confined to the urban women. The politics of violence pursued by the terrorists had a few women. Pritilata Waddedar in men's clothes and Bina Das, both from Bengal, are well-known among these.

By identifying himself with the masses, with the disinherited and the forgotten millions, Gandhiji stirred the depths of Indian national conscience as no leader has done before or ever since. With remarkable foresight and with the experience he gained in South Africa he assessed the strength inherent in women. He realised that the only way to rouse

them from their traditional role of domesticity was to appeal to their sense of patriotism and awaken in them national consciousness and social responsibility. Gandhiji's message offered to the women of India an opportunity to break away from the past with all its frustrations. What is more, Gandhiji by linking women's participation with economic rehabilitation and social reform gave the much desired content to their participation. Women, literate and illiterate, rural and urban swelled the ranks of the freedom fighters, took over positions of responsibility, courted imprisonment, were arrested in large numbers. Such a mass participation under Gandhiji leadership gave women a sense of equality with men, an equality which was unheard of in the tradition-bound Indian society.

The leadership of Gandhiji and the work done by women's voluntary organisations like the Women's Indian Association headed by Annie Besant and the All-India Women's Conference led by eminent patriots and national workers like Mrs. Margaret Cousins, Kamaladevi Chattopadhyay, Muthulakshmi Reddy, Rani Lakshmibai Rajwade, Rajkumari Amrit Kaur, Rustomji Faridoonji, Begum Hamid Ali, followed by hosts of others have given direction and strength to the liberation of women.

Currently many, therefore, more organisations in the forefront, like the Grameen Mahila Sangh, University Federation of Women—national and local, AIWC, YWCA, National Council of Women are making their distinctive contribution in specialised fields of their choice. While the greater part of their activities are confined to the urban areas, the Skippo Committee under the able leadership of Dhanvanti Rama Rao brings medical aid to rural women and children.

Gandhiji made women realise that the 80 per cent or more of Indian women living in rural India are a part of the responsibility of the educated. No programme of development can succeed, if rural areas is not awakened. So he created the Kasturba Gandhi National Trust to train workers for rural

areas and bring the message of free India to the people in our villages. At local and village levels, women are contributing to national development. Today there is no activity, not even a demonstration without women. The women's movement is now national in every sense of the term and is—an indispensable part of normal life and activity of India.

With increasing dependence on government grants and external aid, the old *elan* is fast disappearing from voluntary organisations. There is a lack of identity with the cause and selfless desire to work for national advancement. India's value system is changed beyond recognition. One does not hesitate to say that the future of the country can be assured only if the women recapture the qualities which have dominated the lives of Ahalyabai, Rani of Jhansi, Ramabai Ranade, Sarojini Naidu and Kasturba Gandhi, and many others who inspired women to pursue noble ideals, indifferent to consequence, and boldly and fearlessly work for the redemption of the motherland.

The initiative, courage and leadership women displayed in the political movement towards national independence or liberation from colonial rule assured them a ready and abiding place in India's new resurgent life. Today practically all doors are open to them, and women are seen filling a variety of posts and positions barring probably the army. The early fifties also saw the elimination of their legal disabilities and the adoption of the convention of equal pay for equal work for all. With this the women probably felt that they had indeed arrived. But tragically enough, with this also set in a stalemate which seems to have enveloped them like a heavy pall. It is a though gradually the vigour, drive and adventure had been shed. The majority lapsed back into the old routine. The ambitious ones only sought to reap what fruits they could out of the new opportunities. The reasons are many and complex.

There are not a few who say there has been no real women's movement in this country. What they have in mind is obviously a virulent feminist movement with a streak of

the negative in it that perhaps made excessive dramatisation necessary, which was a feature of some of the movements in the west. There was a women's movement in India which began to take organisational form from the early part of this century, when new influences and fresh ideas began to flow in. It was a positive and broad based social force with a larger vision, not just a narrow circumscribed stream. It was in fact part of a great social upsurge for deep changes, which provided it with a healthy core and a rational demeanour. Society was not divided into two warring parties, women versus men, rather into two segments, the liberal versus the conservative.

The emphasis here was definitely more on equal *opportunities* for women even while demanding equality under the law. It is of interest to note that the Indian women always asked for *adult* franchise, when demanding the right to vote. Even when concessions were offered to them such as enfranchising the *wives* of voters or reserving seats for women in elective bodies, they had firmly declined. It is perhaps also necessary to state here that the vote was not regarded as the only yard-stick of emancipation. Another equally happy feature of the movement was its non-communal, nay cosmopolitan, character. It embraced women of all communities and religions, both in its membership as well as leadership, always opposed sectarian issues such as communal electorates, and pursued larger problems of vital community interest. And thus a many pronged movement took shape.

It attached tremendous importance to education. The All-India Women's Conference in fact began as a crusader for more and better education, then found it necessary to spread out into other fields as family and community affairs are an integral whole that cannot be compartmentalised. The women demanded universal compulsory education at least for the primary to begin with, for all children not just for girls, while seeking certain facilities for girls and women teachers such as special hostels for the former and incentives for the latter. The Women's Conference went further. Most of its branches

set up nursery and kindergarten classes which were very scarce and hardly known in those days. They set up middle, even secondary schools for girls in areas where girls were deterred from joining mixed schools.

Above all, the central body took a very wise and commendable step in setting up a college of Home Science, Lady Irwin College in Delhi, the first of its kind in the country and which it ran on its own through its own funds, as the government would neither recognise it as it was thought an outlandish venture, nor aid with finance. There was also the problem of finding trained teachers for the college as none were readily available. Teachers had even to be sent abroad for the required training. It became in course of time a great landmark in women's education.

A special feature of this period was setting up girls' hostels, especially for the working girls. It was not confined to the elite as is often supposed, but mainly for the working women. It also made on the spot studies of working women especially in plantations and mines through special study teams which led to and were instrumental in getting through appropriate welfare legislative measures, especially protective legislation where necessary.

The women naturally attached great importance to children. Various measures for improving the condition of the child were formulated which ultimately took the form of a children's charter. All this was decades before the birth of the UN and its championing the cause of children.

The problem thrown up by the World War II and its termination, launched the women into new projects. The widespread famine led to the birth of the Save the Children's Committee, a wing of the Women's Conference, which set up Homes for the care and education of the destitute children, some of which took permanent root. The large number of women thrown out of jobs induced the setting up of an employment bureau.

The most spectacular was the running of mobile health vans in remote rural areas where medical care was unknown or scarce. Under the slogan of "Keep the Vans Moving", they were made to serve hundreds of villages from one end of India to the other, a great boon to many remote neglected areas.

Another postwar project championed was the supply of quality milk at reasonable rates. The distress caused by milk scarcity had led the Women's Conference to make a special study of the problem and produce a very telling pamphlet. Later a regular campaign was launched and a great deal of pressure brought on the new State Governments to provide adequate milk. Bombay led the way by responding and organising milk supplies through regular booths which other States soon followed. A worth-while project of far-reaching consequences was conducting of training camps for preparing cadres of social workers, for there were no such institutions then.

The biggest and widest campaign was, however, for a change in the laws. The foundation for this had already been laid by the adoption of the fundamental rights at Karachi in 1931 by the Indian National Congress which declared that in free India there would be no discrimination on grounds of sex. The principle had now been enshrined in the new Constitution. But it was a far harder task to bring the existing laws into conformity with it. Though women had been lobbying for appropriate legislative measures for decades, the total changes now called for saw them launch into a terrific breathless campaign throughout the country and intense lobbying within the portals of Parliament. The fairly easy passage of these enactments was an acknowledgment of the crucial role of the women in the freedom fight and the new India.

Let us now try to analyse some of the contributory factors that have led to the decline and exitinction of a movement among the Indian women. It seems that the political leadership which had so long been denied power with prosperity, who

had for decades been ruled by vigour generated by Gandhiji and an idealism which a long line of venerated leaders had inspired, now felt free to indulge their petty ambitions and often a thwarted greed. The emphasis quickly shifted from idealism to selfishness, as also from the group, community and party to the individual. It was more and more a question of each for himself rather than the nation or community. Many felt that recompense was due to them for what they had suffered or foregone in the past. There was thus a slowing down of that old missionary drive. A certain complacency settled on those who had provided the leadership in the past. The repeated warnings of leaders like Gandhiji or Nehru that life for India had only just begun and in this delicate embryonic stage needed the greatest care and most sensitive handling, went unheeded. Gandhiji with his unerring intuition expanded and finalised the constructive programme to provide content and substance to the idea of a free country. But no one paid much attention to it. No one cared to ask whether the millions who were moved to participate in the great freedom battle, would automatically settle down as disciplined citizens, charged with a high civic sense. Whilst Nehru talked of the great new adventures, most others who were now the rulers of the country were content with a tidy income and a smug abode. Another unfortunate tendency was for all fields of activity to get politicised. Politics, its idiom, technique, values seemed to pervade all national affairs.

On the women the result was even more tragic. The vast concourse of women who had poured into the freedom arena, had slipped back into their old grooves. They now had the vote a most powerful weapon in this hands. They also had several legal rights. But of what avail, for, they were hardly aware of their power and potential strength. The women leaders too had got settled in, though in new social grooves of power and position that independence had thrown up. They forged no links with the wide mass of women, who are only approached briefly at voting time to secure their ballot papers. So the common women at large remained and continue to remain to this day, quite ignorant of their precious rights or

how to use them for their own or public advantage. Thus this human mass with its vast latent power which was once sought after and when harnessed moved the very earth, lies today stagnant and unused for social regeneration or reconstruction.

Where a state assumes the role of a welfare establishment, there is an increasing tendency for the administration to enter more and more areas of activity, assume greater initiative and slowly develop a monopolistic attitude. Has this been responsible for the undermining of that colossal constructive urge and daring initiative which marked the public life of pre-independence days? Slowly a feeling seems to have come over the people that little can be done without government help. These psychological trammels have also had an unhealthy, enfeebling effect on community activity. Yet in England where the Establishment claims to be paternal, individual initiative and community welfare activities are just as vigorous as in the pre-war days.

Gradually, voluntary effort and organisations lost their old mighty prestige and commanding position after independence as the authorities came to look with less favour on them. As some political chicanery also went on under the cloak of social welfare, private effort became more and more suspect, especially in the eyes of the Parliament.

These are significant symptoms of a dangerous malady in the body politic of a country which is wedded to democracy. Democracy has meaning and reality only where the people at large are sensitised to their rights, duties and obligations, and encouraged to exercise them.

We completely ignore the need for voters' *education* which must be distinguished from party propaganda which is freely poured out at election time. Every stimulus has also to be offered for their close participation in the local and national affairs from planning to implementation through various local development projects. Above all the crucial test of a democratic society lies in the imaginativeness of the

citizens, the bold adventure of its own independent leadership, and the success they show. In pre-independence days nearly 75% of the educational institutions and hospitals were provided by the people themselves through their own effort. When we proudly acclaim Indian as one of the largest democracies, we simply count the heads and the ballot papers cast, reducing an institution we wish to respect, to arithmetical figures, not conscious active human minds.

Barring exceptional cases and occasions, women in public life tend to pattern on men and their ways. It seems that in the new India after 1947, while the young got busy qualifying for and pursuing professional careers which were opening before them with fair amount of ease, the elders sought security with all its creature comforts and assured public positions. Under the circumstances championing of needy causes seemed too much of a hazard and got neglected.

There are other reasons too for this lack of social sensitivity, a major one amongst them being the warped kind of education imparted to growing minds. Usually learning is taken as the gateway to a job, its merit being judged by the monetary return accruing therefrom. For, the importance of a professional is evaluated by the "Success" achieved, which invariably is in terms of affluence. The larger functions of professions to embrace the citizens' fundamental rights an duties are never stressed in the imparting of education, nor the obligation to scrutinise, assess and strive to enhance the moral quality of human life. The professionals seem content to remain prisoners in their professional sanctum. So much for the young professionals. Neither does education encourage independent thinking to enable one to sift and sort out the nostrums that are fashionable and the popular ideologies which pour out from all the mass media, and realise that the validity or correctness of a proposition is not determined by the size of the those who propagate or accept it.

Women, as family members or citizens, cannot be isolated from the entire society. The many needs and demands such as adequate facilities in housing, education, water, electricity,

transport and the like apply to all. Also the need for clean air, food, administration and a hundred other factors, in none of which the women's voice is heard any more, because of the ignorance of the masses and the callous indifference of the classes. That the women have not promoted even a powerful consumer movement, a territory so close to them, on their own in a country like India, is proof enough of a deadly complacency. The oppressive problem of price rise is thereby used as a political baton by opposition parties, not as an essential civil need by conscious citizens.

There are other vital issues that touch women even more, like dowry. It is socially a most degrading institution and economically hazardous, making a mockery of both law and human decency. Nevertheless today there is no movement even to stifle it, leave alone exterminate it. Here is an open and consistent violation of a law by all classes and at all levels. Again, child marriages are performed galore and the very Act for which women once fought, is nullified with impunity. Yet the women remain silent.

Similarly women who once showed deep concern over the fate of children and compiled a charter of their rights, seem now to have forgotten the most sensitive and vulnerable section on which rests the future of this nation, the children, comprising nearly 40 per cent of the population, a majority of whom remain undernourished. Nor is any account taken of the large proportion of unwanted children born to parents due to latter's ignorance, negligence or sheer irresponsibility, adding to the burden of poverty and the ranks of the destitute and unemployed.

Is this just a low tide in the usual ebb and flow of the human stream? And will the tide rise again to promising heights launching a fresh flow of powerful volume? Let us not forget however, that the human tide is stirred into motion by human initiative and not by an invisible spring. Will the woman's hand raise that tide again to a crest?

11

Politics of Women and Panchayati Raj

Women have lived in two parallel worlds ever since the first community habitation, shelter or villages. They have occupied positions of eminence and authority, even gone into battle. They have also been objects of repression, uncalled for violence and the petty tyrannies of the male bread winner. The legend has it that men have gone forth to earn bread and provide shelter and clothing to family while women have tended her home, children and family. While the roles have remained by and large traditional, it would seem that external factors such as religion, economic necessity, aspirations for higher life, social demands and increasing stresses of modern times have forced the sexes into positions of confrontation even abuse and violence. This has been so because the attitude of man has been so conditioned that even the finest among them have found little virtue in women. Samuel Butler thought while the brigand gives you the choice between your life and your money. She wants both. Sigmand Freud who spent his life time in baring the inner most recesses of human consciousness finally wrote, "The great question that has never been answered and which I have not yet been able to answer, despite my thirty years of research into the feminine soul, is what does a woman want".

An enigma to be desired, mankind has ever been willing to give women everything but equal status. Even the human rights has been given to them but grudgingly. And today a stage has arrived that she is almost an equal partner in the voyage of life. The fact is that the march of mankind is

irreversibly towards an area of equality and the woman is on the threshold of a life hitherto uncharted. The more rigid among the men can at best delay the process of equality among both sexes which was triggered by the mother of all revolutions. But you cannot draw the masses into politics without drawing the women into politics as well. For, the female half of the human race is doubly oppressed under capitalism... [and] in "household bondage".

India is perhaps the first country to recognize this social fact underlined by Lenin on the International Working Women's Day in 1921, and to have concrete measures to draw women into leadership positions and thereby into politics by giving them one-third reservation in what may now be called the third tier of governance — the Panchayati Raj. The Constitution (73rd Amendment) Act, 1992, Article 2430 (3) reads:

> "Not less than one-third (including the number of seats reserved for women belonging to Scheduled Castes and the Scheduled Tribes) of the total number of seats to be filled by direct election in every Panchayat shall be reserved for women and such seats may be allotted by rotation to different constituencies in a Panchayat."

And Clause (4) of the Act has the following provision:

> "...not less than one-third of the total number of offices of chairpersons in the Panchayats at each level shall be reserved for women:
>
> Provided also that the number of offices reserved under this clause shall be allotted by rotation to different Panchayats at each level."

The constitutional amendment providing one-third representation to women in elected bodies as well as reserving one-third of the offices of chairpersons for them will have far-reaching consequences in Indian political and social life. This is indeed a welcome, though delayed, gesture for we cannot make democracy meaningful in a traditional society like ours without the full involvement of women. But a constitutional provision is only a necessary step which should

be followed by effective measures for women's uplift in the country. To make women's participation in society and politics is reality, enormous work remains to be done, given their present socio-economic condition.

In spite of the provision of reservation for women the real power equations in the village whereby women, if they know what is good for them, leave politics to those who know better—husband, father-in-law or sons. Often they degenerate into party spokeswoman and hardly voice their own opinion on the floor of the house. Most of them remain as silent spectators to the proceedings of the house and rarely participate in its work.

Political parties were and are not serious in fielding women candidates. They often resort to the practice of fielding 'dummy' women candidates just for the sake of statistics in constituencies where male candidates are almost sure to win. In 'safe' constituencies men are normally fielded rather than women. This discourages women aspirants.

Obviously, women-friendly development remains a myth yet to become a reality in India. The indicators for women development show a pathetic picture despite all the rhetoric. It is quite frustrating to see the clock turn back in our country. The glorious traditions of more than a century and a half of the nineteenth century and the Indian national movement of the twentieth century, the Gandhian ideology of women's emancipation, the guarantees provided by the constitution of India for gender equality, everything goes in vain widening the gap between rhetoric and reality.

Women's education is one of the most important preconditions for the silent revolution to be successful. The States which have given importance to women's education, have shown phenomenal increase in all indicators of social progress, like a lower birth rate, higher health standards as well as a higher expectation of life at birth. Thus, women's participation in public life and their leadership has a direct link with the above factors.

Taking the situation in the country as a whole, women's educational levels are abysmally low, to say the least. After fifty-two years of independence, the literacy rate of women in some states is almost at the same point as it was when we began our journey in 1947. Over the years, however, there had been a steady improvement. But noticeably, while the literacy rate had gone up, the total number of illiterates had also increased.

As such the gràmous statement, "Educate a boy and you educate a person. Educate a girl and you educate a nation" goes in vain.

Those who oppose reservation of seats for women in panchayats brandish four main reasons in support of their stand. First, women who become members of panchayats and local bodies will disturb the harmony of homes and of family life. Even those men who tolerate women working in offices for fixed hours donot take kindly to them when their roles change to one of community leadership. This is because then the women have to attend to people's problems as leaders. This means irregular hours of work and a twenty-four hour demand on their time. Therefore, who will look after the children and household chores, the menfolk ask? Second, women will become targets of attacks by anti-social elements when they move of their homes or go outside their villages for work, meetings, and so on. Third, whenever women hold elected offices, the male officers are the ones who 'dictate' what is or is not to be done. They take control of the entire situation and women elected representatives become the helpless victims or mute spectators at the hands of men-dominated environment

Obviously, these and many other problems are the product of a particular mind-set and culture of male dominance. A social transformation aimed at the woman's changing role could be achieved by Panchayati Raj Institutions. But, of course, the task is beset with enormous difficulties for women in its initial phases.

12

Political Dynamics of Women and Congress Constructive Programme

In the history of the Congress movement it is a well known fact that Gandhi had made social uplift and social reform a part of the Congress programme as that was an instrument to serve political emancipation. His programme was that liberty and growth must be based on equality and justice. He said, "freedom, self-rule or salvation of India—call it what you will—consisted not just in political freedom but in political freedom plus Harijan welfare plus rural uplift, plus women's well being and other social reform activities." To him social welfare work on behalf of women was part and parcel of a larger whole namely the remaking of Indian society.

The tempo of the anti-untouchability movement initiated by Gandhi continued to spread throughout the country and Orissa was no exception to that. His Harijan movement roused the people specially the women to a great extent and made them conscious about the social problems of great magnitude. By strenuous efforts he collected large sums for its use. He asked his followers to proceed with the work with utmost patience. G.D. Birala became its President and A.V. Thakkar was selected as Secretary of this Organisation. Its branches were opened throughout India. One of its branches consisting of 28 members was organised at Cuttack. Rama Devi was chosen as one of its Secretaries. The arrival of A.V. Thakkar, Secretary, All India Harijan Seva Sangh at Cuttack in the middle of November 1932 accelerate the movement all the more. He gave great importance to the spread of education among the untouchables.

By the beginning of November 1932, an Anti-Untouchability Committee consisting of representatives from different districts was formed at Cuttack under the Chairmanship of Kabiraj Balukeshwar Acharya its name was "Asprusyata Nibarini Samiti". This committee formed the nucleus of the Orissa branch of the "All India Harijan Sevak Sangha". Rama Devi became the Joint Secretary of this Organisation.

Rama Devi devoted herself whole-heartedly to the cause of the removal of untouchability work among women with Binapani Devi, Kiranbala Sen, Mangala Sengupta, Godavari Devi, Sobha Panda, Annapurna Devi, Tulasi Mohanty, Manik Devi and Susila Devi. They gave increased attention towards these programmes for the uplift of Harijans. Smt. Rama Devi along with her husband established an Ashram known as Sevagar at Ban. The aim was to accommodate the children of the Harijan workers in the Ashram and impart them training in various constructive programmes. Some other ladies after receiving their proper training in this centre started social work as per the Gandhian constructive programme in their respective areas. Smt. Kokila Devi established a Harijan School and in Ashram at Talapada in the Balasore district. There she taught the pupils, reading, writing, spinning, weaving, making of mats, discipline, punctuality, etc. She presuaded the caste Hindus to open the village temples in Bhadrak to Harijans. Similarly Haimavati Devi opened a day School for the Harijans in a small village in the district of Puri.

At Cuttack Rama Devi started to take regular classes of some Harijan girls mostly from the scavanger families. Under the auspices of the Anti-Untouchability Board seven other sisters worked with her for the promotion of social well being of the Harijans. They taught three R's and Bhajanas to the untouchable girls in Rajabagicha, Mathasahi, Kaflabazar, etc. They also attempted to extend their activities to other bazars in the 'same district. They moved from place to place and advised the Harijans to refrain from eating beaf, distributed

medicines among them and explained them to follow simple rules of hygiene and health. Admiring the selfless service of these ladies Gandhiji wrote "I congratulate the sisters of Cuttack on their devotion to the cause of the much desired reform."

On 8th May he announced his novel programme for removal of untouchability from the masses by undertaking 'Padayatra' in Orissa. Like an ancient sage propagating the message by sacred marches on foot throughout the countryside, Gandhiji was determined to root out the evil from the Hindu society by his sacred mission which began from Puri, one of the most famous religious centres of the Hindus in India. On 9th May 1934, the Padyatra began along the Puri-Cuttack road. In the Harijan movement of Gandhi these ladies joined in turn his padyatra on foot. They collected signatures from public to voice against untouchability. They organised meetings and established contacts with Harijans in their dwelling areas-Gandhiji being very much pleased with the selfless and untiring service of women in this regard entrusted the organisation of his seven day foot march to Smt. Rama Devi in 1934. Smt. Malati Choudhary also stressed the need of unity and advocated for the removal of untouchability.

When Bapu's Harijan tour programme was announced, at that time a Committee was made under the presidentship of Swami Bichitrananda Das to welcome Gandhiji. Its membership was rupees three only. To collect its membership fees Sobha Panda, Mangala Sen and Annapurna Choudhary moved to different places by bicycle. At that time people were not willing to be members of this Committee due to police interference. But due to their approach a number of people became its member.

The first Congress ministry in Orissa was formed on 19th July 1937 with Biswanath Das as the Prime Minister. The first session of the Assembly started from 28th July 1937. Sarala Devi and A. Laxmibai were elected as members of the Legislative Assembly. This ministry settled a number of social, economic and political problems of Harijans.

Sarala Devi took keen interest for the development of Harijans. On 7th September 1937 she put questions as to what the Government has done to extend suitable facilities to Harijans in the field of education and employment. She compelled the Government to provide better education and employment to them in order to redress their financial difficulties. Due to poverty the Harijans were borrowing money with high interest from the money-lenders. During the collection of debt, the money-lenders were sometimes applying criminal method to exact as much money as possible from the debtor without taking into account the amount of debt. Sarala Devi challenged the inhuman activities of the money-lenders and asked the Government to open Agriculture Bank and Land Mortgage Bank for these people including the poor farmers.

In Ganjam district most of the Harijans were employed as watchers in the reserve forest. In 1938 some of them were removed from service all on sudden although they had put in services ranging from 10 to 20 years. When these people were thrown out of employment, Mrs. A. Laxmibai as a legislator asked the Government, 'why was such a drastic step taken by the forest department'. She criticised the Government bravely for this type of activities and appealed the Government to give them employment urgently.

Due to the sincere efforts of Sarala Devi and A. Laxmibai the Government of Orissa was forced to sanction funds for the buildings of Kaibalya Kutir, a hostel for Harijans, at Cuttack.

Harijans of Sambalpur were allowed free use of forests for rearing cocoans, Subsidy were paid to the spinner's associations to encourage spinning and weaving among the pans of Angul. Circulars were issued to all departments for appointment of local people with preference to Harijans and tribals in clerical and ministerial grades. By this time under the leadership of Champa Devi and Jayamangal Rath, the Harijan movement spread throughout Ganjam district and crossed the boarder of Orissa. Jayamangal Rath married to

Nayani Devi who later on became an Assistant of Patitapaban Sangha.

Champa Devi stayed with Harijans and took care of Harijan ladies. She read Ramayan and Mahabharat in their streets. She did Sankritan with Harijans at her residence. At her "Women Welfare Ashram" of Ichapur she kept a number of untouchable ladies. In Vaidic way by offering mantra and homa, they were made touchables. Sariamani Devi was one of them.

In this manner the movement spread throughout Orissa and gradually the Harijans mixed freely with the cast Hindus Due to their sincere efforts the caste Hindus employed the Harijans, accepted food and water from them, wells and bathing ghats were opened for them and they were encouraged to participate in the public dinners. This process of socialisation and interaction made a great impact on both rural and urban life of Orissa.

To quote Bapuji, "In this struggle for religious reform, therefore the women of India may be expected to take leading part. I hope there fore, that the example of the women of Cuttack will prove infectious and that the work begun by Smt. Rama Devi and her campanions will be continued inspite of difficulties and disappointments that they might have to face."

With great appreciation he wrote-"I have had the privilege of mixing with ten and thousands of India's women. I have seen them at work. But no where have I seen anything quite like what Smt. Rama Devi and her little band have been found to do so gracefully and naturally."

Kisan Movement

In the meantime a new socialist school of thought and action was coming to the fore-front in the Congress organisation. There was a cry of socialism all round among the youth of the country. Some young men and women were inspired by Marxist philosophy and become ambitious of channelising

the Congress movement along with the lines of class struggle. In Orissa Naba Krishna Choudhry, Surendra Nath Dwivedy, Manmohan Choudhury, Bhagabati Panigrahi, Malati Choudhury Sarala Devi and A. Laxmibai, took the lead of this socialist movement. They in fact were influenced by the Bolshevik Revolution of Russia of 1917.

In February 1933 they met secretly at the farm house of N.K. Choudhury at Anakhia in Cuttack district to discuss the formation of an organisation which would develop class consciousness among the people particularly among the exploited class like farmers and industrial workers. Malati Choudhury was most prominent among them. The meeting was of historic importance as they formed there the "Utkal Congress Samyavadi Karmi Sangh" as a forum to discuss socialist ideas. Thus the first socialist organisation was established in Orissa.

The socialists vowed not to own private property and whatever private property they might possess would be given over to the League." Malati Choudhury set the first example by donating all her orgnaments. Thus the foundation stone of socialist movement in Orissa," was laid down.

The Gajrats were called "Andhari Mulak" as the people were completely ignorant about their rights, privileges and human dignity. They knew nothing about the day-to-day happening outside the world. Their condition was very miserable. Most of the people were dependent on agriculture but they had no right over their land or its product. No ryot could cut any reserved trees from his assessed land without license. No ryot could grow any miscellaneous crops, except fruit trees. The ryot could distribute fruits among themselves only after the chief took his lion's share.

The ryot had to pay the rent property to the landlords. They had to pay the rent in two or three instalments to the headman. If the defaulting tenants did not pay the rent inspite of repeated warning of the state authority, the ruler could recover the dues by instituting a case against him. For

the recovery of arrears the movable and immovable property of the tenants were attached usually and sold at the time of growing necessities.

The agrarian situation in those states became more acute everyday by the enhanced rents. This practice of enhancement was beyond any check. However the sufferings and misery of the peasants for a long time did not come to light. It was Kuntala Kumari Sabat who first came forward and made significant and immense contributions in redressing their grievances through her famous ballad *Gadajat Krusak*. Inspired by the Marxist approach she composed how the peasant 'Gokuli' led a life of suffering and to what extent his economic condition was pitable and social life miserable. In other words she exposed the fact that the ryot was physically tortured, economically harassed, socially humiliated and culturally disgraced. The character of Gokuli was taken as a symbol of peasant's society. In order to champion the cause of the peasants in the province, Malati Choudhury organised the Utkal Provincial Kisan Sangha in 1935 in Orissa. She had read a number of books written on Russian revolution and was greatly influenced by literary works like Maxim Gorky's Mother, George Bernard Shaw's *Fabian Essays*, *An Intelligent Women's Guide to Socialism*, etc. Like Kuntala Kumari, she wanted to make the people conscious of their civic rights and duties, make them aware of their political environment, social setting and economic conditions and provide them inspiration to fight against the Zamindar and the British Raj. She felt that class consciousness must be developed among the masses so that they could involve themselves and activity participate in the struggle for the right of ryots.

Therefore she organised a Kisan Day procession of 15000 Kisans which marched through Cuttack city shouting slogans of down with imperialism, abolish landlordism, etc.

In the meantime the Provincial Kisan Sabha drafted its manifesto which demanded 50% reduction in land and water tax, cancellation of arrears of rent and revenue, tax on

agriculture income, land tax exemption to small farmers, etc. It was submitted to the UPCC to make it a part of their general manifesto. On 12th October 1936, the UPCC met and accepted it as their manifesto.

To strengthen the hands of the Congress ministry for initiating radical change among the peasants Malati Choudhury decided to go from village to village for holding meetings to get Kisans' signatures and asking for remission of land revenue because of crop failure. She moved to remote villages on foot or by bullock carts propagating against oppression of Zamindars and money-lenders.

On 12 April 1935 a Krishak Sammallani was held at Ramasahi, P.S. Balasore and it was presided over by Malati Choudhury. She readout a leaflet on the aims of the peasants associations. The leaflet contained urgent demands of the peasants relating to the remission of taxes debts and land revenue, education of water tax and fixation of the wages of the day labourer.

Another meeting was held on 4 May 1936 at village Mururia (Ersama P.S.) in the district of Cuttack. Malati Choudhury urged the villagers to report the acts of oppression on the part of the zamindars and those might be referred to the Board of Revenue. Besides this a local Krushak Sabha was formed and its members were exhorted to strive for the success of the forthcoming Kisan Conference.

To submit a true report Malati Choudhury with her high educational background, gave up all her comforts and marched from place to place carrying her own bedding and singing patriotic songs to collect the correct informations. She remained in the poor peasant's cottages and created faith among them. On the basis of the collected informations she prepared and submitted the report to the Editor, All India Kisan Bulletin, Bombay. Moreover she started a weekly named 'Krushak' (peasant) in order to create awareness among the peasants and people alike.

Gradually under her able leadership the movement spread like wild fire and crossed the boarder of Orissa. She even received a petition signed by the Oriya peasants living in Calcutta.

In the District of Puri a meeting was held at Delang on 9 May 1937 under the Presidentship of Smt. Sarala Devi, M.L.A. After two days another meeting was held where she protested against the Bethi (forced labour) system prevailing in the Zamindari of Delang.

When the Assembly started its business Sarala Devi bravely asked the Government regarding the steps taken by the Government to prevent flood and appealed the Government not to collect land revenue from the flood effected areas. She also strongly argued for the development of agriculture education and free utilisation of jungle by the people of feudatory states. She warned the Government not to delay in this regard and forced the ministry to look into the matter without delay as the peasants interest lies in it.

At that time land revenue was not very high, it was about two or three rupees per acre. Still the farmers considered it a burden. They were unable to pay it in time. When they failed to pay the land revenue to the Zamindars, they were severely punished.

Sarala Devi was the first lady to object the system and draw the attention of the Government to take stern action against it. The sufferings of the peasants was only due to their poverty. So she demanded, "every effort must be made to increase the wealth of the peasant".

In order to increase the financial condition of the poor farmers Mrs. A. Lakshmi Bai suggested the Government to take immediate steps to eradicate unemployment and to improve the cottage industries, and to impose no tax on collection of wood from the jungle.

Due to the women socialist leaders and M.L.As. the peasant movement made rapid progress even in areas like

Ganjam formerly constituting parts of Madras. Malati Choudhury, Hemalata Samant and A. Laxmibai established contacts with the Ganjam 'ryot' movement. They toured those areas and addressed big gatherings of ryots and also collected lady members for the movement.

Due to the sincere efforts of Gandhi Krishnamurty the ryot movement spread throughout Badakehmandi Zamindari in Ganjam. He moved from village to village and called the ryots to join the movement. His wife T. Arabalu inspired him to do the work like Bapuji. She joined the meetings along with her husband. The women of Badakhemandi Taluk were also attracted and gradually a large number of women joined it and offered membership. They were Uma Devi, Ahalya Devi, Manakya Devi, Bishnupriya Devi, Sumana Devi, T. Annapurna, Sulakhyama Devi, Tarini Devi, Padmavati Devi, Sita Devi from Kumarode, and V. Kumudini Devi, from Davar.

Due to the strong protest against the 'Bethi' system by the women leaders and the other Kisan leaders the system was partly abolished in some of the states and the rulers were not in a position to abolish it completely because the, "total abolition of the Bethi system would entail an amount of expenditure that the state was not in a position to incur without additional taxation which would cause greater hardship to the people." Still they had taken steps to confine the 'Bethi' labour in future only to the repairs of the road, required by the villagers themselves to instill a proper sense of responsibility in them."

On 11 April 1939 the All India Kisan Committee met under the presidentship of Narendra Dev. Malati Choudhury was elected from Orissa to the Executive Council of Central Kisan Council. There she met the top Kisan leaders of India and explained them the condition of peasants of Orissa. Due to her sincere efforts pressure was exerted from Central Kisan Council on the Government of India to look into the matter. Series of negotiations started with the Government representatives and Kisan leaders of Orissa. The representatives felt that the matter had been badly handled by the feudatory

chiefs and therefore they thought of abolishing the system of Bethi and Bheti ultimately.

The mass movement in the states of Orissa was spontaneous and the involvement of women in it from top to bottom was complete. The British imperialism was condemned every where and the whole agitation was considered a part of the National movement. The success of the peasant movement was largely due to the tireless efforts of women leaders, particularly of Malati Choudhury. In this movement she came to be known as 'Johan of Arc'. The entire movement was based on the Marxist philosophy to bring out a socialistic pattern of society in which workers and peasants will be the true rulers of the society.

Women's Movement

Being inspired by Gandhi in ideas of emancipation of women, the small band of women leaders also made courageous efforts for the uplift of women in Orissa. The most promiment in this group were Reba Roy, Sailabala Das,* Kuntala Sabat, Sarala Devi, and Malati Choudhury. As the 'women problem' had very rightly been visualised by them in the form of seclusion, restriction on movement and lack of education, etc., popular lectures, writings, education, etc. were first undertaken by them as a method of attack to overcome these problems. They created a sense of self-reliance and self-confidence in women and restored them their rightful position in the society by encouraging their education and participation in political, social as well as national activities.

The first Woman's Association was founded at Puri known as the *Mahila Bandhu Samiti* by Labanya Mayee Devi. This association gave recognition to women's creative talent. Chanchala Devi, Yamuna Devi, Radhamani Devi were the other members of this association. Mahila Bandhu Samiti discussed various problems related to Oriya literature, society, etc. On 13th March 1925 these members admiring and appreciating the worth of the literary works of Kuntala Kumari conferred on her the title "Utkal Bharati".

Gradually having understood the importance of political movements as well as associations, the Oriya women organised a conference known as the "Utkal Women's Conference". The initiative was taken up by the women of South Orissa. A couple of ladies like Rasamani Devi and Swarnalata Devi met at Swaraj Ashram, Berhampur and founded the *Utkal Women's Conference* (UWC) which held its first session in June 1924.

In the midst of great enthusiasm women from all over Orissa mot in the Swaraj Ashram at Berhampur on 30th June 1924. Acharya Prafulla Chandra Roy of Bengal presided over the conference which was attended by many celebrities like Mudhusudan Das and Gopabandhu Das.

The occasion created excitement among women belonging to different classes. Ladies of aristocratic origin who would not otherwise come to the public gathering also attended it. There were representatives from all religious groups and sects and the participants took keen interest in the discussion. The credit for making the meeting a success went to Sarala Devi, the most important leader of Orissa of that period. She was ably assisted by Rasamani Devi, Haimabata Devi and Kishorimani Devi.

On 28th December 1926 Kuntala Kumari presided the *Madhu Pyari Samitani* which was organised by "Sanskar and Sevasangh" of Berhampur. Many reputed personalities like Jayamangal Rath, Saisbhusan Rath, Chandra Acharya Lingaraj Panigrahi, Balakrishna Rao, Sadasiva Bidyabbusan, Baisbnaba Charan Das, Anand Acharya, Kripasindhu Narendra Dev and Iswar Sahu, etc. participated in that meeting. Kuntala Kumari delivered a powerful speech there.

There after she went to Surala to see the work of patitapaban Sangha. The fishermen and women of Surala welcomed her with much pomp and ceremony and they addressed her as "Mother"'. She addressed there a vast gathering narrating them the greatness of their ancient culture and tradition including the story of Karubaki. From there Kuntala Kumari

came to Berhampur and addressed the *Berhampur Mahila Samaj* where a number of Telugu women and Oriya women were present. This visit of Kuntala Kumari to Ganjam had great impact on the women of South Orissa. The letter of Jayamangal Rath the founder of "Sanskar and Sevasangh of Utkal" to Kuntala Kumari testifies the fact.

Another poetess of the period Annapurna Devi also moved from place to place and organised meetings for women's freedom. She organised a number of Pathasalas in the villages for the development of women education. She established a Nari Seva Sadan at Berhampur with the help of Parsuram Patra a famous advocate of Berhampur.

To quote Gandhiji "our first task in the country is to educate women. Education will help them to safeguard their virtue". It had great impact on Sailabala Das who organised the *Orissa Women's Education Reform Conference* which was to encourage female participation in schools and colleges. Eminent women of that time like Rukmini Devi, Nirmala Nayak. Sarojini Choudhury, Suprava Kar, Sudhansubala Hazara and Binodini Sadangi participated in the conference. They took all possible steps for the spread of education among women. Smt. Reba Roy also made good effort, at reforming society and raising the standard of education of women to the level of the educated community of men. She did a lot of work for the uplift of women education and opened a girls school at Cuttack. She also edited a paper named "Prabhat" and published a number of articles in it regarding the development of womenhood.

In 1929 Sarala Devi, Jahnabi Devi, Rasamani Devi and Rama Devi went to attend the *Prabasi Utkal Samilini* which was organised with the aim of helping the Oriyas at Cuttack.

In the meantime the Civil Disobedience movement was called off by the Congress followed by Gandhi-Irwin pact on 4th March 1931. Then the Congress took interest on the Fundamental Rights and Socio-economic development as per the resolution passed in the Karachi Session.

For the Fundamental Rights of the women, *Orissa Provincial Women's Conference* (Nikhila Utkal Mahila Samilani) met at Balasore on 3rd and 4th August 1931. It was presided over by Kuntala Kumari Sabat. Where as on the first day one thousand women participated, the next day nearly twelve hundred women participated in that meeting. The Conference was held in the town hall of Balasore. Male persons were not allowed to enter into the hall excepting the press reporters. Strictly speaking the conference was exclusively of women, for women, by women. On the very first day thousands of women marched in a procession and in the evening by 7.30 P.M. another meeting was held under the presidentship of Rama Devi where Kuntala Kumari delivered a fiery speech which created a spirit of revolt among the women of Orissa. The grand success of the conference attracted a number of delegates from different parts of the state to join it.

A Central Executive Committee named *Nikhila Utkal Nari Parisad* was formed with thirty members. Among them eight members were from Cuttack eight from Balasore, five from Puri and four from Ganjam. Rest were the office bearers such as President, General Secretary, Additional Secretary and Cashier. Kuntala Kumari was elected as the President to the Council and Basant Kumari Devi, the General Secretary, Sarojini Choudhury and Kokila Devi as Additional Secretary and Janhabi Devi as the Cashler.

A number of proposals were put fourth and passed to inject into the mind of worsen, a sense of political conscious ness and a spirit of revolt. Among them Janhabi Devi offered a proposal to condemn the atrocity of the police action against the women satyagrahis of Scijang campaign and to pay sympathy to the victims. Apart from this she raised her voice against dowry, untouchability and purdah system. Kokila Devi offered a proposal to from Committee to promote khadi and charkha in each district. Besides this she suggested the participation of women in district boards, local boards, and municipalities. Sunamani Devi putforth a proposal to form one *Pradesik Nari Karma Mandir* (Provincial Workshop for

women) to promote health science, prevention of liquor, charkha, child welfare, women awakening and welfare, etc. Rama Devi suggested to collect women satyagrahis to make the Congress a success. Sarala Devi offered the proposal for compulsory education in schools and to workout "Sarada Act" immediately. Chaya Devi proposed to promote widom remarriage system. Haramani Devi offered a proposal to set up a National School for girls. At the end, Kuntala Kumari read out a Declaration of five rights of women. All these proposals were unanimously accepted by the women present there. As a result Orissa witnessed a new era of revolt and reform in her history.

Meanwhile under the leadership of Sribasta Panda Jayamangala Rath, Brajasundara Panda, Nandakishore Mishra, Sasibhusan Rath, Ananda Das, Kasinath Pala, Digampur Rath and Madhusudan Das, a meeting was held at Berhampur Utkal Ashram on 19th April 1931 to discuss about the social evils like drinking of liquor, inequalities of men and women in social status, untouchability, untouchability of women during their mense and delivery period, child marriage and dowry system, etc. They took a resolution to form one *Utkal Mahila Niketan* for the upliftment of women. A Committee was formed with the above persons in which Chandramani Devi became the Secretary of the Committee and Sarala Devi a member for the executive body.

Being a member of the Legislative Assembly Sarala Devi fought for the dignity and rights of women on many occasions. To cite a case the ruler of Alee a feudatory state of Orissa murdered a girl of 13 years. He was charged of rape and murder but with the help of some English officers he escaped. Sarala Devi strongly opposed it and bravely criticised the British Government in these words— "it is not one case, number of cases like it are still in dark. For it the local officers are highly responsible. These matters are suppressed by the police department too due to their weakness. I feel it is an insult to the women society. I defend it on behalf of the women society and I feel for the protection of women a Estate

Women's Protection Act should be passed." In this manner she started a movement for the emancipation of women.

Political dynamics of women shows how thus women participated in all aspects and phases of nationalist activity including the constructive programme. They proved their worth and genius as good organisers and great reformers on that occasion, when this programme was launched by Gandhi. Gandhi believed that the nationalist movement was not merely a political struggle but also a means of rejuvenating and regenerating the society. Therefore respecting his ideas and theories women campaigned for the uplift of the Harijans and kisans and as well as their own community. In working out the constructive programme and making it a success, women left no stone unturned. For their multifarious activities they deserve all praise and appreciation.

13

Women Representation in Political Life

> One of the evils of democracy is that you have to endure the man you elected, whether you like him or not.
>
> —*Will Rogers*

Despite the fact that females make up approximately 50 per cent of the world's population, researchers agree that throughout the world the female representation in public life is remarkably similar—very small. Women simply have not moved beyond the ballot box into local and national office. The political arena appears to be where women have made the least headway in the contemporary world; politics appears to be the last male stronghold (Chaney, 1973; Baiter and Lansing, 1980; United Nations, 1980b).

A major segment of the research concentrates on the fact that few women achieve political standing, and the diversity of female participation. The literature documents the variety of ways in which women have exercised political power (Jacquette, 1973; Van Allen, 1974; MacCormack, 1975; and Boulding, 1977). The researchers generally agree that the most thorough evidence for a change in the position of women is the number of women who are actively pursuing political careers (Lansing, 1979). Haavio-Mannila (1972) suggests that a change in sex role ideologies is not as clearly seen in the voting "of" women, but rather in the voting "for" women. Researchers agree that women have not achieved equality with men in any part of the world.

As late as 1966 only 55 out of 144 member states of the UN had women members in their respective parliaments (Phadnis and Malani, 1980:5).

Coser (1980) suggests that women' "cluster at the bottom". In other words, when they appear, they are lower level participants.

Researchers—who have examined trends in women's participation in political office have found mixed results: it is rising in some countries, stagnating in others and declining in others (Newland, 1979; Phadnis and Malani, 1980; and United Nations 1980b). For example, the participation of women in Finland at the local and national level is increasing (Haavio-Mannila, 1972 and 1978). However, an examination of historical data for the United States of America since 1921 shows a mixed picture (Werner and Bachtold, 1974). Kohn (1980) concluded that participation of women in national legislatures has been increasing in for the six countries he had studied. For these countries, increases appear to be more likely at the lower than at the highest centers of decision-making (Phadnis and Malani, 1980). These data suggest that female representation appears to be increasing at the local level and is either totally absent or minimal at the national level.

At the international level, researchers differ in their evaluation of progress toward equality for women since the appearance of the current women's movement in the 1960s (Epstein, 1981). Tolchin and Tolchin, (1974) suggest that politics in the United States is open to women's contribution because of the major social and political upheavals of the 1970s including the women's movement. Some researchers, however, are skeptical about whether change has occurred and whether it is continuing to improve or whether women will lose the gains they have achieved. Lipman-Blumen (1973) suggests that crises result in only temporary improvement for female participation. At the same time, major ideological changes expressed through some kind of social movement

have been documented to have significantly improved women's options (Safilios-Rothschild, 1975). Epstein (1981) suggests that pressure from women's groups result in an increased female representation in public office. In fact, she suggests more improvement for women in appointive than in elective office.

The rebirth of the current women's movement at the international level was manifested by the United Nation's establishment of International Women's Year in 1975. In fact, IWY and the resulting Plan of Action for the Decade for Women (1976-1985) were responses to pressure from women's organisations throughout the world, many of whom have observer status with the United Nations as non-governmental organisations. Despite the existence of a body of literature which suggests improvement in the social as well as political position of women in response to the women's movement (Safilios-Rothschild, 1975; Haavio-Mannila, 1972; Lansing, 1979; and Epstein, 1979), few researchers outside the United Nations system attempted an evaluation of progress since International Women's Year (United Nations, 1980b).

This research attempts such an evaluation. Data collected by the United Nations to evaluate progress in the political representation of women during the first half of the Decade for Women by the World Conference of the United Nations Decade for Women are utilised (United Nations, 1980c). These data make possible an assessment of change in female representation since International Women's Year. The countries examined are more representative of the global picture than the current literature since previous cross-national analysis focussed predominantly on the developed countries. Hence, a special feature of this analysis is the incorporation data from the developing countries of Africa, Asia, and Latin America, and North Africa and the Middle East along with data from the developed countries of Europe and North America. These data are examined to determine the significance of changes in several Indices of Female Representation in political life during the 1975-78 period with an eye toward the future of

women in political life. Indices of Female Representation are used in this study to evaluate the following trends: How did female representation change during the 1975-78 period ? Were the changes greater at the local than at the national level and were they greater for appointive than elective office? Finally, what do these changes mean for future progress toward equality for women in political life? In essence, it assesses whether International Women's Year and the first half of The Decade for Women (1976-1985) made a difference in the political representation of the female, half of the world's population.

Method

The data analysed in this article were collected by the United Nations from member nations for the World Conference of the United Nations Decade for Women (Copenhagen, Denmark, 14-30 July, 1980) as part of a review and evaluation of progress made by women since 1975, an evaluation which was mandated by the UN General Assembly (United Nations, 1980d : 4).

In 1978, member nations were sent a 53-page questionnaire on the implementation of the World Plan of Action adopted at the World Conference of International Women's Year (United Nations, 1978). Countries were asked to report for 1975 and 1978 the percentages of women out of the total of women and men who: were elected to public office at the local-level, were elected to public office at the national level, held office at higher levels in the executive branch of government, were officials in foreign affairs departments at higher levels, and were officials in diplomatic service at the level of first secretary and above (United Nations, 1978: 21 and 23).

Data from the responses are used in this article as Indices of Female Representation in Elective Office at the Local and National Levels and in Appointive Office in the Executive Branch of Government, Departments of Foreign Affairs, and the Diplomatic Service. Of the United Nations member nations, 93 responded to the questionnaire (United Nations, 1980d :

68). These responses were used in the preparation of review and evaluation documents for the World Conference (United Nations, 1980b). These data were also published for the Conference to facilitate further analysis like that undertaken here (United Nations, 1980c).

The data available for 1975 and 1978 are percentage point, not per cent. Percentage point change focuses our attention on how much of an increase (or decrease) in the representation of women was accomplished by the addition (or deletion) of one or several women. Hence, the data measure the result of any efforts to change the representation of women during this period. In fact, it is a better measure of progress than percentage increase where the addition of one woman may represent a 100 per cent increase over no women. Data in percentage point form address the issue of how much the addition of one (or several) woman changes the proportional representation of the female population in political life.

Comprehensive upto-date information on the subject of elected women are not kept by any international organisation and is extremely difficult to obtain (McLean, 1980). In fact, researchers have written about the great difficulty in collecting data on women's political participation (for example, Blay, 1979). While these data are the largest set available, they are not without limitation.

Despite their limitations, these data are the most extensive available for global evaluation of female representation in political life (Boulding et al., 1976). Hence, the data are used, but are used with caution.

To accomplish the purpose of this investigation, median indices are employed to examine the range of changes during the 1975-78 period with a particular focus on declines, stagnations, and moderate and high levels of change; changes in these indices are evaluated in terms of low, medium and high levels of 1978 representation; and finally, the indices for 1975 and 1978 are evaluated for possible significant changes during this period using the Wilcoxon Matched-

Pairs Signed Rank test. These data provide the basis for an assessment of change during the first half of the Decade for Women as well as the basis for a discussion of prospects for the future.

Findings

Indices of Female Representation for 62 countries are examined in this article. These countries include 33 developing and 29 developed countries. They represent 11 African, 10 Asian, 10 Latin American, 2 Middle Eastern, 1 North American, 17 Western European, 4 classified as other (Australia, Israel, Japan, and New Zealand), and 7 Eastern European countries including the erstwhile Soviet Union. Hence, Indices of Female Representation are examined for a number of countries which have not previously been subjected to comparative analysis, in particular the developing countries of Africa, Asia and Latin America. At the same time, the data include a larger number of developed countries than have heretofore been examined.

Indices of Female Representation for 1978 yield the following medians: appointive office in the executive branch of government of 10 per cent, elected office at the local level of 8.3 per cent, elected office at the national level of 6 per cent and, finally, appointive office in foreign affairs departments of 6 per cent and in high levels of the diplomatic service of 4.6 per cent.

Efforts to improve female representation since International Women's Year resulted in a median increase of female officials elected to local office of 2 percentage points for the 23 countries for which data are available for both 1975 and 1978 (United Nations, 1980c). The data for this period, however, indicate that several countries reported actual declines or no change in contrast to the several countries which reported substantial increases. Percentage point declines were reported for Columbia, Cuba, Dominican Republic and India. No change during the 1975-78 period was reported for several countries including Botswana, Israel, Paraguay and

Swaziland. Increases between 0.4 and 3.4 percentage points were reported for nine countries. Substantial increase, above 4.5 percentage points were reported for six of the 23 countries: Belgium, Denmark, Kenya, New Zealand, Poland and Sweden.

An examination of Table 1 indicates that countries with low levels of representation in 1978 experienced low levels of change during the 1975-78 period. In contrast, countries with high levels for 1978 experienced either moderate or high levels of change for the same period. Countries with medium levels experienced a mixture of declines, stagnations, and moderate and high levels of increase during the evaluation period.

TABLE 1: PERCENTAGE POINT CHANGE IN INDICES OF FEMALE REPRESENTATION IN ELECTED OFFICE AT THE LOCAL LEVEL BY LEVEL OF REPRESENTATION

1978 Level of Representation (Percentage)	*%age Point Low (–2.2 to 0.4)*	*Change between Moderate (1.1 to 3.4)*	*1975-78 High (4.5 to 8.0)*
Low (0.0 to 64%)	Dominican Republic India Israel Madagascar Paraguay	Iceland Papua New Guinea	
Medium (7.1 to 17.7%)	Botswana Columbia Cuba Netherlands Swaziland	Austria Jamaica New Zealand United States of America	Belgium Denmark
High (20.0 to 49%)		Byelorussia Romania	Kenya Poland Sweden

Source: Statistical Abstract (A/Conf. 94/26), World Conference of the UN Decade for Women, 1980. New York: United Nations, as supplemented by Women in Socialist Society. Moscow: Council for Mutual Economic Assistance Secretariat, 1980.

As expected, female participation at the national level changed less than female participation in local elective office (United Nations, 1980c). Here, the median change during

the 1975-78 period was an increase of one percentage point. As was the case at the local level, some countries reported a decline, others stagnation and still others reported an increase in percentage point. Declines were reported by Columbia, Israel, the Netherlands, and the United Kingdom of Great Britain and Northern Ireland. No change was reported by Botswana, Dominican Republic, Iceland, New Zealand, Singapore, Swaziland, and the United States. Slight or moderate increases were reported for 10 countries. Percentage point increases above the median were reported by Belgium, Finland, the German Democratic Republic, the Philippines, Poland, Norway and Vietnam.

TABLE 2: PERCENTAGE POINT CHANGE IN INDICES OF FEMALE REPRESENTATION IN ELECTED OFFICE AT THE NATIONAL LEVEL BY LEVEL OF REPRESENTATION

1978 Level of Representation (Percentage)	*Percentage Point Change between 1975-78* *Low (–1.8 to 0.5)*	*Moderate (1.0 to 20)*	*High (29 to 8.0)*
Low (0.0 to 5.0%)	Botswana India Iceland Madagascar New Zealand Singapore United Kingdom United States of America	Ireland Jamaica Papua New Guinea Paraguay	
Medium (5.5 to 13.2%)	Columbia Dominican Republic Israel Netherlands Swaziland	Austria Germany, Fed, Republic of Kenya	Belgium Philippines
High (15.5 to 33.6%)		Denmark	Finland German Democ. Republic Norway Poland Vietnam

Source: Statistical Abstract (A/Conf. 94/26), World Conference of the UN Decade for Women, 1980, New York: United Nations, as supplemented by Women in Socialist Society. Moscow: Council for Economic Assistance Secretariat, 1930.

The pattern is similar for appointive positions. The median change in appointments to high office in the executive branch of government is 0.2 percentage points for the 19 countries for which data are available for both 1975 and 1978 (United Nations, 1980c). Two countries reported percentage point declines: the Netherlands and the United Kingdom of Great Britain and Northern Ireland. Five countries reported no change during the period (Botswana, Denmark, Finland, Iceland and Swaziland), increases of less than two percentage points were reported for seven countries, and five reported comparatively substantial percentage point increases above five percentage points (Belgium, Ireland, Ivory Coast, Sweden, and the United States of America). Countries with low levels of representation for 1978 experienced low or moderate levels of change during the 1975-78 period and, again, countries with high levels for 1978 experienced high levels of change, with the exception of Botswana which reported a low level of change during the evaluation period.

Changes in appointments to high office in foreign affairs departments are similarly low: the median change here is also 0.2 percentage points (United Nations, 1980c). Percentage point declines were reported for six of the countries including Barbados, Cuba, Ecuador, Ireland, the Netherlands, and the Philippines. No change between 1975 and 1978 was reported for Iceland. Israel, Mali, Nepal, Papua New Guinea, Singapore, Sri Lanka. Swaziland and Uruguay. Increases above three percentage points in the same period reported of seven of the 32 countries: Botswana. Eeypt, Greece, Jamaica, Kenya, Mauritius and New Zealand. Again, countries with low level of representation for 1978 experienced a low or, in some cases, a moderate amount of chance during the evaluation period. Changes for countries with a high level of representation for 1978 varied from low to moderate to high levels of change between 1975 and 1978.

Women appear to have fared better during this period in being appointed to the diplomatic service at the level of first secretary and above. Here, for the 32 countries during the

1975-78 period, the median change was an increase of 0.8 percentage points. Only two countries reported declines : New Zealand and Uruguay. No change was reported for Barbados, Botswana, Israel, Nepal, Papua New Guinea, Singapore, Sri Lanka, Swaziland and Togo. By comparison, substantial increases were reported for seven countries; Cuba, Ecuador, Egypt, Jamaica, Kenya, Paraguay, and the Philippines.

Countries with low levels of representation experienced low or moderate levels of change, countries with medium levels experienced a moderate level of change. In sharp contrast, countries with high levels of representation experienced a variety of changes ranging from low to high

Changes in the Indices of Female Representation during the 1975-78 period yield the following hierarchy:

Index of Female Representation	*Median Change (Percentage Point)*
Elective Office, Local	2.0
Elective Office, National	1.0
Appointive Office	
Diplomatic Service	0.8
Executive Branch of Government	0.2
Foreign Affairs Departments	0.2

Greater changes were reported for women in local than in national office. Change in elective office at the local level exceeds the percentage point change for national elective office which, in turn, exceeds appointive office. Appointive office in the diplomatic service exceeds the two other appointive offices Contrary to expectations (Epstein, 1981), changes were greater for elective than for appointive office. The application of the Wilcoxon Matched-Pairs Signed-Ranked test assesses the degree to which groups of countries improved the representation of females in political life in these five areas during the 1975-78 period. At the local level, significant progress was reported at the global level for women elected

to political office ($Z=-3.02$, $p=.003$). The developed countries experienced significant improvement in this area, whereas the developing countries did not ($Z=-2.8$, $p=.005$ and $Z=-.4$, $p=.67$, respectively). Europe is the only region with significant improvement in this area ($Z=-2.7$, $p=-.008$).

Global progress was also significant for women being elected to national office ($Z=-3.0$, $p=003$). Here again, thc developed countries experienced significant progress in contrast to developing countries ($Z=-2.5$, $p=.01$ and Z—1.7, $p=.08$, respectively). Again, Europe is the only major region reporting significant improvement ($Z=-2.5$, $p=.01$).

Progress for women is less for appointment than election to political office. Significant improvement is reported for women in the diplomatic service at the global level ($Z = -3.4$, $p=.001$). However, the developed but not the developing, countries reported significant progress ($Z=-2.7$, $p=.006$ and $Z=-2.2$, $p=.03$, respectively). Again, Europe was the only region to experience significant progress ($Z=-2.9$, $p = .003$). In Departments of Foreign Affairs, women did not experience significant improvement in the developed countries (Z–2.0, p.05). No regions reported significant improvement in the participation of women in this important decision-making post. Global progress also was not significant for female appointment to the executive branch of government ($Z=-2.4$, $p=.017$) nor were improvements characteristic of either developed or developing countries or any particular region.

Discussion

This analysis presents three major findings. First, how did female representation in political life change during the 1975-78 period? Median indices yield a greater change at the local (2 percentage points) than at the national level (1 percentage points) and a greater change in diplomatic service (0.8 percentage points) than in the executive branch of government (0.2 percentage points) and departments of foreign affairs (0.2 percentage points). These findings tend to support Phadnis and Malani (1980) who suggest that female

representation increases at the local level rather than the national level. However, it only partially supports this trend since there is an increase at both the local and national levels: an increase for election to local office is twice that of national office.

Progress since IWY in these five areas is statistically significant for females elected to political office at both the national and local levels. Progress for appointive office is significant for women in the diplomatic service, but change in Departments of Foreign Affairs and the Executive Branch of Government during the 1975-78 period are not significant. Where found, significant changes are characteristic of the developed, rather than the developing countries, and in Europe in contrast to other regions.

Findings which demonstrate improvement since International Women's Year, suggest success during the first half of the Decade for Women. Increases in female representation support the suggestion of Haavio-Mannila (1972) of a change in sex role ideology during the first half of the Decade for Women as evidenced by change leading to an increased voting "for women". The findings also support the suggestion of Epstein (1981) that pressure of women's groups result in increased female representation in public office. Contrary to her suggestion, this improvement is greater for elective than appointive office. The findings also support Safilios-Rothschild (1975) by suggesting that social movements are successful in improving women's political options. It appears that women's groups have been able to pressure the various political parties to nominate and, ultimately, elect women candidates. Overall, the data suggest that in the area of political representation, the first half of The Decade for Women was most successful in the developed countries, particularly those in Europe. In sum, the findings suggest success of the Plan of Action since International Women's Year for Europe, in contrast to other parts of the world.

A closer examination of these trends suggest important consequences for the futue. Despite the overall increase in

female representation, in no country are women represented at a level near their actual numbers. Moreover, country reports varied from increases to stagnations as suggested in the literature (Newland, 1979; and Phadnis and Malani, 1980). At the same time, countries with low levels of female representation in 1978 experienced low rates of change during the 1975-78 period. At the same time, countries with high levels in 1978 experienced high levels of change.

Female appointment to diplomatic service is the only deviation from this pattern. Here, countries with high levels in 1975 experienced varying changes ranging from high to low. Such findings suggest little hope for significant progress in countries where female representation is already low. If present trends persist, these findings suggest an increasing gap in female political representation between the developing and developed countries and between Europe and other regions of the world. In fact, if one were so bold as to assume that the rate of change during the 1975-78 period represented a trend for the future, it would take decades, if not centuries, for women to achieve equality with men in political life. For example, if present trends persist, the year of equal representation for the median country will be 2,041 for local office, 2,110 for national office, 2,578 for the executive branch of government, 2,638 for the foreign affairs departments, and 2,148 for the diplomatic service.

Current research provides only hints about what patterns seem to be forming and what their courses may be. A great deal remains to be done to provide the information necessary for these special efforts. If the full integration of women into political life is important for the international development strategy (United Nations, 1980a), recognition is given to both the importance of a greater participation of women in policy-making positions at the local, national and international levels (United Nations, 1980a: 11) and the special efforts needed to increase the participation of women in public and political life at every level.

As a contribution to improving the political representation of the female population, a number of important questions are on the research agenda. For example, do women have a greater chance for advancement when the economic sphere is part of the political sphere as suggested by Epstein (1981)? Do women fare better at the local than at the national level as a consequence of movement of major decisions from the local to the national level as suggested by Blay (1979)? Historically, women in the Congress seem to be assigned to less prestigious committees and, hence, are cut off from power sources (Gehlen, 1969). What are the variations in this trend at the international level? Has it changed since International Women's Year. Others suggest that when women are in office, they tend to concentrate on social questions such as health, education and the conditions of the female population (Duverger, 1955). In this the case are there variations by region or stage of development?

The suggestion that European women have been the major beneficiaries of changes in female representation since International Women's Year, necessitates further cross-national research in all these and other areas which encompass the developed along with the developing countries. Rather than focusing on why there are so few women in positions of power, it might be fruitful to address the question raised by Stacey and Price (1981) and Stacey (1982). How has it come about that in such a short period of time so many women have become involved in politics? At the same time, it is important to assess the success or failure of national strategies based on the Plan of Action and the Programme of Action developed by the World Conference of the United Nations Decade for Women for the second half of the Decade for Women. These are only some of the questions which need to be answered if efforts to increase the political representation of women are to be successful throughout the world.

REFERENCES

Baxter, Sandra and Marjorie Lansing (1980), *Women and Politics: The Invisible Majority*. Ann Arbor: The University of Michigan Press.

Blay, Eva Alterman (1997), "The Participation of Women in Brazil: Female Mayors" *Signs: Journal of Women in Culture and Society* 51:1 (Autumn): 42-59.

Boals, Kay (1975), "Review Essay: Political Science.' *Signs: Journal of Women in Culture and Society* 1: 161-174.

Boulding, Elise, Shrley Nuss, Dorothy Carson and Michael A. Greenstein (1976), *Handbook of International Data on Women*. New York: John Wiley and Sons (Halsted Press, Sage Publications).

Boulding, Elise (1971), *Women in the Twentieth Century World*. New York: John Wiley, and Sons (Halsted Press Division, Sage Publications).

Chaney, Elsa M. (1973), *Women in Latin American Politics: The Case of Peru and Chile*. In Ann Pescatello (ed.), *Female and Male in Latin America: Essays,* pp. 103-104, Pennsylvania: University of Pittusburgh Press.

Duverger, Maurice (1955), *The Political Role of Women*. Paris: United Nations Educational, Scientific and Cultural Organisation (UNESCO).

Gehlen, Frieda L. (1969), "Women in Congress,' *Transaction* 6: 36-40.

Githens, Marianne and Jewel C. Prestage (eds.), (1977), *A Portrait of Marginality: The Political Behaviour of American Women*. New York: David McKay.

Haavio-Mannila, Elina (1972), "Sex Roles in Politics." In Constantina Safilios-Rothschild (ed.), *Toward a Sociology of Women,* pp. 154-172. Lexington, Massachusetts: Xerox College Publishing.

Harkess, Shirley (1980), "Colombian Women in Party Politics: A Token Role." In Helena Znaniecki Lopata (ed.), *Interweave of Social Roles: Women and Men,* Vol. 1, p 1-31. JAI Press, Inc.

Jacquette, Jane (1973), "Women in Revolutionary Movements in Latin America," *Journal of Marriage and the Family,* 35:2:344-354.

Kattakayam, Jacob John (1982), Women, Power and Innovation: A study of Women's Organisations and Social Change. Paper

Presented at Tenth World Congress of Sociology, International Sociological Association, Mexico City.

Kohn, Walter, S.G. (1980), *Women in National Legislatures: A Comparative Study of Six Countries.* New York: Praeger (Praeger Special Studies).

Lansing, Marjorie (1979), "The American Woman: Voter an Activist." In Jane L. Jaquette (ed.), *Women in Politics,* pp. 5-24. New York; John Wiley and Sons.

Lee, Marcia Manning (1976), "Why Few Women Hold Public Office: Democracy and Sexual Roles." *Political Science Quarterly* 91: 297-314.

Lipman-Blumen, Joan (1973), "Role De-differentiation as a System Response of Crisis: Occupational and Political Roles of Women." *Sociological Inquiry* 43 : 105-129.

MacCormack, Carol (1975), "Sande Women and Political Power in Sierra Leone," West African *Journal of Sociology and Political Science* 1: 42-50.

Margolis, Diane Rothbard (1979), "The Invisible Hands: Sex Roles and the Division of Labour in Two Local Political parties." *Social Problems* 26 (February): 314-324.

McLean, Scila (1980), The Role of Women in the Promotion of Friendly Relations Between Nations, Unpublished Manuscript.

Newland Kathleen (1979), *The Sisterhood of Man.* New York: W.W. Norton and Company

Nyonyitono, Rebecca (1982), Women as Agents of Change in Developing Countries: The Case of Kenya, Paper presented during Tenth World Congress of Sociology, International Sociology Association, Mexico City, August.

O'Barr, John F. (1975), "Making the Invisible Visible: African Women in Politics and Policy." *African Studies Review* XVII: 3 (December): 19-27.

Phadnis, Urmila and Indira Malani (eds.) (1978), *Women of the World: Illusion and Reality,* New Delhi: Vikas Publishing House Pvt. Ltd.

Safilios-Rothschild, Constantina (1975), "Sex Role Socialisation in Selected Countries." In Marlaine E. Lockwood (ed.), *Research on Women's Acquaintance of Professional and Leadership Roles,* Princeton, New Jersey: Educational Testing Service December.

Secretariat (1980), *Women in Socialist Society:* Moscow: Council for Mutual Economic Assistance.

Sharon, Raka (1982), Working Women as Agents of Social Change in India, Paper presented at Tenth World Congress of Sociology, International Sociological Association, Mexico City, August.

Stacey, Margaret and Marion Price (1981), *Women, Power and Politics.* London: Tavistock Publications.

Tolchin, Susan J. and Martin Tolchin (1974), *Clout: Manpower and Politics.* New York: Coward, McCann and Geoghegan.

United Nations (1978), Questionnaire on the Implementation during the Period 1975-1978 of the World Plan of Action Adopted at the World Conference of the International Women's Year (79-41341), New York: United Nations.

United Nations (1980a), World Plan of Action for the Implementation of the Objectives of the International Women's Year. New York: United Nations.

United Nations (1980b), Review and Evaluation of Progress achieved in the Implementation of the World Plan of Action: Political Participation, International Cooperation and the Strengthening of International Peace. (A/Conf. 94/13 and Corr. 1) New York: World Conference of the Untied Nations Decade for Women.

United Nations (1980c), Statistical Abstract (A/Conf. 94/25). New York: World Conference of the United Nations Decade for Women.

United Nations (1980d), Report of the World Conference of the Untied Nations Decade for Women: Equality, Development and Peace, Copenhagen, 14 to 30 July 1980 (A/Conf. 94/35). New York World Conference of the United Nations Decade for Women.

Van Allen, Judith (1974), "Memsahib, Militante, Femme Libre: Political and Apolitical." In June L. Jaquette (ed.), *Women in Politics,* pp. 304-321, New York: John Wiley and Sons.

14

Women in Politics and Trade Unions: Global Scenario

Of late, women's participation in public and trade union activities has recorded a phenomenal growth. This chapter gives a vivid account of women in political and trade union life.

UNESCO's *Second Medium-Term Plan (1984—1989)* states that:

> The difficulties women encounter in attaining positions of responsibility strongly emphasize the fact that equality is basically a political problem and that it is related to the balance of power. The participation, or rather non-participation, of women in political life is a fundamental part of the problems surrounding the status of women.
>
> In many countries, women are still excluded, in practice, from high-ranking positions such as head of state, government, political party, military hierarchy or judicial authority.
>
> Stress should accordingly be laid on the need to interest women in these matters to a greater extent. The role played by women's associations, past or present, in this connection should be borne in mind, especially where, faithful to a long tradition, they remain a hive of initiative and concentration.

Since the right to vote and the right of association are among those to which, in democratic countries, every individual is entitled, it would be of interest to examine how, and to what extent, women have managed to exercise these rights and also to look at the extent to which a woman in a position

of power—head of government, minister—may influence the policy of her country in order to abolish inequalities between the two sexes.

The participation of women in trade-union life as ordinary members or officials is very important for their individual development, for a trade union is also a meeting place where a woman who is employed for the first time will lose a little of her shyness and self-effacing manner as she is urged to give her opinion and take part in discussions. She will have a fuller awareness of her personality and her responsibility for the defence of her rights and participation in trade-union action.

In order to gain a clearer picture of women in elected assemblies, it would be useful to discover their representation percentage in the various political parties.

In *Belgium,* in the legislative elections of November 1981, with 212 seats to be filled in the Chamber, 12 women were elected; they lost 4 seats in relation to the previous legislatures. In the Senate, there are 14 women among the 106 members elected on a national basis; of 50 senators elected by the provincial councils, only 5 are women.

It seems that through the 'preferential votes' procedure, the electoral system has enabled women to progress in the opinion of the electors; unfortunately, this development has not been reflected in their position in the party lists.

In *Denmark,* legislative elections were held in December 1981; there are 47 women in the Danish Parliament among the 179 members; this is the highest proportion registered in the ten EEC countries. Once again as a result of the voting system, the greater preference expressed for women was not reflected by an increased number of seats, as it is the men who decide about places on the lists.

In *Spain,* at present, 30 women sit in the two assemblies out of a total of 558 elected members (20 of 350 in Congress, and 10 of 208 in the Senate).

In *France,* the comparison between the number of women deputies and senators reveals a curious development over the years.

Between 1946 and 1968, their number continued to drop in the National Assembly—from 5.4 per cent to 1.4 per cent—and in the Senate from 3.6 per cent to 1.7 per cent. At present 28 women (out of 491 members) sit in the National Assembly and 9 women (out of 316) in the Senate.

And yet the political role of women has constantly developed, and their position within the political parties has been consolidated—but not, it seems, to the point of establishing a position for them on the lists of candidates which would offer them a level of representation commensurate with their actual political strength.

In *Ireland,* at present, there are 14 women among the 166 members of Parliament; this is the highest proportion ever reached in this country.

In *Italy,* there are 49 women among the 630 members of the Chamber of Deputies and 16 out of 322 members in the Senate.

In the *Federal Republic of Germany,* there are 51 women out of 520 members of Parliament.

In the *United Kingdom,* the proportion of women Members of Parliament is low; at present, only 25 of the 636 Members are women.

In the *European Parliament of the EEC,* women received greater support from the electorate at the 1979 European elections than in the national elections; 67 were elected among the 434 members of the European Parliament. Following the 1984 elections, the figure rose to *75.*

In the *developing countries,* some of which have relatively young political and administrative structures, there are states where women occupy very important functions or positions in national political life. Unfortunately, there are no statistical

data that would enable detailed information to be provided in this respect.

In order to enable women to play an active part in politics, certain political parties and countries are considering the introduction of a quota system that would fix a minimum number of places to be occupied by women.

Women in Government

Male politicians realized a long time ago that it was in their interest to give women a share in government, long before the latter had obtained the right to vote. In France, for example, three women were appointed secretaries of state in the Popular Front government of 1936. This was an innovation which was well received.

It should be pointed out that a number of very capable women are currently presiding over the destinies of their countries. Countless countries throughout the world now have women ministers, and not only in ministries concerned with social matters. They are no longer an exception and they exercise their responsibilities to the full. But their number still remains relatively small.

Women and Trade Unions

The basic function of a trade union is to defend the rights of its members and to monitor the application of the laws that protect them with regard to remuneration, working conditions, accident prevention, etc.

Under the collective bargaining system, it is hardly possible for an employer to talk to each of his employees. A delegation is therefore required consisting of one or several representatives of the co-operate body and/or of each of its constituent categories. It is the trade unions that assume this role of representing the workers.

Every worker therefore has a material interest in belonging to a trade union, as a means of defending his own interests; and he may also feel a moral obligation to express solidarity

with his fellow workers. What is more, the experience of trade-union life is intellectually rewarding and provides opportunities for the development of the individual.

The position of women in the trade unions. Statistics are lacking for many countries, especially in Latin America and Africa, and where they do exist, relate only to an international federation and not those trade unions that are not affiliated to it.

A study provided by the European Trade Union Confederation (ETUC) provides a few percentages in relation to the total number of members. In six countries, the proportion of women in the trade unions affiliated to ETUC range from 40 to 30 percent; these are, in descending order, Denmark, Italy, France, the United Kingdom. Ireland and Belgium. Next are the Federal Republic of Germany and the Netherlands where the levels are between 20 and 11 per cent.

It must also be stated that women are far from being represented in proportion to their numbers within the governing bodies. Thus for the seventeen organizations that replied to the ETUC survey, five have slightly over 10 per cent of women among their executive officers, eight have fewer than 10 per cent and four have none.

Women are most strongly represented in Finland: 30 per cent on the Executive Committee.

The Trades Union Congress (TUC) in the United Kingdom provides more precise figures: there are 2,265,000 women among the 6,022,000 trade-union members, almost 38 per cent. The distribution of women within the governing bodies is as follows: permanent trade-union representatives, ninety women for a total of 1,636 seats; delegates to the TUC, sixty-six women for a total of 418 seats; and members of the executive bodies, forty women for a total of 316 seats.

It has been noted that the level of union membership for both men and women varies greatly with the category of worker.

Trade-union action on behalf of women. In general, the trade unions' commitment to women has been rather weak.

They did not really grasp the fact that there was a female employment problem for a considerable time. For some years now, however, their leaders have been establishing commissions for the study of female employment and placing questions relating to women on the agenda of their discussions. But no real action on any scale has been taken to tackle this issue which, in spite of its occasionally specific and circumstantial nature, has to do with the rights of workers as a whole. Nevertheless, this situation is changing, as a few specific example will show.

In British Columbia, Canada, the civil service union has inserted clauses in a collective agreement whereby female workers benefit in terms of maternity leave, resumption of employment with recognition of the period worked prior to the leave taken in order to bring up a child, and retraining courses to assist them in returning to their occupational activity.

In the United Kingdom, at TUC instigation, an equal-opportunity clause is to be inserted in all collective agreements, to the effect that equal opportunities in employment are established without regard to the sex, matrimonial status, beliefs, racial or ethnic origins of the worker.

Bibliography

Almond, Gabriel A. and G. Bingham Powell, Jr. (1978), *Comparative Politics*: Second Edition, Boston, Toronto: Little Brown and Company.

Almond, Gabriel A. (1974), *Comparative Politics Today: A World View*. Boston: Little Brown and Company.

Aparna Basu (1976), 'The Role of Women in the Indian Struggle for Freedom', in *Indian Women: From Purdah to Modernity,* edited by B.R. Nanda Vikas Publishing House Pvt. Ltd., New Delhi.

Barker, Anthony, and Michael Rush (1970), *The Member of Parliament and His Information*. London: George Allen & Unwin Ltd..

Baxter, Sandra and Marjorie Lansing (1980), *Women and Politics: The Invisible Majority*. Ann Arbor: The University of Michigan Press.

Blay, Eva Alterman (1997), "The Participation of Women in Brazil: Female Mayors" *Signs: Journal of Women in Culture and Society* 51:1 (Autumn): 42-59.

Boals, Kay (1975), "Review Essay: Political Science.' *Signs: Journal of Women in Culture and Society* 1: 161-174.

Boulding, Elise (1971), *Women in the Twentieth Century World*. New York: John Wiley, and Sons (Halsted Press Division, Sage Publications).

Boulding, Elise, Shrley Nuss, Dorothy Carson and Michael A. Greenstein (1976), *Handbook of International Data on Women*. New York: John Wiley and Sons (Halsted Press, Sage Publications).

B.R. Nanda (1976), *Indian Women—From Purdah to Modernity* Vikas, Publishing House Pvt. Ltd., Delhi.

Carl N. Degler (1965), "Revolution Without Ideology: The Changing Place of Women in America" in Robert Jay Lipton, ed. *The Women in America,* Boston, Houghton Miffin.

Chaney, Elsa M. (1973), *Women in Latin American Politics: The Case of Peru and Chile*. In Ann Pescatello (ed.), *Female and Male in Latin America: Essays,* pp. 103-104, Pennsylvania: University of Pittusburgh Press.

Channana, Karuna (1988), *Socialisation and Women: Explorations in Gender Identity*. New Delhi: Orient Longman.

Desai, Neera and M. Krishnaraj (1987), *Women and Society in India*. Delhi: Ajanta Publications.

Duverger, Maurice (1955), *The Political Role of Women*. Paris: United Nations Educational, Scientific and Cultural Organisation (UNESCO).

Epstein, Cynthis Fuchs (1981), "Women and Elites: A Cross-National Perspective." In: Epstein, Cynthia Fuchs and Rose Laub Coser (eds.), *Access to Power: Cross-National Studies of Women and Elites,* pp. 3-15. London: George Allen and Unwin.

Gehlen, Frieda L. (1969), "Women in Congress,' *Transaction* 6: 36-40.

Ghadially, Rehana (ed.) (1988), *Women in Indian Society*. New Delhi: Sage Publications.

Githens, Marianne and Jewel C. Prestage (eds.) (1977), *A Portrait of Marginality: The Political Behaviour of American Women.* New York: David McKay.

Haavio-Mannila, Elina (1972), "Sex Roles in Politics." In Constantina Safilios-Rothschild (ed.), *Toward a Sociology of Women,* pp. 154-172. Lexington, Massachusetts: Xerox College Publishing.

Harkess, Shirley (1980), "Colombian Women in Party Politics: A Token Role." In Helena Znaniecki Lopata (ed.), *Interweave of Social Roles: Women and Men,* Vol. 1, p 1-31. JAI Press, Inc.

Hazel D'Lima (1983), *Women in Local Government,* Concept Publishing Company, New Delhi.

Jacquette, Jane (1973), "Women in Revolutionary Movements in Latin America," *Journal of Marriage and the Family,* 35:2:344-354.

John Stuart Mill (1960), *On Liberty, Representative Government, The Subjection of Women*, Oxford University Press.

Kamaladevi Chattopadhyay (1958), 'The Struggle for Freedom', in *Women of India,* T.A. Baig (ed.). New Delhi, Publication Division, Government of India.

Kattakayam, Jacob John (1982), Women, Power and Innovation: A study of Women's Organisations and Social Change. Paper Presented at Tenth World Congress of Sociology, International Sociological Association, Mexico City.

Kohn, Walter, S.G. (1980), *Women in National Legislatures: A Comparative Study of Six Countries.* New York: Praeger (Praeger Special Studies).

Lam, Mithan J. (1988), *Women in India: A General Survey of their Conditions, Status and Advancement*. New Delhi: All India Women's Conference.

Lansing, Marjorie (1979), "The American Woman: Voter an Activist." In Jane L. Jaquette (ed.), *Women in Politics,* pp. 5-24. New York; John Wiley and Sons.

Lee, Duke T. (1977), "Law and the Status of Women: Introduction." In Columbia Human Rights Law Review (eds.), *Law and the Status of Women: An International Symposium,* pp. 3-8. New York: Centre for Social Development and Humanitarian Affairs (United Nations).

Lee, Marcia Manning (1976), "Why Few Women Hold Public Office: Democracy and Sexual Roles." *Political Science Quarterly* 91: 297-314.

Lipman-Blumen, Joan (1973), "Role De-differentiation as a System Response of Crisis: Occupational and Political Roles of Women." *Sociological Inquiry* 43: 105-129.

MacCormack, Carol (1975), "Sande Women and Political Power in Sierra Leone," West African *Journal of Sociology and Political Science* 1: 42-50.

Margolis, Diane Rothbard (1979), "The Invisible Hands: Sex Roles and the Division of Labour in Two Local Political parties." *Social Problems* 26 (February): 314-324.

Mari, Lucille Mathurin (1985), *International Women's Decade: A Balance Sheet.* New Delhi: Centre for Women Development Studies.

McLean, Scila (1980), *The Role of Women in the Promotion of Friendly Relations Between Nations*, Unpublished Manuscript.

Mitra, Asok et al. (1979), *The Status of Women: Shifts in Occupational Patterns 1960-71*. Delhi.

Newland Kathleen (1979), *The Sisterhood of Man*. New York: W.W. Norton and Company

Nyonyitono, Rebecca (1982), Women as Agents of Change in Developing Countries: The Case of Kenya, Paper presented during Tenth World Congress of Sociology, International Sociology Association, Mexico City, August.

O'Barr, John F. (1975), "Making the Invisible Visible: African Women in Politics and Policy." *African Studies Review* XVII: 3 (December): 19-27.

Omvedt, Gail (1986), *Women in Popular Movements: India and Thailand during the Decade of Women*. UNRISD.

Phadnis, Urmila and Indira Malani (eds.) (1978), *Women of the World: Illusion and Reality,* New Delhi: Vikas Publishing House Pvt. Ltd.

Safilios-Rothschild, Constantina, (1975), "Sex Role Socialisation in Selected Countries." In Marlaine E. Lockwood (ed.), *Research on Women's Acquaintance of Professional and Leadership Roles,* Princeton, New Jersey: Educational Testing Service December.

Secretariat (1980), *Women in Socialist Society:* Moscow: Council for Mutual Economic Assistance.

Sharon, Raka (1982), Working Women as Agents of Social Change in India, Paper presented at Tenth World Congress of Sociology, International Sociological Association, Mexico City, August.

Sipila, Helvi (1976-77), "Changing Roles of Women in the Developing Regions of the World." *Journal of International Affairs* 2:30 : 183-190.

Stacey, Margaret (1982), "Masculine or Feminine Power. Action in the Public Domain. Paper presented to Session 6, Women's Politics: Theoretical Considerations, Research Committee on Women and Society, International Sociological Association, Mexico City.

Stacey, Margaret and Marion Price (1981), *Women, Power and Politics.* London: Tavistock Publications.

Tolchin, Susan J. and Martin Tolchin (1974), *Clout: Manpower and Politics.* New York: Coward, McCann and Geoghegan.

United Nations (1978), Questionnaire on the Implementation during the Period 1975-1978 of the World Plan of Action Adopted at the World Conference of the International Women's Year (79-41341), New York: United Nations.

United Nations (1980a), World Plan of Action for the Implementation of the Objectives of the International Women's Year. New York: United Nations.

United Nations (1980b), Review and Evaluation of Progress achieved in the Implementation of the World Plan of Action: Political Participation, International Cooperation and the Strengthening of International Peace. (A/Conf. 94/13 and Corr. 1) New York: World Conference of the Untied Nations Decade for Women.

United Nations (1980c), Statistical Abstract (A/Conf. 94/25). New York: World Conference of the United Nations Decade for Women.

United Nations (1980d), Report of the World Conference of the Untied Nations Decade for Women: Equality, Development and Peace, Copenhagen, 14 to 30 July 1980 (A/Conf. 94/35). New York World Conference of the United Nations Decade for Women.

Van Allen, Judith (1974), "Memsahib, Militante, Femme Libre: Political and Apolitical." In June L. Jaquette (ed.), *Women in Politics,* pp. 304-321, New York: John Wiley and Sons.

Warner, Emmy E. and Louise, M. Bachtold (1974), "Personality Characteristics of Women in American Politics," In Jane L. Jaquette (ed.), *Women in Politics.* New York: John Wiley and Sons.

Index